T0110088

209 Fast Spare-Time Ways to Build Zero Cash into 7 Figures a Year in Real Estate

209 Fast Spare-Time Ways to Build Zero Cash into 7 Figures a Year in Real Estate

TYLER G. HICKS

WILEY

John Wiley & Sons, Inc.

Copyright © 2004 by Tyler G. Hicks. All rights reserved.

Published by John Wiley & Sons, Inc., Hoboken, New Jersey.
Published simultaneously in Canada.

No part of this publication may be reproduced, stored in a retrieval system, or transmitted in any form or by any means, electronic, mechanical, photocopying, recording, scanning, or otherwise, except as permitted under Section 107 or 108 of the 1976 United States Copyright Act, without either the prior written permission of the Publisher, or authorization through payment of the appropriate per-copy fee to the Copyright Clearance Center, Inc., 222 Rosewood Drive, Danvers, MA 01923, 978-750-8400, fax 978-646-8600, or on the web at www.copyright.com. Requests to the Publisher for permission should be addressed to the Permissions Department, John Wiley & Sons, Inc., 111 River Street, Hoboken, NJ 07030, 201-748-6011, fax 201-748-6008.

Limit of Liability/Disclaimer of Warranty: While the publisher and author have used their best efforts in preparing this book, they make no representations or warranties with respect to the accuracy or completeness of the contents of this book and specifically disclaim any implied warranties of merchantability or fitness for a particular purpose. No warranty may be created or extended by sales representatives or written sales materials. The advice and strategies contained herein may not be suitable for your situation. You should consult with a professional where appropriate. Neither the publisher nor author shall be liable for any loss of profit or any other commercial damages, including but not limited to special, incidental, consequential, or other damages.

For general information on our other products and services, or technical support, please contact our Customer Care Department within the United States at 800-762-2974, outside the United States at 317-572-3993 or fax 317-572-4002.

Wiley also publishes its books in a variety of electronic formats. Some content that appears in print may not be available in electronic books.

For more information about Wiley products, visit our web site at www.wiley.com.

Library of Congress Cataloging-in-Publication Data:

Hicks, Tyler Gregory
209 fast spare-time ways to build zero cash into 7 figures a year in real estate / Tyler G. Hicks.
p. cm.
Includes index.
ISBN 0-471-46499-6 (PAPER)
1. Real estate investment. I. Title: Two hundred and nine fast spare-time ways to build zero cash into 7 figures a year in real estate. II. Title.
HD1382.5.H528 2004
332.63'24—dc22

2003017895

10 9 8 7 6 5 4 3 2 1

For my wife,
Mary,
with many thanks for her wise counsel
and guidance based on
her astute publishing know-how.

Contents

INTRODUCTION

How This Book Can Make You Rich on Zero-Cash Borrowed-Money Real Estate

THIS BOOK SHOWS YOU HOW TO BUILD YOUR REAL ESTATE RICHES IN YOUR spare time on zero-cash—that is, borrowed money.

"How can you," you ask, "show me how to get rich in real estate on zero-cash borrowed money?" My answer to you, given very politely, is:

- **For years** I've owned valuable residential real estate and have watched it grow in value—every month of the year, and every year I've owned the property.
- **For years** I've been President, and am now Director, of a large lending organization that has made—and continues to make—many millions of dollars in real estate loans every year. During this time I've searched for ways to make more real estate loans, while approving thousands of applications for these loans. So I've sat—and do sit—on both sides of the Loan Officer's desk.
- **For years** I've written—and had published by major publishers—books and newsletters on real estate borrowing and business finance procedures. Users of these books and newsletters write me thousands of letters, e-mails, and faxes telling me how they're earning big money in real estate using my suggestions and ideas on zero-cash spare-time methods. And thousands more of these readers call me

on the phone to tell me what they're doing in real estate or to ask questions on how they should proceed with a particular deal.

So—good friend—I'm in, and I've been through, the entire real estate "scene"—I've survived and prospered. So, too, have many of my readers. And you can likewise start and build your wealth in real estate today using zero cash, possibly even with poor or no credit.

If you're a Beginning Real Estate Wealth Builder—we call such people ***BWBs*** for short—this book is for you. Or if you're an Experienced Real Estate Wealth Builder—***EWB*** for short—this book is also for you.

This book shows both BWBs and EWBs how to build wealth in real estate on zero-cash borrowed money. Thus, using this book, you can get started in real estate without using money from your own bank account. Instead, you will get started on zero cash—namely borrowed money.

And you are shown how to get started even if your credit is not the best. So people who've had personal problems—illness in the family, divorce, loss of job, or other problems—can get started in income-producing real estate on zero cash by using borrowed money. It isn't always easy but it CAN be done—and this book shows you exactly how to get started.

To help you understand what you can do—and how you can do it—you are given dozens of actual letters from readers telling exactly what they're doing to acquire—and profit from—income real estate today, using what we call zero cash—no money from their own pocket or pocketbook.

If you want to examine these actual letters in the same condition that we received them, you have an open invitation to visit my Manhattan office to see the letters. All we ask is that you give us a day's notice so we can arrange desk space for you—to make you comfortable while you read the letters that interest you.

As you read this book you'll get hundreds of smart, proven, practical ways to take over income real estate using borrowed money—zero cash. And I show you exactly how and where to get the money you need for these takeovers.

Using this book, you'll learn how to "figure the numbers" of a property. You'll see how much ***MIF***—Money in Fist—you'll have at the end of each month. MIF is money you can spend on your own needs—your home, food, entertainment, vacation, children's education, etc. And—if you take my suggestions—you'll use a large part of your MIF to buy more income property to increase your MIF and real estate assets!

"Why have you written this book?" you ask. "Aren't you giving away your money-making secrets?" My courteous answer to you is: "I've written this book because I want you to have a better quality of life, which comes from a larger income in real estate—most of which is tax-sheltered."

There's so much real estate in this world that no person could ever own it all. So I'm really not giving away secrets. I'm just sharing with you some of my real estate experiences that—hopefully—will make you a happier and more productive person in your own real estate endeavors. Thus, in this book I show you how:

- **An airline pilot**—laid off after 9/11 because of the drop in air travel—was able to buy three properties after his layoff and is now "doing better financially than ever before." See Chapter 1.
- **A reader bought 4 properties** in 3 months with zero cash down and "received several thousand dollars back at the closing on each one." See Chapter 2.
- **Another reader "bought 6 rental houses** without putting in a penny of his own cash"—he was broke but had excellent credit and experience. See Chapter 3.
- **In just one year a reader** "acquired over one million dollars of property with zero cash down, and pulled a considerable amount of cash from the transactions." See Chapter 4.
- **A reader, passed over for a deserved promotion in her job,** resolved to get into real estate. Just 30 days later she bought her "twins"—two identical side-by-side houses for $80,000 with zero cash down, and received cash at the closing. See Chapter 5.
- **A beginner bought his first apartment house** with zero money down. Then he bought a second one the same way. See Chapter 6. Subsequent chapters tell similar real-life stories. Finally:
- **An overworked, two-job-holding restaurant waiter** built a 7-figure (that's millions of dollars a year) spare-time income in real estate

starting with zero cash and less than $500 in his checking account. See Chapter 12.

Lastly, I'm as close to you as your telephone. The last line in the last chapter of this book gives you my telephone and fax numbers, as well as my e-mail address. Just call me—I'll answer you on the first ring and try to help. Or fax or e-mail me. I'll answer as soon as I can, after taking care of all my newsletter subscribers!

Good luck to you in your real estate ventures!

TYLER G. HICKS

CHAPTER 1

Build Your Real Estate Wealth on Other People's Money

MORE FORTUNES ARE BUILT IN REAL ESTATE ON BORROWED MONEY THAN in any other popular business. And *you* can build your fortune in real estate using borrowed money—if you follow the tips given in this book. How can I make such a statement?

Thousands of my readers write, call, fax, or e-mail me telling how they're building their wealth in income real estate using borrowed money to start. Many of these readers do this by following the tips in one of my books, newsletters, or courses. Their letters, calls, faxes, or e-mails prove to me that you ***can*** make big money in real estate today, starting with money you borrow from others.

Here are three letters showing how ***Beginning Wealth Builders*** (*BWBs* for short) get started in income real estate on borrowed money. (*The state or country in which the BWB letter writer has his/her real estate is given at the end of each letter.*)

Twenty Units in One Year

"I talked to you briefly last night and I want to thank you from the bottom of my heart for the courage you gave me in your books one year ago. I read two of them one year ago by accident. I ventured out to buy my first fourplex with zero money down. Thanks a bunch for those books. I now have 20 units in my portfolio, one year later. I gross $98,000 a year with a net of $30,000. I am now seriously considering quitting my job and doing this full time. The biggest miracle is that I have been in this country for 15 years and was starting to feel unsure about what to do with the rest of my life at age 35 when I read your books. Again, thanks a bunch."

—Rhode Island

Cashing Out at Your Closing

"I just bought a 3-bedroom house with an attached garage at 50 percent of appraised value and cashed out $5,100 at closing. This is my fourth straight zero down deal."

—Virginia

(Note: "cashed out" means the buyer received $5,100 at the closing of the purchase.)

Airline Pilot Finds a New Career

"I read your book out of a desire to become involved in real estate investing. I'm an airline pilot and September 11 caused a huge disruption in my industry. Luckily, I have been able to purchase three properties since my layoff and I am doing better financially than ever. Thank you for your words of wisdom; they definitely helped motivate and inform."

—Pennsylvania

If you'd like to examine any or all of the letters cited in this book, just give me a call on the phone. You'll find my telephone and fax numbers listed in the last paragraph of the last chapter (Chapter 12) in this book. Please allow us a day to assign you a desk in my Manhattan office where you can spend as much time as you wish examining the actual letters—just as we received them.

Invest in an Item of Lasting Value—Income Real Estate

Buying a piece of real estate or dealing with a piece of real estate allows you to work with an item of lasting value. Why is this? Because the land on which the real estate value is based will never go away. It is there forever. So, too, is its value.

I know you can tell me that in some sections of the world the land falls into the sea and disappears. This is true. But the amount of land to which this happens is such a small percentage of the world's total that this event can be ignored. (And I assume that you have enough sense not to buy such land!)

Recognize the Many Pluses of Real Estate

All real estate has a certain basic monetary value that usually rises as time passes. But there are other advantages, besides the usual rise in value, to making your fortune from real estate. Here are some typical advantages:

- **In real estate,** you are in a "borrowed money" business; this means that it is easier for you to start by using Other People's Money (OPM)—even if your credit is not the best when you start.
- **In most real estate deals,** little of your labor or time is required for the usual piece of income property.
- **As a property owner,** you are entitled to and can enjoy enormous legitimate and legal tax savings on your real estate income.
- **Almost all real estate** is an excellent asset on which you can borrow more and more money as your property rises in value (money to buy more and more income-producing property!)
- **Nearly the entire world** is in the midst of a real estate boom; hence your property will almost always rise in value with the passage of time.

- **You can wheel and deal** in hundreds of ways in real estate to reduce the amount of money you need to borrow to get started.
- **When you pick your properties carefully,** failures are almost unheard of in real estate income property holdings.

You'll tell me, I'm sure, that there are many other advantages you will enjoy while you build your wealth in real estate using borrowed money. Good. This shows you know your goals and you are ready to work towards those goals.

Speaking personally for a moment, I have been a real estate investor/entrepreneur for a number of years while at the same time I run several other businesses and work as a consultant for a Fortune 500 firm. Although I make good money from my other businesses and earn comfortable consulting fees from my regular career, nothing can equal the advantages that my real estate investments give me. I own real estate, while at the same time I:

- **Serve as director** of a large money-lending organization annually making millions of dollars of real estate and other types of loans.
- **Regularly do writing services** for some major firms.
- **Plan and publish** two internationally circulated and respected monthly newsletters covering real estate and business financing.
- **Author—that is, write—**one or two new books a year.
- **Market** some 15 marine products to boat owners all over the world.
- **Give lectures** in many parts of the world to businesspeople and Beginning Wealth Builders (BWBs) and Experienced Wealth Builders (EWBs) on real estate and business.
- **Enjoy** a great family and leisure life.

And I am fully convinced that you, too, can have many of the above joys. So I am giving you in this book what I believe are the essential keys to becoming rich in real estate using borrowed money to finance your fortune.

The tips I give you in this book are based on my years of personal experience in the fields of borrowing money, lending money, investing in real estate, and seeing that real estate rise in value, year after year. You, too, can do the same—or even better than I have done!

Build Your Real Estate Riches Minute by Minute

As I mentioned earlier, hundreds of people contact me each year to tell me of their adventures in real estate. Here are several more typical letters written to me by some of my readers. One of these BWBs was able to take over property worth more than $1,400,000 with zero cash down! Read these letters now to see how you, too, might do the same for yourself!

11 Units with No Cash Down

"Your books have been a major influence in my real estate investing success in the past 11 months. I have a total of 11 units (1 single-family, 1 fourplex and 1 sixplex), all purchased with no cash down. My money-in-fist (MIF) is $1,300 per month.

—Ohio

(MIF = *Positive Cash Flow you can bank with no claim on it other than yours!*)

$2,000 to $120,000 in Two Years

"I started using your techniques two years ago and built $2,000 borrowed money into $120,000 net worth in two years. I have a real estate corporation, a trout farm, and a sports store."

—Washington

Averaging $167,777 per Year on Borrowed Money

"The result of reading your books speak for themselves: In 4.5 years I took over four properties with these values: No. 1 = $525,000; No. 2 = $550,000; No. 3 = $275,000; No. 4 = $135,000. Total value today = $1,485,000. My mortgages total $730,000. So I built a $755,000 net value in 4.5 years, or averaged $167,777 per year on borrowed money. It's not easy but it's well worth it. And I think this is not bad for a Scottish immigrant!"

—New York

Personal Cash Flow over $8,000 per Month

"Thank you for talking to me on the phone. Your book has sure changed my life. Since I first read your 'three-year' real estate book, I have amassed over one-half million dollars in real estate and two other rapidly growing businesses. My personal cash flow is now over $8,000 per month, and my two businesses will do over $350,000 cash flow in the next 12 months. All in less than two years and part-time—I still have my 40-hour per week salaried job." —Texas

What do these letters show us, my good friend? They show you and me a number of important concepts that I've been preaching for many years, namely:

- **Income property** can be bought on zero cash.
- **BWBs** can make money with 100 percent financing.
- **You can get help** as a Beginning Wealth Builder.
- **Wealth-building deals** *are* available today.
- **Any BWB** can wheel and deal on prices.
- **Knowledge** *does* pay off in real estate—I told YOU so!
- **Finding a good property** encourages you to look for more.
- **You have a great future** in real estate—if you work at it!

By including the letters above, I am trying to show you what actual, real people are doing these days. And you, too, I believe, can do the same! But YOU must work at it and YOU must:

- **Keep trying** to build your real estate wealth—never give up!
- **Plan to achieve** what you want in real estate—and then work your plan!
- **Know there *is* a property for *you*.** You must keep looking until you find it!

- **Wheel and deal** whenever you can—it's fun and profitable!
- **Decide to learn** all you can about the real estate business!

Now you know that it ***is*** possible to take over real estate for very little money down. Or, in some cases, you can take over real estate for zero cash down. This is one of the greatest advantages that real estate offers the BWB today.

Please keep in mind that all the examples you will read about in this book are drawn from the actual experiences of living, breathing BWBs. So they reflect real-life experiences. What's more, I keep the actual letters in a bank safe deposit box. But you are welcome to read them in New York City any time you wish. Just give me a few days' notice and you can study them as long as you want.

Start-Ups Win in Almost Every Real Estate Deal

Forget about needing a college education to make it big in real estate. I know thousands of people who are actively earning big money in real estate today. Few of these people have ever seen the inside of a college classroom. Many of them have never even been on a college campus, and a number of them could not produce a high school diploma if asked to do so. Yet they are earning large incomes from their real estate investments. I firmly believe that you, too, can do the same—with or without a formal education.

You do, of course, need some basic know-how in real estate. It would be foolish to try to take over income property, make real estate deals, or start a real estate investment company without knowing what you are doing. But in real estate, you ***can*** learn while you earn, because:

- **Most income properties** are easy to buy and run.
- **By hiring an accountant and an attorney** to help you with the business and legal aspects of your real estate you can avoid problems.
- **Help is easily and readily available** from thousands of people in real estate who are ready to assist you when you have questions about your real estate plans.
- **You will gladly learn** more about how to increase your income when money is flowing into your bank from your rental properties.

Do not call me, e-mail me, or write me to say, *"I don't know what I am doing; hence I can't make money in real estate!"* This is a give-up excuse that only annoys me. Please *do* call or write me, and I will be glad to try to help you, if you're trying to build your real-estate holdings. But I will refuse to try to help you if all you want to tell me is about the number of times you tried to do something and failed. What I want to hear about is the number of times you tried to do something and succeeded, like these readers who wrote:

Triplex with No Cash Down and Cash Back at Closing

"Purchased a triplex with no money down and cash back at settlement for rehab. Seller said it was the best deal he had ever seen!" —Maryland

Three Pieces of Real Estate with Zero Money Out of Pocket

"I just purchased my third piece of real estate with zero money out of my pocket. Two properties are rental homes with about $200 positive cash flow per month each. Third house is our dream house. All these have a value of $160,000 and were purchased with zero money out of my pocket—well almost, the last home I put about $300 out of my pocket for $80,000. I am presently employed as a firefighter and I found rental properties are a great second job. I am starting my 22nd year as a firefighter; so retirement is not far away. I plan on taking your advice and double my real estate holdings every two years or sooner. I am only 43 years old and will be in my early fifties when I retire. I will need the extra income!" —Oklahoma

I'm the First to Say Zero Down Deals DO Work

"After reading several of your books I purchased several real estate units. I currently own three up-and-down doubles and I'm working on a deal to buy two townhouses. The owner is willing to refinance these townhouses and sell them to me on a land contract. Some people say 'no money down deals' don't happen. I will be the first to say they do!"

—Ohio

From $1,000 Borrowed to $225,000 Value

"I read two of your books and followed your advice for the purchase of two beautiful properties in New Jersey. I bought the first one, now worth about $225,000, with a borrowed $1,000 down payment. I am now ready for more substantial propositions."

—New Jersey

Apartment Building for $500 Down

"I purchased one apartment building for only $500 down and $500 closing (it was a repossessed building) using the method Ty gave in a recent issue of his Newsletter. I am now negotiating for four more buildings from the same bank."

—Texas

Another $500 Down Nets $8,000 Profit

"I have three of your books. Because of your inspiration my wife and I bought a building eight months ago for $500

down and recently sold it for a net of $8,000. Thank you for your help."
—Minnesota

Speedy Results Are Possible in Real Estate

My education is as a mechanical engineer. After graduating from engineering school, I obtained my license as a Professional Engineer. For a number of years I worked as a consulting engineer. During my education and my consulting engineering activities, I always enjoyed working with numbers. All of my business life has been directed toward numbers, such as the six classes of numbers I look for in real estate, namely:

1. **The four numbers I need from you** to advise you on whether a proposed real estate investment in income real estate will be profitable for you. These numbers are: ***The Price, The Income, The Expenses, The Down Payment.*** I call these numbers the P, I, E, and D of investment real estate.
2. **The precise numbers of making a fortune** in real estate using borrowed money (you will see these numbers later in this book).
3. **The average number of hours** it takes to build a real estate business that has $1 million worth of income property.
4. **The usual number of weeks or months** it takes to acquire a typical income property.
5. **The happy number of dollars** you can "walk away with" each month from each income property you own.
6. **The very small number of errors** I have seen BWBs make in the income real estate business.

When you analyze an investment in advance and have good legal advice, these numbers are all in favor of you, the BWB in real estate. Why do I say this? Because the numbers that give your time input, money input, energy input, and "worry" input are all very small. But the numbers that give your chances of being successful and the income that you can earn are very large! Listen to the following BWBs who wrote to me:

$1.2 Million in Assets on Little or Zero Cash

"I have benefited substantially from many of your real estate books. I now own 20 properties (78 units) with a value of over $1.2 million. All these properties were bought with little, or zero money, down." —Nebraska

From Rentals to Sales

"Your books and inspiration helped me buy five houses with absolutely no cash! I now have $425 per month positive cash flow and $1,000 in security Also, three tenants want to buy their houses with over $10,000 profit in each to me!"

—Virginia

Get the Seller to Carry

"Thank you for the time you spent with me on the phone. By answering my questions and explaining to me how to structure a zero-cash-down deal, I was able to buy a $300,000 building for $240,000 while putting up none of my own money. I got a first mortgage for 80 percent of the purchase price and the seller carried the rest. After all expenses and debt service I have an annual cash flow of $7,100. Not bad for the first one!" —Florida

Home Equity Loan Gets a BWB Started

"I started out to become a millionaire 19 months ago with the idea of making it in five years. So far I've acquired about $200,000 in income properties and lakeshore raw land. I had no cash when I started this venture, but acting on the advice in one of your books I borrowed $10,000 in the form of a mortgage on my home. Since I had an excellent credit rating, I was able to buy two income buildings for $1 down on each. I just sold one of them for a net profit of $2,000 after owning it a year. I bought another building with 8 apartments for $63,000 with $1 down; I could sell it now for a $10,000 net profit. There is no possible way I could put a price on the value your books have been to me in the past year and a half." —California

Get in on Zooming Worldwide Growth

Traveling throughout the world, I watch real estate deals being made by various people, many of whom are beginners. These deals are often truly fantastic! Here are a few recent ones I've seen reported in the media:

- **A real estate BWB in California** made some $200,000 in 10 months from a property he bought using borrowed money and sold after making some minor repairs to the landscape.
- **A Canadian real estate BWB** bought four pieces of property valued at $4 million for just $4—one dollar on each!
- **A young BWB** took over eight houses and one building lot in his first eight months in the real estate business. His holdings are valued at $350,000 and he mortgaged out with $27,000 in tax-free money. The $650 he put down was borrowed money!
- **Many other mortgaging-out deals** exists in which the BWB put down zero cash and came away with the ownership of the property plus money in amounts from $5,000 to $35,000.

Since such deals are being made almost routinely, I have full faith that you, too, can do much the same if you follow the ideas and hints I give you in this book. I have nothing to sell you, good friend, except your success in income real estate!

Good Financing Can Be Yours Even with Bad Credit

It would be great if you could spend a day with me in my lending activities to see how much money is available to BWBs seeking real estate of some kind. For some years I have been Director of a rapidly growing lending organization. Prior to becoming Director, I was President and Chairman of the Board of the same lending organization. During these years, we have been "busting at the seams" with money.

Ever since our lending organization was granted the right to make real estate mortgage loans of various types, the Board and I have spent hours discussing why we could not find more people to borrow our money for real estate purposes. Yet when we checked with other lenders of a similar type, we found that they, too, had the same problem—they could make only a few loans when they wanted to make many.

Why does this situation exist? We have come up with a number of reasons for our lending organization and for similar ones. These reasons are as follows:

- **We are competing with many other lenders.** Since there is a lot of money around for real estate purposes (actually, billions of dollars), our prospective borrowers go to them for the money they need.
- **Qualified (and many unqualified) borrowers** find it easy to get money from various lenders. So they seem to think of us last.
- **Borrowers who have a good income property** or any other attractive type of real estate are a magnet to most lenders who are anxious to make a loan. This means that there are probably more lenders than borrowers at certain times. So we lose out.

While you may doubt what I say, the situation I detail is not unusual in my experience. Many other lenders to whom I speak on a regular basis tell me they run into the same problem. They just cannot find enough qualified borrowers for the money they have available to lend for real estate.

Take the Billions Being Offered to Real Estate Investors Today

Your reaction to the heading directly above might be intense laughter. If so, please don't call me to tell me you tried 116 lenders and they all said no. I know what our situation is; I wrestle with the problem of finding more borrowers for our real estate money. Plenty of my friends in the business tell me they, too, have the same problem.

Since I have actual, daily, experience in lending money for real estate purposes, I know that you ***can*** find the money for your real estate deal that involves attractive and "lendable" properties. A lendable property is one that has a value somewhat greater than the amount of the loan you seek. Of course, if the property is worth a lot more than the loan you seek, your borrowing will be made much easier.

Because I struggle daily to find more real estate borrowers, I am convinced there is plenty of money around for ***your*** real estate deal. All you need to do is go out and look for the real estate money you need! You can look for this money in a number of ways, such as:

- **Writing** to various lenders asking them if they would be interested in your real estate loan.
- **Calling** lenders in your area who might be interested in lending on your real estate proposal.
- **Visiting** in person lenders whom you think would be willing to help you.
- **Looking** on the Internet for real estate lenders who might work with you on the deals you have.
- **Reading** the Real Estate Section of your local large-city Sunday newspaper, looking for ads run by lenders in your area.
- **Consulting** the various directories of real estate lenders listed at the back of this book to find the names, addresses, and telephone numbers of many lenders. One of these lists contains 2,500 names of active real estate lenders.

So please believe me—good friend of mine—when I tell you that real estate money ***is*** available to you. What you have to do is look for it in a way that you find is suitable to your lifestyle and method of looking! And by using the smart and proven methods we give you in this book, *you can borrow your way to real estate riches!* Take it from someone who works both sides of the street as:

- **A borrower** for real estate investment purposes.
- **A lender** who loans to real estate investors.

Forget about a Real Estate License When You're an Investor

Many BWBs I talk to think they must have a broker's or salesperson's license to invest in real estate. You do ***not*** need a real estate license of any kind to invest in real estate for a profit! Most brokers and salespeople I know do not invest in real estate. Instead, they're more interested in earning commissions than they are in investing. True, while I do know some BWBs who are licensed, the main reason they got their license was not to earn money selling real estate.

Instead, the purpose in getting the license was to save the commissions they otherwise would have had to pay a broker. Some of these readers use sales commissions in place of the down payment on a piece of income real estate. Having the license permits them to take over certain properties with zero cash down.

Again, you do ***not*** need a license of any kind to make your fortune as a real estate investor. Keep this fact clearly in mind at all times as you read the remaining chapters in this book. And your age makes no difference, as the following BWBs told me in recent letters:

Become Carefree about Money Early in Your Career

"At present I own six of your books. Using the principles explained in them, I have gone from zero to owning

$250,000 of profitable, well-located income property in less than two years. My income allows me modest comforts of living, debt retirement, plus a healthy surplus. I was offered a $250,000 project for $20,000 down, which I borrowed. I feel the hardest part is now behind me. Thanks to your books, in no small part, I became financially independent on my 25th birthday."

—Iowa

Trailer Park Success

"I'm glad to inform you we bought a 102-space trailer court with 21 acres of land, a complete water system, a lagoon, laundry with machines and four trailers for $109,000. We raised the money using your methods, borrowing $78,000 from a local Savings and Loan Association. Then we got a $10,000 mortgage from the seller and $21,000 of borrowed money was put up by my partner. When we closed the deal I became half owner of the property without making any payments from my pocket. In fact, I received a $3,000 finder fee for locating such a nice deal for my partner."

—Illinois

Get into Non-Ownership Income Real Estate

Most BWBs thinking of building their fortune in real estate assume they must do so by owning income-producing property. Such ownership is not necessary! You can make a fortune working deals on property you do not own.

Still, you might ask: "Do I need a license to work on non-ownership deals?" You do *not* need a license to work real estate deals on property you do not own. There are many activities that can make you money in the world of real estate that do not require a license. Typical money makers you can use are:

- **Income property management** for a fee.
- **Real estate Limited Partnership formation** for a fee and a piece of the partnership, with proper legal guidance.
- **Holding special properties,** which are needed for a large project, for selected clients and assembling the properties into a larger parcel.
- **Money finding** for real estate investors for a fee by acting as a financial consultant.
- **Buying and selling** real estate options for big profits.
- **Acting as a Second Mortgage Lender** for real estate investors.
- **Flipping** (selling) desirable properties you buy with an option and sell for a profit. NOTE: Recently, new terms have been used for flipping, including: Fast resale, Swift resale, Rapid resale, Prompt resale, and Speedy resale.

There are many other ways you can earn money in real estate without owning property. Activities listed above are just a few in which you can make big money today. In none of these will you own property. Instead, you will deal with properties that other people own. The money you earn will usually be free of any real estate property taxes, points, or fees.

Furthermore, as your fortune grows, you may find it profitable to:

- **Invest some of your money** in real estate stocks and bonds. (I have done especially well investing in local public real estate project municipal bonds.)
- **The money you invest** in these projects helps provide good living space for people needing it.
- **The interest you receive** on the money you invest in municipal bonds is free of income taxes.
- **Both the owner of and the investor (you) in** the properties benefit financially.

You can also earn money in many other ways in real estate that do not involve the ownership of property. These ways will be given to you later in this book. I'll show you how to use each of them.

Plenty of Free Advice and Assistance Can Be Yours

Income real estate is not a complicated business. You'll find that many attorneys and accountants know the ins and outs of real estate. So you do not have to run around looking for people who know things about a business that is highly complicated. How can we say this? Because:

- Experienced real estate attorneys can easily draw up the papers you need to buy or sell real estate.
- Documents such as leases, security agreements, and maintenance contracts are almost what attorneys call "boilerplate." Nearly every document you'll ever need can be found in the standard reference books containing often-used documents for real estate attorneys.
- However, *you must always have the advice and guidance of a competent real estate attorney whenever you buy or sell any real estate.* Likewise, you should also have the services of a competent Certified Public Accountant (CPA).

Your accountant will not have much of a problem with the average real estate deal. Why do I say this about accountants? Because the arithmetic aspects of real estate are well known to accountants. You can easily learn them yourself if you wish.

I suggest that you get to know the "numbers" of real estate because doing so can mean a big difference in your income. Later in this book you will get you started on the numbers you'll need to know to borrow your way to real estate riches.

Grow Rich with Tax-Sheltered Real Estate Income

Regulatory agencies constantly revise the tax laws. Various loopholes are closed soon after they're discovered. Result? A larger bill for most taxpayers. But real estate has hardly been affected by these changes. You will always have major tax-saving advantages as the owner of income real estate. Why?

- **Because most governments encourage** the construction and operation of safe, clean, and affordable housing.
- **If you can provide such housing,** you can easily get the financing you need and you will be allowed generous tax advantages.
- **Thus, the depreciation allowance alone** can shelter your cash income from a piece of real estate. This means that the money you receive after having paid your expenses, real-estate taxes, and mortgage is free of both federal and state income taxes.

Can you ask for any better break? And you get these breaks by using borrowed money as your starting capital! So get to know the numbers of real estate tax savings. Truly, good friend:

- **You cannot make big money** today on a salary from a job!
- **The only way** you can build a fortune today is with a business of your own.
- **And, in my opinion,** real estate is the best business anywhere for a BWB.
- **It is almost impossible** to fail in this great business if you choose your properties carefully.
- **And the tax savings** that you are often offered is one of the reasons why the failure rate is so small!

National governments encourage real estate wealth builders by offering them enormous tax savings. Why don't you get some of these savings by getting into real estate today? I am certain you will never regret it!

Winners Are the Real Estate Norm

Studies by respected organizations show that about 80 percent of the new businesses formed by people fail within the first two years. But these figures do not apply to real estate because very few new real estate projects fail. Why? Because:

- **Adequate, well-maintained housing and commercial and industrial space** are avidly sought by renters in almost every area of the world.

- **Highly desirable properties** are hard to come by since construction rarely keeps up with demand.
- **Proving the maxim,** "Location, location, location," good locations are often rented long before a building is completed.
- **Businesspeople** know that a good location can mean the difference between failure and success for a business firm.
- **Property vacancy rates,** often assumed to be 5 percent for financial analyses, are typically less than half a percent in well-located property.
- **Desirable properties** that have been rented for years become popular, and almost as soon as a vacancy occurs someone shows up to rent the space. (The vacancy rate in some properties I know of has been 0 percent for 10 years!)

Thus, it really is almost impossible for you to lose money in well-located real estate. Also, if you buy an existing building—as I always recommend for your first purchase—your chances of success are even higher. Why is this? Because if a building has been operating for, say, 10 years, you can easily check its records for the entire period. Also, you can check the income tax returns of the building to learn what the true expenses were. With such information on hand, it is hard to make a major mistake. What all of this amounts to is this important fact:

Income real estate is probably the safest investment you can make. Also, income real estate is probably the best investment you will ever make in your entire life. And you can make this investment without putting up a cent of your own if you use borrowed money!

My friends and I in the real estate field are so enthusiastic about our business that we try to convince almost everyone we meet that it is a worthwhile way to earn their living. I want to convince you of the same because real estate has been good to me and to thousands of other people I know.

This is why I am ready to help you start building your real estate fortune using borrowed money for your starting capital. Here's what two highly enthusiastic BWBs wrote me about using borrowed money in real estate.

Zero-Cash Real Estate

"I bought my first building (an 8-family). I snatched it from a seller who wanted out quickly. The price was a bargain, with a $60,000 annual rent income. I applied for a $300,000 mortgage. **I did not have any money for the down payment, so my only option was a zero-cash deal.** Several banks offered me a $225,000 first mortgage because the rent roll was high. That meant I had to come up with a $75,000 down payment. (I never had this much money in my life!) I got the seller to hold a second mortgage for $30,000 and I took a second mortgage on my mom's house and my grandfather's house for $45,000. At the closing the seller gave me a 'Seller's Concession' for $20,000 which covered my closing costs. **The rents have paid for all loans and I have never missed a payment.** Since most of my tenants are Section 8, my money comes directly from the Government.

I recently refinanced the building to take cash out. Since the building was bought under market value, I had 'built in' equity. Also, the equity in the building has risen in the two years I've had the building and the property is appraised at $430,000. I refinanced the original loan that was at 8.5% to 6.38% and **I was able to take out $108,000 in cash.** I plan to use the money to make improvements and for the down payment on other income property." —New York

"Plastic" Wealth Building Is Popular in Real Estate Today

"I started out a year ago with an old, but sound, four-family [house] that had been run down. I bought it for $35,000, the seller holding a $30,000 first mortgage at 8.5% for 20 years. I borrowed $5,000 from my credit card for the down payment and took out home improvement loans from five different

> banks to renovate the building quickly. A week after work started, the large double next to my house came up for sale. I couldn't pass this one up. I borrowed $12,000 for the down payment. The purchase price was $55,000, commercial zoned. During all of this my wife and I bought a 55-acre farm for $28,000.
>
> Opportunity kept knocking and I kept taking it. I bought another double for $30,000 with $1,000 down. I am also in the process of buying a four-family and a six-family, all with excellent terms."
>
> —Illinois

Talking on the phone with this reader, he told me that the present worth of these properties, just a year after he started, is about $340,000. And he did it ALL on money he borrowed! Who says YOU can't start using borrowed money—OPM (Other People's Money)?

Getting Real Estate Funding the Smart Way

Another young reader told me: "We took over a 48-unit apartment house costing $100,000 for $7,500 down. The owner took back a mortgage. Our income is now $2,000 a month, after paying ALL expenses and mortgages. We had a clause put into the contract saying all the past-due rents we collected would become ours. So far we've collected about $5,000 in back rents. This means our cash investment is only $2,500!"

And, to see what goals can do for YOU, look at what this young man is doing. He:

- **Runs the building** from 9 A.M. to noon.
- **Goes to school** in the afternoon.
- **Drives an auto** as a chauffeur at night.

Take the First Step to Your Real Estate Wealth

By now you have many of the convincing facts you need to help you decide if you want to make real estate investments your way to wealth.

I truly hope that you do decide to do this because I think your chances of success are really enormous. And you can succeed without putting up a penny of your own money, if you use my ideas!

Since I'm so dedicated to helping you succeed quickly and easily, I am giving you hundreds of easy-to-use ideas in this book. You'll find these ideas in the how-to chapters that follow this one. These chapters show you how to build your real estate fortune in the shortest time possible and with the most fun—using borrowed money to get started and to continue your wealth-building!

Naturally, I can't guarantee the results. But I am so convinced that you will earn big money in real estate that I am ready to help you in every way possible. By this I mean that I will:

- **Answer any letters** you write to me as soon as I can.
- **Talk to you on the telephone** when you call me, answering you on the first ring when you call.
- **Give you information** that you seek—if I have it.
- **Try to find** one or more lenders for you.
- **Supply you** with information on my books, newsletters, and courses, which are designed to get you ahead faster in this great real estate business.
- **Meet you** in New York City, or in your area if I'm there on a business or seminar trip, if you can spare the time to talk to me.
- **Visit you** in a large city near you if you are a 2-year, or longer, subscriber to one of my newsletters.
- **Serve as a private lender advisor** on your real estate project if it has promise from a "numbers" standpoint.

None of the above will cost you a penny, if you exclude the cost of the postage stamp or telephone call. And if you don't have the postage stamp or the money for a phone call, I will send you a stamp—and then you can call me on my toll-free number, if I suggest that you do so. While it is not necessary to do so, I truly hope that you will read my newsletter, *International Wealth Success.* I have been publishing it for years, and it has helped many Beginning Wealth Builders around the world get started in earning money from income real estate. For more information, see the back of this book.

Again, it is not necessary that you read the newsletter to get advice from me. But I must admit that I believe my newsletter readers are better able to use my advice than are people who have not followed my ideas for a number of months.

Further, since my Newsletter subscribers are my paying customers, I do—naturally—give them preference when it comes to answering real estate business questions and on matters concerning private lenders.

Your Keys to Real Estate Riches

- ❑ **Real estate is a borrowed-money business;** as such, it is an ideal business for Beginning Wealth Builders (BWBs).
- ❑ **There is plenty of loan money** around for good real estate deals. You can make some of this money yours if you look for it and apply using a well-prepared business plan for your real estate purchases.
- ❑ **It is almost impossible to fail** in well-located real estate; you can earn money from a well-located piece of property for as long as you live.
- ❑ **There are many tax advantages** available to people who own real estate; all or almost all of the income from your real estate can be completely free of income taxes for many years.
- ❑ **There are plenty of people** in the real estate business who are willing to help you when you are starting.
- ❑ **These days, real estate is probably the safest business** for you to build your fortune in—quickly and with lots of fun.
- ❑ **Real estate is booming almost everywhere in the world today;** you would be foolish now if you did not take advantage of these boom times to build your fortune in real estate quickly and easily, using borrowed money.
- ❑ **You always have a friend** in me—Ty Hicks—if you just ask for help! I'm ready to help when you need help!
- ❑ ***YOU CAN USE BORROWED MONEY*** to build your real estate fortune quickly and easily!

CHAPTER 2

How to Base Your Real Estate Riches on Borrowed Money

TODAY THERE ARE THREE TYPES OF REAL ESTATE PROPERTIES YOU CAN invest in to make your millions:

1. **Residential properties.**
2. **Commercial properties.**
3. **Industrial properties.**

We will consider each of these in a section of this book. In this chapter we will talk about residential properties, such as apartment houses, duplexes, triplexes, fourplexes, garden apartments, etc. The important point to remember about residential property is that you are renting it to people who are living in the property as their home.

Dozens of residential properties can be taken over by you with zero, or very little ($100 or so), of your own cash—that is, with borrowed money. Let's see how—right now. Truly, you ***can*** borrow your way to real estate riches in residential zero, or very low-cash, properties!

"How can residential property make me rich?" you ask.

- **Because more than 5 million families** seek a new or different home each year.
- **Hence, there is an enormous and growing market** in residential properties of all kinds.

- **The home people seek** today might be an apartment, a single-family residence, a condo, a co-op, or a furnished apartment.
- **But regardless of what type of home** these 5 million+ families are seeking, there are only about 4 million new units built in a typical year!

Thus, there is a shortfall of some 1 million units per year. So you can easily see that apartments and homes are in great demand. And this demand continues to rise each year as more families are formed, people move to other areas, and people enter the United States from other countries. This is why you can make millions in residential income real estate property, using borrowed money to start and expand your holdings. Everyone needs a home!

Know Why Income Real Estate Is So Good for You

In the recent past, we figured the average apartment in a large city would bring in $500 per month in rent. Today, the average large-city apartment brings in considerably more than that. For example, here are a few rents I have seen in just the last few weeks:

- **An ordinary three-room apartment,** $1,800 per month.
- **A "swinging" area studio apartment** (2.5 rooms), $2,500 per month.
- **A four-room apartment** in an upper-middle class area, $4,000 per month.

Thus, my good friend, the day of the $500-per-month apartment is basically gone in many large cities. Today we should figure on at least an average of $1,000 per month. What does this mean to you?

Higher rents mean you can build your riches faster! Yes, I know that all costs related to a building have risen. Fuel, labor, insurance, and repairs all cost more. But all these expenses are provable and tax-deductible.

As the rents for residential real estate rise, your income will almost always increase. In many desirable large-city areas of the country, it is basically impossible to find an attractive apartment or home at a rent of $1,000 or less per month. You may find this situation a turnoff, but this is what is happening in the world of residential real estate today. I want you to take advantage of this situation.

> **So recognize, here and now, that the rent numbers of residential real estate have changed. And I am delighted to say they have changed in your favor!**

Let's see how you can start building your millions in residential real estate on borrowed money, starting right now.

Pick the Location for Your Future Properties

Your first step in making your millions in residential income property is to decide where you want to have your real estate property. A delightful aspect of real estate is that you can own property either in a local area or in a distant city or town. It really makes no difference so far as your income is concerned. Why is this?

Because income property is much the same, no matter where it is located—be it in New York, New York, Dubuque, Iowa, or San Francisco, California. People will happily rent, and pay for, clean, neat apartments. And if you attract families with two or three children, families in which the husband is at least a sub-professional, you will probably keep them as tenants for many years. Such tenants regularly pay their rent on time and do not give you any problems.

Let's start you with local properties in the area in which you live. We'll talk later about distant properties and how you can invest in them.

Local Properties Are Ideal for Beginners

I strongly recommend that for your first few properties you pick buildings near you. Why? Because then you can watch them as time goes on to see and learn about the typical problems you will meet. You will also learn how to solve these problems so you can apply the methods to buildings far from you at a later date.

It's easy to pick properties near you. Just read the Real Estate Section *For Sale* ads in your local Sunday papers to see what is available. Make a list of :

- **Typical prices.**
- **Cash down payment.**
- **Income.**
- **Expenses of these properties.**

You can get this information by calling the seller or by asking the real estate broker who is selling the property to provide you with an Income and Expense Statement for the property. By preparing a simple Summary Sheet, such as that shown in Table 2.1, you can become a local expert for income properties in your area. With this information in hand, you can easily judge how much money you will earn from a potential income residential property that you might buy.

If you are thinking of investing in distant properties, you can construct Summary Sheets, similar to Table 2.1, for them. Construct these in the same way—by getting information from the seller or from the real estate broker handling the sale of the property. Start with a few properties close to you and then you can, within six months to a year, branch out to distant properties should you desire to do so.

Figure What Down Payment You'll Need

"How much of a down payment will I have to make?" you ask. The amount of money you may be asked to put down on a property can vary

Table 2.1
Summary Sheet

Property Name	Price ($)	Down Payment Asked ($)	Annual Income ($)	Annual Expense ($)	Annual Debt Payment ($)	Annual Profit ($)
State Street	150,000	30,000	24,000	12,000	9,000	3,000
Bay Avenue	325,000	60,000	45,000	20,000	18,000	7,000

from as little as nothing (zero cash) to as much as 29 percent of the asking price. (The reason why people ask 29 percent of the selling price is to come within the IRS guidelines for an *installment* or *time sale.*)

Take my advice: Use my ideas and you will put down either zero cash or very little money (about $100.) Why do I suggest that you put down zero cash or just a few hundred dollars? For a number of proven reasons, including these:

- **Putting zero cash down** forces you to work harder to make your real estate business succeed.
- **Working harder** improves your chances of success in your real estate business.
- **With zero money down,** you leverage your time or money (or both), allowing you to get a more profitable property.
- **Zero money down forces you** to learn more about the income property business because you are compelled to be creative.

Compute Your Needed Starting Cash

Figure out how much money you can or should put down on your first property. To do this, take these five lucky steps. They will work for any type of residential income property, from a duplex to a building having 100 or more units. Your steps are:

1. **Count up** how much money you have available.
2. **Study your Summary Sheet** of available properties to see if the amount of money you have is in line with the asking down payment in your area.
3. **If you do not have any money,** try to take over a property for zero cash down.
4. **Even if you have enough money** for a down payment, try to get the seller to reduce his or her asking down payment, so you conserve your cash.
5. **Negotiate as much as you can.** Keep talking until you get an agreement on the down payment (be this zero cash down or an acceptable sum for you).

Money in hand gives you power! Knowing how much money you can put down places you in a power position. Why? You, and only you, know how much (or little) money you have to put down on the property. The seller does not know. So the seller is working from an unknown position, whereas you know all about the deal.

To build your wealth in real estate on borrowed money, follow this rule which works everywhere in the world:

> **Keep your down payment as close to zero as you can on every property you buy. Allow the seller or the mortgage lender to put as much money into the property as possible. By keeping your down payment as low as possible, you increase your leverage enormously.**

And apply my Success Rule for every property you buy, namely:

Never pay all cash for any piece of income property.

You can, if you wish, pay all cash for your home because you want to get away from the monthly mortgage payments. Doing this will give you more time to think about your real estate business. But do ***not*** ever pay all cash for an income property. It ties up too much of your money. Let another person or lender put their money into the property! That's how you can get rich in real estate on borrowed money.

Many of my readers get their first few properties with zero cash down. How do they do this? By:

- **Analyzing** their cash situation so they know exactly how much money they have (or do not have) for their future real estate investments.
- **Recognizing** they have to get property for zero cash down because they don't have much cash.
- **Studying** their Summary Sheet for their local area and deciding that some properties could be obtained for ***zero money*** down.
- **Reviewing** their Summary Sheet for other local properties. Some required ***very little*** money down.

- **Negotiating** with different owners to the point where some of them agreed to allow you to take over their properties for zero money down. Most such sellers are elderly and are anxious to move to another area.

Thus, as you can see, the three keys to getting residential income real estate for zero cash down are to:

1. **Do your best** to analyze the seller's situation. Put yourself in the seller's place and try to understand why he/she wants to sell the property.
2. **Work to give the seller** what he or she desires, provided the deal can be done on zero cash from you.
3. **Try to give the seller** the asking price, a higher rate of interest, large monthly payments, or any other "sweeteners" while reducing your down payment to zero.

Keep in mind at all times that the most a seller can say is ***no!*** But even after a seller says no, you may find that the seller calls you a few weeks later to say yes! This happens again and again. Never be afraid to negotiate! It will eventually pay off in big savings to you.

Negotiate Your Way to Success

Here are some letters I've received from readers telling how they bought income real estate for zero cash down:

Four Properties with Zero Down

"In the last 3 months I bought 4 properties with zero cash down and received several thousands back at closing on each one. I now have assets totaling over $1 million and a net worth of $360,000. I could not have done it without the information in your books. I no longer work my job. I stay at home with my wife and teach my kids." —Missouri

Two Properties for $100 Down

"I would like to let you know that I will be acquiring two properties this week (August 11) for a low down payment of $100 because of the advertisement I placed in the July issue of 'IWS.' Last month I bought two older doubles for zero down payment. I have read three of your books and they have helped me to gain a lot of knowledge about real estate. And the 'IWS' newsletter has been a tremendous help also. I can now start working for myself and stop working for other people. Thank you again for your help. —Illinois

So, it does pay to negotiate! The above reader, by the way, is a woman in the Midwest. So you see it really does not make any difference whether you are a man or woman; you still can make a fortune in real estate starting with zero or very little cash.

Again, a reader writes:

Second Home with Zero Down

"I just bought a second home with zero cash down (thanks to your information) after a number of people told me 'No way.' I haven't even closed yet and the value has already gone up about $10,000. I've enjoyed your books very much and hope to make great use of them in the immediate future." —Texas

So you can see that it is possible to negotiate your way to a zero (or nearly zero) down payment. Truly, it can be done!

Bootstrap Your Way to Real Estate Ownership

You'll often hear the word ***leverage*** when people talk about real estate. ***Leverage is the use of a small amount of money to control a large amount of value—that is, money.***

Thus, if the reader in the above example took over a building worth $50,000 for $100, her leverage = $50,000/$100 = 500 to 1. This means that this BWB is controlling $500 of real estate value for every $1 she invests. This is excellent leverage.

But when you borrow your down payment, or when you do not put any of your own money down on a real estate property, your leverage is infinite! The reason for this is that any number—such as the $50,000 in the above example—divided by 0 is infinity. This is why I recommend that you try to get real estate property for zero cash down, or for as little money down as possible.

Money you borrow for real estate using the property as collateral is called a ***mortgage.*** A mortgage is one of the oldest types of loans used in the world today. We won't go into the history of mortgages because it will not help you get the loan you seek.

But knowing that millions and millions of people have successfully borrowed money on mortgages should make you more certain that you, too, can get the mortgage you seek. And you should try to get your property with zero money down, or as little as possible down—and preferably with none of your own money!

REMEMBER: Try to get into every income property with zero cash. Then your potential for rapid growth will be enormous!

Leverage has been used for centuries in real estate. You can use it also—if you set your mind to doing so. I will continue to give you other real-life examples of the actual use of leverage for various types of properties as we move through this book. Be sure to keep an eye out for them.

Find Rental Income Assistance Everywhere

While you may not like to hear this from me, you ***do*** need a real estate attorney and an accountant for every one of your real estate deals. The help and advice you get from these professionals need not be expensive. You can easily hire a good attorney and a good accountant on an hourly basis. Be sure to use their advice in all your real estate deals. You will have fewer problems and you will sleep better!

IMPORTANT SUCCESS TIP: ***When you cannot afford to pay a real estate attorney and an accountant while you are working on your first few properties, give them a "piece of the action." To do this you give each a 2 percent or 3 percent ownership in the property. Then all your legal and accounting services will be free of any cash outlay.***

Be sure to get an attorney and an accountant who have experience in income real estate. The reason for this is that such people can give you a great deal of help in a short time. They can become your "college professors" of income real estate!

Remember this: Take my advice here and now. Do not enter a real estate deal of any type unless you have:

- **An experienced attorney** who knows real estate and who has your future well-being and safety in mind.
- **A competent accountant** who believes in what you are doing and who knows real estate.
- **Specific goals and a clear plan** of where you want to go with your real estate investments.

Begin Your Income Real Estate Ownership Journey Now

You have now reached the point in your real estate education where you have three favorable factors working for you:

1. **You have contacted good professionals** to guide you in your investing from the legal and the profit-making aspects—both of which are important for your future.
2. **You have prepared a comprehensive Summary Sheet** of properties available in your area.
3. **You have developed the motivation** to try to get your first property for zero cash or very little money down.

Having prepared yourself this well, it should be easy for you to take over your first property. ***Do not be frightened.*** Many BWBs become nervous when they come face-to-face with their first deal. This is not the time to get nervous!

(As an aside, let me say that many real estate investors start to worry when faced with a new investment opportunity. Welcome such worry. Why? Because worrying about a new real estate deal alerts you to the pluses and minuses of the transaction and prevents you from making serious mistakes!)

With a carefully picked income property, it is almost impossible for you to lose money on it. Also, if you cannot pay for the property after you buy it, the lender can always repossess it and you will be freed of the burden of having to pay for it.

But I do not want you to ever have a property repossessed. If you follow my rules, you will never get into this situation! Taking over your first property involves these five simple steps:

1. **Make an offer on the property.** If the seller wants cash, offer the asking price for the property but zero cash down. You can also offer to pay a ½ or 1 percent higher interest rate on the mortgage if the seller is holding (that is, giving) the mortgage and is willing to sell for zero cash down.
2. **Negotiate with the seller to get what you want**—namely, as low a down payment as possible—preferably zero cash—and as long a duration for your mortgage as possible. Keep plugging away at the price that you want and the zero cash down payment you seek from the seller. Do not give up!
3. **Get one or more lenders** who might give you the mortgage on the property if the seller does not plan to hold the mortgage. Having these lenders ready in advance can make your deal go through faster. It can also save you money if one lender will make a loan at a lower rate than the seller is seeking. Having a second lender ready to work with you can make the seller more eager to put through a deal with zero cash down.
4. **Have your attorney and accountant** ready to work with you on the deal. Don't wait until the last minute when they may be busy on other deals and unable to help you.

5. **Try to have the deal go through as quickly as possible.** This way you will have less time to be scared! Also, there will be less time for the seller to change his or her mind.

Stay Focused on Your Plan

You are trying to become a professional real estate investor. And you can easily do this if you prepare yourself, just as an athlete prepares for a big event. Since taking over your first property (or any property) is a big event in your life, you should be ready for it.

Keep your main goal—taking over the property for zero cash or as little money down as possible—in mind at all times. To accomplish your goal:

- **Be sure the seller understands** that you want the property for zero cash or very little money down.
- **Do not go to the first meeting** for the sale of the property and have the deal fall through because the seller suddenly finds that you want to pay less cash than he/she wants.
- **Avoid wasting your time** and that of everyone else at the meeting by not having your goal fully explained to the seller.

My goal is to make you the best real estate investor anywhere! And I think I can do this by giving you specific ideas to show you what steps have proven to be helpful to BWBs everywhere. For instance, here are seven letters BWBs sent me:

Take Over Property and Get Cash for Yourself, Too!

"Less than two weeks ago I closed on my second investment property, 45 days after closing on my first one. Using 100 percent financing (zero cash) enabled me to cash out $5,010 at closing with zero cash down. Enclosed is a copy of my mortgaging-out check from the attorney for $5,010.89. In addition, I received favorable financing from the seller, who took back an assumable Second Deed of Trust at 10 percent interest, 30-year amortization, with a 5-year call. I also have the first option to purchase the note and/or sell the note. Thank you, Mr. Hicks. I am growing as a BWB." —Virginia

Multiple Career Success in Real Estate

"I'm a veterinarian, rancher and mother of four sons. I invest in real estate and have done one major development. I have managed to take my Net Worth from $200,000 to $2 million in six years, despite losses in livestock and agriculture." —New Mexico

33 Rental Houses as a Side Hobby

"I have purchased all your books through the years. I'm in full agreement with everything you write regarding the ability to accumulate wealth with rental property. We have 33 rental houses as a side hobby while enjoying an excellent professional career. I know of no other business where the risks are low, the rewards great, and there is plenty of time to be with the family for vacations and social activities. Keep up the good work!" —Michigan

Full-Time Jobs and Five Rental Units

"As a small investor, my wife and I have full-time jobs as well as owning five rental units. We would like to expand this to make it a full-time endeavor for both of us. We have done well on our rentals and have a monthly positive cash flow of about $1,000." —Ohio

Fresh Out of College, Gets His Start in Real Estate

"I graduated from college in May and spent almost a month looking for a job. Then I went to the library and started reading a book a week. I picked up your 3-Year book and was impressed. I bought a 4-plex with no money down. After paying a manager, I make about $200 a month from the property. Now I'm getting a 7-unit building." —Arizona

Townhouse with No Money Down

"I just bought a townhouse with none of my own money. But I needed to have 5 percent down. I bought the townhouse while it was being rented out for $685 per month. Right before closing I took one of my credit cards and took a cash withdrawal for the down payment and it worked great! The rent pays for the mortgage, condo fee, property manager, taxes, and—of course—the monthly credit card payment and I have a positive cash flow of $68 per month. When the credit card is paid off I will be in clover." —Pennsylvania

Zero Cash Down While in Prison

"As you can see from my letterhead, I am in prison—incarcerated as they say. I will be released in November of

> this year. I recently bought, and read your book, How to Make Millions in Real Estate in Three Years Starting with No Cash. I have always wanted to buy real estate and make a good profit. My wife and I just bought our first home. We bought a one-family unit valued by the County at $93,000. We got it for $79,000 with zero cash down, with the owner holding the note at 6.25 percent. Not a bad deal. My credit is way less than perfect. Now I'm considering buying a few foreclosed properties."
>
> —New York

As the letters above show, ***you can buy income propery for zero cash down!*** Plenty of people do it every day of the week. And right now is the time for you to start!

Manage Your Holdings for Maximum Income

When you buy a piece of income real estate, you must go through what is called the ***contract*** and ***closing*** steps. These two steps are called the ***passing*** in some states. Both these steps are easy for three reasons:

1. **Your work** is little more than showing up and having your papers ready.
2. **Your attorney and accountant** will know exactly what to do and will give you this information.
3. **The average contract signing** will take only about one hour of your time. The average closing will take about 1.5 hours. So you will invest about 2.5 hours, during which your attorney will be present to tell you which papers to sign and to explain the various details of the contract signing or closing.

Since the contract and closing stages are so routine in the purchase of income real estate, I am skipping the details here. Also:

- **Your attorney will be at your side** to explain every step in the process, should you ask.

- **Your attorney can explain** what's going on much better than I can. So I am sticking to the business and cash flow aspects of your income real estate deals in this book.
- **Your attorney is an expert** on the legal aspects of your transaction. And your book's author is an expert on the business and cash flow aspects of your income real estate investments.

After you buy your income property, you will probably receive some rent security deposits. These can range from $1,000 for a small property to as much as $50,000 or more for a large property. But you are not allowed to spend these security deposits; instead, you must keep them in a bank account where they are safe and secure for your tenants.

You can, if you wish, transfer your rent security deposits to another bank that might be more inclined to grant you a loan to improve the property you just bought. If you shift your rent security deposits around—a procedure which you are entitled to follow—you will probably learn this fact:

Most bankers are glad to take care of those customers who do business with their bank. So you may find that transferring your rent security deposits to your bank will get you more attention and larger loans than you have ever had.

To make your income real estate property earn a profit for you, take these easy steps:

1. **Take immediate action to clean up the public areas**—lobby, halls, yard, etc. Unkempt and neglected public areas will turn off prospective tenants and may cause your present tenants to move elsewhere. Most public areas can be cleaned up for $100 or so.
2. **Have a contractor paint the exterior of the building,** where needed. It is amazing how cheaply a building can be made to look new, neat, and clean by simply applying one coat of a good grade of paint. Many owners report that painting the exterior can halve your vacancy rate. (The usual average vacancy rate is 5 percent; many buildings operate with 0 percent vacancy.)

3. **Clean and paint the interior halls of your building,** if paint is needed. Use a bright color so you do not have to use large electric bulbs to light the halls. Switching the paint color can reduce your electric bill. And a light-colored paint does not cost any more than a dark-colored one! (Many 100 percent occupied buildings are painted a light color on both the inside and outside. Lots of owners find this really pays off.)
4. **Visit and inspect each apartment in your building;** offer the tenants in the apartments that need work the right to do minor cosmetic repairs with materials supplied by you. Using this approach, you will often find that tenants are delighted to clean up their apartments using your materials. Since the materials normally cost only about one-third of the total job of painting, carpentry, repairs, etc., you will be saving two-thirds of the cost. Meanwhile, you will find that most of your tenants happily accept your offer to supply the materials.
5. **Inspect the other parts of your building that may need work**—roof, basement, windows, wiring, etc. I suggest that you employ off-duty police officers and fire department personnel for these jobs. You will find they do good, honest work for about half the usual cost.

Increase Your Profits from Every Property

Having made the improvements suggested above (which will take about two months), you are ready to raise the rents in your building. Here are a few guidelines I find work well in all types of apartment houses:

- **Tune in to today's economy** by ridding your mind of ancient rent guidelines. Rents have risen enormously! Be sure you raise your rents to reflect the increases that have taken place.
- **Never be afraid of losing tenants.** You can always rent an apartment to someone else.
- **The bottom line always is:** You ***must*** make money on the property; otherwise you will have to get rid of it. So you must take action to raise the rents as soon as possible.
- **Your tenants will usually be willing to pay higher rents** if you improve the property. Thus, their sympathies will be with you when you take steps to improve your building.

- **Be certain you know the numbers** (income, expenses, profit) of your buildings before you raise any rents.
- **Make careful computations** so you're sure that the increases cover all your expenses and give you a profit and positive cash flow (PCF). Never support a building by putting cash into it each month.

Learn All You Can about Your Holdings

During your early days as a BWB—when you first take over an income property—particularly a residential one—there is a period during which you are getting comfortable with your property. Here is what I mean by "getting comfortable:"

- **Happily (we hope) or unhappily (we hope not)** you are learning the truth about the building (this is usually somewhat different from what the seller might have told you).
- **During your visits** to your building (and you will make many visits at the start), try hard to get to know your tenants.
- **The actual expenses** of your building will become clearer to you because you're paying the bills! These expenses may be somewhat different from what the seller told you—they may be more, or they may be less than you were told. Usually, they'll be more!
- **Your income and expense calculations** show you changes to make to improve your income from your building.

You will find the "getting comfortable" time is longest with your first building. Why is this? Because you are learning a great deal, as listed above. For your second and future properties, you will feel comfortable sooner.

Take my advice: ***for your first property, take your time to get comfortable with it.*** If you rush this process, you may find you do not learn as much as you should about your building. After you are comfortable with your building, you are ready to expand your real estate holdings, should you wish to do so. Here's how you can do this:

The proven method for making money in real estate is with large holdings. Why is this? Every rental unit (such as an apart-

ment) you control in a residential income property gives you a certain profit per month. So, to increase your profit, you have to acquire more rental units. And it follows that the more rental units you have, the higher your positive cash flow and profits.

Real-Life Examples of Fast Buildup of Ownership Assets

Here are seven real-life examples of building wealth in residential real estate. But before you read the letters below,

REMEMBER:

- **Once you have your first building,** you are in an excellent position to get the second, third, fourth, or more.
- **Your first building is an "asset."** This asset will be valuable. It will show on your financial statement as an asset that is worth money.
- **Every asset you own** will make it easier for you to get money for your second property, your third, or more.

Now here are seven letters showing how BWBs are building wealth today in residential buildings.

Zero-Cash Takeover of a 38-Unit Building

"I just got my loans. It took only three days to get $20,000. I combined four $5,000 property improvement loans on a building I don't even own yet. I took over a $200,000 38-unit apartment building and borrowed the down payment. The cash flow pays all the loans, too. By carefully timing the close of escrow, pro-rations of rents and payments, I walk away with $3,000 cash and a building! I'm putting students and alcoholics to work as apartment managers, painters, carpet layers and plumbers. And I'm giving Senior Citizens a good place to live. I'm thrilled and delighted." —California

100 Percent Financing of a Duplex

"We have 100% financing for a duplex priced at $179,900. We have an 80% first mortgage at 7.25% and a 20% loan [second mortgage] at 12.875%. The seller is in a hurry because he wants to move to a dryer climate." —Oregon

Investor Loan for Zero Cash Down

"Thank you for your publications. I subscribed to your IWS Newsletter in November and bought my first income property, a duplex, with no money down the same month. I got an investor loan from a Savings Association and the seller paid all closing costs and took back a second mortgage for the balance of the purchase price. This duplex gives me about $100 per month profit after the two mortgage payments and all expenses. Not bad for no cash investment of my own. Now this same property owner wants to sell me four other properties under the same terms. I'm on my way to building my wealth in real estate!" —Florida

Zero Cash Works Again and Again

"I have read several of your books and have been most impressed by your methods. I did start investing in rental real estate and purchased a total of 33 units the first year with just $10,000 borrowed from the bank. We did—of course—put some of our profits back into these purchases before we were through acquiring the first 33 units. Most of these properties are single-family homes. I do have one duplex, one triplex and one 5-unit apartment building." —Colorado

Big Value on Little Cash

"In the past six months we have purchased four pieces of real estate totaling $2,650,000 in value for $4.00 down payment—$1.00 on each deal. While not exactly zero cash, it comes close to it." —Canada

100 Percent Financing of a Flip House

"As a BWB following your expert instructions, I just closed on my first income property—a 5-bedroom Victorian single-family dwelling in surprisingly good condition. The seller agreed to hold a second mortgage for $11,000, including interest and $24,000 was financed through a mortgage company, giving me 100% financing! The house is currently rented and the rent covers both first and second mortgages. I plan to renovate the house which could bring the house to $80,000. I'm already working on a similar deal on another house—can't stop now!" —Virginia

More 100 Percent Financing for BWBs

"Five months ago I bought a house with 100% financing. I got lucky. After going to several banks, none wanted to loan me the money I needed because I was self-employed. By luck I found a broker who was advertising 100% financing. They gave me an 80/20 loan for the first and second mortgages. I bought the property below market value. I now have $50,000 equity in the property." —California

How to Acquire More Residential Income Properties

To acquire your second residential income property, follow the same steps you did for your first purchase of income property. The five steps are:

1. **Start by preparing a Summary Sheet** of offerings in your area. You can also refer to your earlier Summary Sheet to see if it has good properties still remaining in it.
2. **Get out and visit the buildings** that interest you. Carefully inspect each. If you feel at all doubtful about a building, but think it would be a good buy, get a building inspector to go through it with you. This will cost you a few dollars, but it is worth it.
3. **Keep looking until you find** the building you want. Negotiate to take it over for zero cash down. Concentrate on deals in which there has been some kind of loss—divorce, death, or illness in the family owning the building. You will find many buildings in such families are often available for no or very little money down.
4. **When you cannot buy a building for zero cash down,** try to borrow the required down payment. When you list your first building as an asset on your financial statement, you should be able to get a loan for a large enough down payment for your second building.
5. **Use the services of your attorney and accountant** to guide you on the takeover of your second building.

Once you have your second building, you'll find you are much more relaxed than you were with the first. Why is this? Because you learned many valuable lessons from your first takeover. Likewise, the same will be true, of course, of your third, fourth buildings.

"Mud Flats" Can Be Money Machines

Daily, on my way to my New York City office, I pass a group of residential buildings that are sometimes called "mud flats." The owner of these buildings never refers to them as his mud flats. Instead, he calls them his rental income "money machines." His 1,000 apartments in these money machines each give him a Positive Cash Flow income of

$300 per month, ($300,000 per month). And—I'm sure—he is eating very regularly!

"But," you say, "I don't want to take over as many as 1,000 rental units. Just 100 units at $300 per month each will give me an income of $30,000 per month. That's enough for me because the yearly income (before expenses) will be 12 × $30,000 = $360,000! I don't need any more income than that!"

That's fine with me, your friend, Ty Hicks. All I want for you is a good, dependable income from your real estate. And that income should be large enough so you can have all the good things you want in life.

Expand Your Ownership to Larger Properties

You have an unlimited potential, good friend, in what you can do in residential income real estate! For instance, you can start with single-family units, as many of my readers have. Or you can start with 10-unit buildings. Either way, you can earn an excellent income every month of the year.

Given this, here's what—as your good friend—I want you to do:

- **Get out a pencil and piece of paper** and write down what you want in life.
- **Specify the exact income you want**—a net income of $8,000 per month, $15,000 per month, or $90,000 per month, for example.
- **After you decide** exactly how much income you want from your residential real estate, convert this into the number of rental units you need.
- **Do this by dividing** your desired monthly net income by the amount of Net Positive Cash Flow you can expect from each rental unit in your area of the country. A good number for most areas today is $100.
- **Adjust it upwards**—or downwards—to reflect your personal experience.

Thus, in rural areas, the $100 might be accurate. But in large-city areas the number might more accurately be $200—or even $300—per month. Use your knowledge of your area to choose your number!

The \$100 number is suggested because by using it you will be on the safe side. It will give you a result that will probably show a higher number of rental units than you actually need. So if you acquire the number of rental units indicated by dividing by \$100 per month, you will have an income higher than you expected! And—good friend—I'm sure you won't criticize me for this. Now, let's see how this might work for you.

You want, we'll say, a net income of \$10,000 per month, or 12 × \$10,000 = \$120,000 per year, from residential income property you will rent to people. Exactly how many rental units do you need to obtain this net income?

Trusting me, and using the above rule of thumb, you figure the number of rental units you need this way:

Number of rental units = \$10,000 per month / \$100 per unit = 100 units. If your average building has 20 rental units, then you will need 100/20 = 5 buildings. You can probably take over 5 buildings in about two years.

And—good friend—note that your \$10,000 net income per month is what I call MIF, "Money-in-Fist." By MIF I mean money that you can spend after paying all expenses associated with your income real estate buildings, including the mortgages. If you want to know where the \$100 per month per rental unit comes from, it is the average net profit per unit for "talking and figuring purposes" at the time of this writing. And, if in your area your units will pay a higher monthly net profit, then you'll need fewer units!

Forget "Advanced Education" for Your Success

Some people I know who have done well in residential real estate—and I know lots of them—do not have a college education. And some of them didn't even graduate from high school! Yet the lack of formal education does not seem to hold them back in their real estate activities.

This is one of the reasons I'm so enthused about income real estate of any kind. A person can come from nothing and achieve great success. And I want you to be an outstanding success in income real estate! (And—good friend—I'm not saying that you came from nothing! I'm simply urging those people who do not have much now in the way of money and hard assets to start working so they can have a real estate fortune in the near future.)

Don't let the scarcity of money worry or bother you. Just read this letter from a reader who says:

Cashing Out with $20,000 on Zero Cash Put Up

"I want to thank you for helping me get started in real estate investing. We negotiated a 3-family house purchase with the idea of fixing up and selling 2 units while holding on to the third unit. I read your real estate book and became very excited. We had no collateral and very little cash at the time. We applied to many conventional banks, private lenders and mortgage companies, using a loan package such as you recommended. (We received many compliments on the professional appearance of our package.) The purchase price was $140,000, with rehab costs of $80,000, for a total of $220,000. The seller took a $40,000 second mortgage subordinate to the rehab money and we put $5,000 down, which came from our credit card line of credit. So we needed $175,000 ($95,000 to close and $80,000 for rehab). Also, we wanted to finance our monthly expenses. Based on the market value at completion, the property would be worth $330,000. So we applied for a loan of $195,000, $20,000 more than we needed. I knew that if we applied at enough lenders we would eventually get the loan. After getting 20 rejections we finally got a commitment for $195,000—2 days before closing. In summary, we own a piece of property worth $330,000 with $90,000 equity and have $20,000 cash left to help with any expenses. One further point: I was a part-time newspaper driver. Now I am a full-time investor. Thank you, Ty!" —Massachusetts

Now what does this letter tell you about your future in income residential real estate? It tells you:

- **Zero cash deals can be done today**—almost everywhere BWBs want to invest in income residential real estate.
- **You CAN get the loan you want**—if you apply at enough lenders and do not get discouraged when you're rejected.
- **A well-prepared loan package can get positive results from lenders**—if you show your package to enough real estate funders.
- **You CAN mortgage out**—that is, get cash at the closing if you arrange your financing in advance to get what you want and need.
- **Getting know-how in income real estate** CAN pay off for you by helping you get the property you seek with the income you want.

You ***can*** earn an enormous amount of money in income real estate today. I see this every day of the week amongst my real estate friends and in my own activities. And you don't have to be a genius to earn BIG MONEY in income residential real estate today.

Start by looking for good residential properties in your area. Take action to acquire your first income property. Then go on to your second, third, fourth property. Your friend—me—Ty Hicks is here to help you every step of the way.

Quick Steps to Make Money in Distant Real Estate

"Distant" real estate is any income property more than 25 miles from your home. Why do I pick 25 miles to define distant real estate? Because:

If you must drive or travel more than 45 minutes to see and inspect your income real estate, the drive or travel becomes a chore, unless you've knowingly chosen to invest in distant real estate and have accepted the travel time as a necessity.

To choose distant real estate, use the same steps given above for local real estate. Also:

- **Try to get** distant real estate in areas offering you the type of recreation you enjoy—golf, boating, hiking, swimming, etc. Then you'll be happy to visit your distant income properties.
- **Run the same profit numbers** for distant real estate that you do for local real estate. You should also include travel expenses to and from your distant properties.
- **Keep in mind** that your travel expenses to and from your distant properties are fully tax-deductible if you make these trips to collect rent, supervise repairs, find new tenants, for example.

You can, if you wish, make money from distant real estate. But you'll need the help of a local manager to supervise the property while you're not there.

On the plus side, you'll find that the price of distant real estate is often lower than local real estate. So your profit margin and Positive Cash Flow (PCF) can be higher with distant real estate than with local properties.

Your Keys to Real Estate Riches

- ❑ **You *can* earn a fortune** in residential real estate because everyone in the world needs a place to live.
- ❑ **Good, neat, clean housing** in apartment houses, garden apartments, and single-family homes is almost always in demand because the population is growing faster than the number of available living units.
- ❑ **Getting your first residential income property** on zero cash is easy—if you plan your moves carefully and follow the guidelines in this book.
- ❑ **Your residential income property** can either be in your local area or a distant area—it all depends on what you like to do.

- ❑ **Use the services of a competent attorney and accountant** in all your income real estate deals. The cost is nominal and you'll be protected from possible problems.
- ❑ **Don't delay your takeover deals**—work quickly. You'll get faster results and your fortune will arrive in your bank sooner!
- ❑ **Make any needed repairs** to your first income property immediately after you take it over. You can then raise rents and increase your cash flow from your property earlier than if you delay.
- ❑ **Get to know the going rents in your area.** Then raise the rents in your property as soon as you can. Clean, well-maintained income real estate commands higher rents. Be sure you get them!
- ❑ **Work hard to get your first income property** into the condition where you—and your tenants—are proud of it. Then start looking for your next property. Don't rest on your laurels!
- ❑ **Increase your income real estate holdings** until you reach an income level that meets all your needs. Keep expanding your income real estate holdings until you reach your income goals!

CHAPTER 3

Start Your Real Estate Empire Without Using Any of Your Own Cash

THOUSANDS OF REAL ESTATE BWBS CALL ME, WRITE ME, FAX ME, E-MAIL me, or visit me each year. And almost every one of these ambitious, bright BWBs has found an ideal income property they want to buy. They lack just one ingredient—that beautiful five-letter word—MONEY!

Without money, how can a BWB get started? He or she (and there are many thousands of ambitious female real estate BWBs) has to borrow the money needed for the down payment on their ideal income property. When you don't put any of your own money into an income real estate property I call it a ZERO CASH DEAL.

Defining the Zero-Cash Deal

A zero cash real estate deal is one in which you borrow money for the long-term first mortgage and for the down payment on the property. None of the money you put into the deal comes from your savings or other assets. Your down payment loan might come from credit card lines of credit, a personal loan, or a Purchase Money Mortgage (PM), which is a loan made to you by the seller.

Who Uses Zero-Cash Deals?

Zero-cash techniques are used by thousands of real estate BWBs every year. You, too, can use zero-cash techniques if you follow the advice of your author and friend—Ty Hicks. You will start your real estate empire using OPM—Other People's Money—to pay for the entire real estate transaction that will generate a monthly income for you. And you can even use borrowed money to pay the closing costs on your deal. Happily, the sources for your borrowed money are increasing in number every year! You'll find many of them later in this book.

Here's a reader's letter showing how you can build a fortune in real estate on zero cash—that is, borrowed money:

Six Houses Without a Penny of Cash

"I bought our first six rental houses without putting in a penny of our cash (I was broke, but had excellent credit and experience). For our seventh house I used $1,500 from my investment pool in the other houses to give the seller enough cash to pay her real estate agent's commission, then assumed her mortgage. We own two other investment properties and our personal residence. We haven't put a penny of our own money into any property except our personal residence. I never buy a property unless it will return 20 percent after assuming the borrowed money had been my money. Further, the property must return at least $100 per month Positive Cash Flow after all expenses, including mortgages. We live on the proceeds of our investments in a private residential/recreational community. All properties are free and clear, except about $30,000 owed on a former residence we turned into a rental. Our assets are a bit over $1 million." —Arizona

Focus on the Down Payment You Need

When you find your first income real estate project you'll note two aspects of it, namely:

1. **The property is probably in reasonably good condition.** Otherwise, you would not have been attracted to it unless you're a "builder type of person" who likes to fix up (rehabilitate—rehab for short) older properties. For the moment we're assuming you're an owner type who's interested in monthly rental income.
2. **Your future property probably has an existing first mortgage on it.** For most properties the lender will probably be glad to issue a new mortgage for anywhere from 75 percent to 90 percent of the property's selling price. So you do not have to worry about the long-term mortgage. With reasonably decent property it's easy for you to get the long-term or first mortgage. It's the down payment that challenges most BWBs.

Given that your long-term first mortgage is easy to get, your focus should be on your down payment. Why? Because:

> **If you are able to borrow the down payment for your first income property, you will have a zero cash deal! As such, you have infinite leverage, meaning that you can bootstrap yourself to wealth on zero cash!**

Use Borrowed Money to Begin Your Empire

"Then how can I get started on zero-cash deals?" you ask. The easiest way is to explore the loans that might be available to you for the down payment on your selected property because your first mortgage is readily available. If you explore the various types of loans available, you'll find that there are at least seven different types of loans you might be able to get for the down payment on your income real estate, namely:

1. **Personal loan** from a bank, credit union, or finance company.
2. **Secured loan** using stocks, bonds, or other assets as collateral.
3. **Home-equity loan** on property you already own.
4. **Credit card line of credit** on one or more credit cards.
5. **Second (PM) mortgage** from the seller of the property.
6. **Loan** from family members using a gift letter.
7. **Partner's loan** from people interested in real estate deals.

You—with my help—will explore each of these seven types of loans to see how you might use it in your wealth building in real estate. And you will succeed in real estate because it's the safest business for you to enter. Why? Because real estate has fewer failures than any other business you might start. People—and companies—all need safe, secure, heated, and air- conditioned space to live their lives in or conduct their business in. When you provide such space that's clean, neat, and well maintained, your income will be steady and rising year after year. And the value of the building you own will—in general—increase while you sleep! Could you ask for a better deal?

A reader writes, telling about her experience with zero cash for real real estate:

Two Properties on No Cash

"I read your Three Year book and thanks to you I am truly excited about my future. I am off to a slow start, but at least I got started! So far I own two properties purchased with no cash. One property is rented and the other is being fixed up getting ready to rent. I am working on another deal with money taken out of the second. It's great. Thanks again for all your help!" —North Carolina

Start with a Personal Loan

Personal loans you can use for income real estate down payment are made by banks, credit unions, finance companies, insurance companies, and other lenders. With a personal loan you do not offer any hard collateral. Instead, your signature on a promissory note, along with your credit history and expected earnings, becomes your "collateral."

Lenders use various measures to judge whether you're a good risk for a personal loan. Such measures include:

- **Income** you have from your job or your own business.
- **Credit rating**—often called your FICO® score—named for the developers of the credit rating system used to figure your score (Fair, Issac & Company, of California).
- **Payment history** you have for paying off loans on autos, home, credit cards, medical and dental, boats, for example.
- **Ownership of hard assets**—such as your home, other real estate, a boat, an airplane, business equipment, to name a few.
- **Miscellaneous financial dealings**—such as your payment records with telephone, fuel (gas, oil, and gasoline), electric and travel companies, education (school loans), or others.

Personal loans can range up to $50,000. Large loans—above $25,000—are often called "Executive Loans" because they're intended for people holding high-level positions in business. But when lenders are pushed to "put out money" as we say in our lending business, Executive Loans will be made to non-executives!

Where and How Your Personal Loan May Be Made

Your personal loan for your real estate down payment may be made at a face-to-face meeting in a bank or finance company. Or you can get a personal loan via the mail or the Internet. Almost all the lenders who formerly made personal loans by mail now do so on the Internet. Here are Web site addresses and telephone numbers of several personal loan lenders you might wish to try:

- **CitiFinancial—800-995-2274—www.citifinancial.com**
- **E-Loan Inc.—888-533-5333—www.eloan.com**
- **GetSmart—415-543-0404—www.getsmart.com**
- **LendingTree Inc.—704-541-5351—www.lendingtree.com**
- **LoansAmerica—866-577-5363—www.loansamerica.com**
- **LoanWeb—800-410-1955 Ext. 155—www.loanweb.com**
- **Wells Fargo Financial—800-346-3009—www.wellsfargo.com**

For a monthly listing of many personal-loan lenders, see my newsletter, *International Wealth Success.* You'll find full details on it at the back of this book. New subscribers are entitled to a free *New Subscribers Lender List* that I developed to help real estate BWBs.

Secrets to Getting Personal Loans More Easily

You'll use part of your personal loan as the down payment on the income real estate you buy. This will give you your zero-cash real estate. But to get your personal loan you must—in general—have a good credit rating.

Today, your credit rating will usually be expressed in terms of your FICO® Score. The three major credit rating agencies use FICO® scores, or variations of it, to rate your credit. FICO® scores can range between 350 and 850. The higher your score, the easier—in general—it is to get a personal loan.

Knowing this, you'll want to raise your score to as high a level as possible. Then you'll find that getting personal loans is much easier. To raise your credit score, take these easy steps:

Seven Steps to Better Credit

1. **Pay ALL your bills ON TIME!** Never let a bill payment be late. It can hurt your score when you have late payments.
2. **Establish a steady job, or business, history.** A long history on a job, or in business for yourself, is good for your credit score because lenders feel comfortable with long service.
3. **Do not change your street address too often.** Again, the longer you live at the same address, the better it is for your credit score. Stability and solidity are loved by lenders!
4. **Hold several credit cards.** Make payments on your balances every month—on time! Never—as we said earlier—be late.
5. **Try to keep the amount you owe**—your balance—to less than half your credit line on each credit card. Thus, if you have a $5,000 line of credit on a credit card, try to keep your balance to less than $2,500 (= $5,000/2). Why? Because lower balances look good for your score.

6. **Use your credit cards regularly.** Make on-time payments on each. Pay ahead of time to avoid mail delays and holidays.
7. **Concentrate on building your credit score** every day of the week. Good credit is one of the most important assets you'll ever have in building your real estate wealth. So guard your credit rating the same way you guard your good reputation.

Where a Good FICO® Score Will Get You Your Loan

Once you have a good credit score—a FICO® of 650 or better—start looking for your personal loan. Look for your personal loan at:

- **Commercial banks**—some offer the *2-minute loan,* the *60-minute loan,* the *anything loan,* to name a few. You get the idea—the banks want to make personal loans so they make it as easy as possible for qualified signature-loan borrowers.
- **Finance companies** are in the business of making personal signature loans to borrowers needing money for a variety of purposes—education, vacation, debt consolidation, medical, dental, or miscellaneous. Their interest rate is somewhat higher than banks but their lending criteria are—in general—somewhat less stringent than banks.
- **Credit unions** are member organizations that make millions of personal loans every year for billions of dollars. You can join a credit union free of charge in the area where you live, at the firm you work for, or at the religious group you attend. Again, credit unions are more compassionate than both banks and finance companies and may make a personal loan to you with a lower credit score than a bank or finance company will. And it doesn't cost you a dime to join a credit union! Further, credit unions often charge a lower interest rate on loans than other lenders and pay a higher interest on savings! So you win both ways when you deal with a credit union.

Use a Secured Loan for Your Down Payment

With a secured loan, you offer your lender something other than the ink on paper which is the "collateral" for a personal loan. Your secured loan pledges stocks, bonds, or other assets as collateral that the lender can attach in the event the down payment loan is not repaid. So the lender feels more comfortable making the loan to you.

If you wonder why I talk about how a lender feels about the loan he/she is making, there is a simple reason, namely:

> For a number of years I've been president, chairman, and director of a large lending organization making personal, real estate, business, and many other types of loans. Every month, at our Board of Directors meeting, we spend hours trying to figure out how we can "put out," that is, make more loans to qualified borrowers. Why? Because our largest income comes from the interest we earn on good loans we make to borrowers. And sometimes the Board hints to me that if I don't figure out how we can make more loans they'll find someone who can do this. So far it hasn't happened!

How Lenders React to Solid Collateral

When you, a borrower, go to a lender (and I hope you'll think of us) with some solid collateral, most lenders rush to make a loan to you. Why? Because we lenders know that if the loan goes bad, we can sell the collateral and get our money back. And—as you probably know—every lender loves money and wants to have every loan repaid in full and on time!

Meanwhile, of course, we're earning interest on your loan. And earning interest is our biggest goal in life, after helping our borrowers.

"But," you say, "I don't have any stocks or bonds to pledge for my down payment loan. And I don't have any other assets. What can I do?" Here's your quick, practical answer:

- **Find someone** who has suitable collateral and who is sympathetic to your real estate ambitions. This person could be a friend, a relative, or a business partner. To find such a person, sit down with pencil and paper and list friends, relatives, and businesspeople who have assets—stocks, bonds, and other holdings—you could use as collateral to get your down payment loan for the income real estate you want.

- **Contact** each "target" person who might be willing to pledge their collateral for your down payment loan. Show them a short business plan detailing how much money you need, for what purpose, and how you would repay it. If you don't have anyone you can contact, then take the next step.
- **Advertise** in local papers, newsletters, and real estate publications saying:

  Collateral needed *for real estate purchases. Will pay good interest rate. Collateral secured by well-located real estate. For info, call 123-4567 after 8 P.M. daily.*

  Show your business plan to interested investors. You may find a mentor who will fund all your real estate deals. It has happened to some BWBs I work with. And it could happen to you! You never know until you try!
- **Ask any stock brokers you know** if they have wealthy clients seeking to earn a higher return on their holdings. When presented with a good business plan showing details of your real estate business, such people may be willing to pledge their assets as collateral for your loan. The typical one-time fee for such a service is 5 percent of the face value of the pledged assets. Thus, with $100,000 pledged, the one-time fee is $5,000.

Knowing and working with thousands of BWBs, I'm convinced you ***can*** find collateral for your secured down payment loan. But you must look for it in a dedicated way. People write or call me—again and again—saying, "Hey, Ty, I found the collateral I was looking for and I did get my down payment loan! You said it would work and it really did!"

Enhance Your Credit with a Guarantor

Another way to get a secured loan is to offer a guarantor who has collateral that can be pledged. Thus, when your credit is not the strongest—with a 500 or lower credit score—you'll need help to get your secured down payment loan. You can make your credit stronger—called *credit enhancement*—by getting a person to guarantee the repayment of your loan, while pledging some type of asset to make your lender feel more secure. Thus you present a much stronger credit picture to your lender. Why?

> **Because your lender has two signatures on your loan application—yours and your guarantor's—plus a pledge of some type of asset. Your chances of getting your loan increase enormously with a guarantor. You can find guarantors using the methods given above for finding people to pledge stocks and bonds for your down payment loans.**

Use a Home Equity Loan for Your Down Payment

A home equity loan is money you borrow using your ownership portion of your home as collateral for your loan. For example, let's say you have a home with a current market value of $100,000. You owe $40,000 on your first mortgage on the house. Thus:

Market value	$100,000
Existing mortgage	40,000
Your equity = $100,000 – $40,000 =	60,000

Today, some lenders will loan up to 125 percent of your equity in your home. Thus, you could borrow:

$$1.25 \times \$60{,}000 \text{ equity} = \$75{,}000$$

Having $75,000 available for the down payment on a good income property puts you in an excellent position to get the building or land of your choice. And it allows you to get income real estate on zero cash—a method giving you infinite leverage in this great business of building your wealth in real estate.

If you don't own real estate on which you can get a home equity loan, consider:

- **Asking a relative or friend** to get a loan for you using their property as equity for the loan.

- **Asking a business associate, partner, or acquaintance** to pledge their home for your loan, rewarding them financially or in some other way they feel is worthwhile.

The good news for you about home equity loans is that we lenders love them because the real estate collateral just goes up in value as time passes. We used to lend only 75 percent of the equity in a house. But now some of us go as high as 125 percent of the equity. Why? Because:

Real estate is one of the best types of collateral for any loan. Hence, lenders love to make home equity loans on well-located real estate almost anywhere in the world.

So if you can arrange to get a home equity loan for your down payment on income real estate, go for it! Your interest rate will be lower than a personal loan and you can get a much longer term—15 years as compared to 5 years. You really can't beat real estate secured loans for down payment money!

Here's a letter from a reader showing you how powerful a home equity loan can be in building your real estate wealth on borrowed money:

Equity Loans Can Get Big Results

"Thank you for sharing your expert knowledge about buying investment property that enabled us to buy a six-family income property. We purchased this property last June by taking an equity loan of $30,000 from my Credit Union on our primary residence which is a duplex that did not require an appraisal. To get the remaining 25 percent of the $45,000 down payment needed for the purchase, we took credit card advances. We have since had an appraisal of our primary residence which we bought for $192,500 three years ago and the value came in at $275,000, allowing us to pay off the first equity loan and credit card cash advances on the new equity line of $60,000. Starting January of this year, after paying the mortgage, equity line, insurance, and allowing $300 per month for repairs, we are showing a positive cash flow of $1,200 per month, which should increase in the months ahead."

—Massachusetts

The letter you just read nicely illustrates several important principles we're recommending to you in this chapter, namely:

- **Home equity loan** for a partial or complete down payment
- **Credit card credit line** for partial or complete down payment.
- **Income from property** to pay off the borrowed money.
- **Expected increase in property value** over time.
- **A reserve for expected expenses**—$300 per month for expected (and unexpected) maintenance.

Get Property Improvement Loans for Your Down Payment

A "cousin" of the home equity loan is the Property or Home Improvement Loan. Such a loan is usually based on the equity you have in a property. And you figure it in the same way as shown above for the home equity loan.

A property improvement loan can easily give you the down payment you need for an income property you want to buy. Here's a reader letter showing how property improvement loans can be used today:

Example of Property Improvement Loans for Down Payment

"I have all your books. I'm now driving a new Cadillac and enjoying the better things of life. Several weeks ago I bought a 40-unit apartment building for $200,000 with a $20,000 down payment. I got five $5,000 36-month Property Improvement loans for the down payment. It took only three days to get the money. I'm thrilled and delighted. __________ Bank told me to bring them more professional people (like myself) and they would loan them down payments all day long. I'm getting ready to buy my second $200,000 building across the street. Many thanks for a better way of life and an opportunity to put into practice principles that really work." —California

Tap into Your Credit Card Lines of Credit

Many times readers call me to say: "I took over a 5-family income property using my credit card line of credit. I got $25,000 in credit card advances and used the money for the down payment on this income real estate. The rents pay my first mortgage, my credit card loans, and my property expenses. I have a positive cash flow of $300 a month, after ALL expenses! Thank you for showing me how to do this."

Here's a reader letter showing how credit cards are being used to acquire income real estate today:

Put Credit Cards to Work

"My wife and I started investing in income producing property about 20 months ago. Our goal has been to acquire as many properties as needed to provide a comfortable lifestyle for ourselves. Our first, and succeeding properties, have been 3- and 4-unit apartment complexes. Our total is now 10 rental units. The down payment has always been obtained from a cash advance on our credit cards. After paying all expenses, including mortgages and credit cards, we have a positive cash flow of $350 per month. This is in line with your recommendations in one of your real estate books. Thank you." —Arizona

If you were to ask me the most common source of down payment loans for income real estate today, I'd have to say it is credit card lines of credit. No other source is ever mentioned as often.

So what does this mean to you, my good BWB friend? It means you should:

Get the Credit Cards You Need

- **Check out which credit cards** you can easily qualify for, based on your income and your credit history. The more the better, as they say!
- **Apply at your bank** to see if they'll issue you a credit card with a line of credit of at least $5,000. Again, the higher the line of credit, the better for you!
- **Respond to any credit card solicitations** you get in the mail. Many such offers include a line of credit up to $100,000 for businesses. With such a line you can really get into big income properties.
- **Establish a company name** for your business. Then check out business credit cards. There are dozens of offers in the mail today promoting business lines of credit from a minimum of $20,000 to the current maximum of $100,000 per business. Several such business credit cards can give you a large amount of cash ready for use when the right deal comes along for you! And you don't pay interest on this available cash until you use it!

Now don't say to me, good friend, "Credit cards are OK, but the interest I'll have to pay is too high!" Not so, good friend. Remember this:

The interest you pay on credit card lines of credit is provable and tax-deductible if the money is used to produce real estate income. Hence, with your income real estate paying your credit card debt, the interest rate has no effect on you, other than to temporarily reduce your profit.

So, good friend, *go with the flow!* Get yourself credit cards that give you:

- **The highest line of credit** available from the card issuer that you can negotiate.
- **The longest payoff period** you can work out with the card issuer. Just be sure you can pay off early if you want to do so. This is important.
- **The greatest number of cards** that one issuer can give you—that is, one for you personally and one or more for your business.

Having a large number of cards may depress your credit score. But the lines of credit will make your lowered score very, very sweet! Believe me, good friend, it *does* work.

Get the Seller to Finance Your Down Payment

When an income property has been on the market for six months or longer, you will find that the seller becomes a bit anxious. He/she worries every day—wondering if the property will ever be sold.

Knowing that these forces are at work in a seller's mind can help you get your down payment financed. This relieves you of having to come up with cash. And it gives you your Zero Cash deal! Here are letters showing this to you:

Office Building on Zero Down

"I'm buying a medical office building. The owner of the property agreed to hold a second mortgage for 20 percent of the price. The lender for the first mortgage required this of me before giving me zero-cash down [no money down] financing."

—Florida

Another letter says:

Second Mortgage for Down Payment

"I just bought your book and it has changed my life very quickly. Two weeks after buying your book I was at the bank and in early February I closed on a $43,000 duplex for which the seller held a second mortgage for the down payment. The seller will be paid over five years during which I will make payments. My positive cash flow, after all payments, is $248 per month. In July I bought another duplex (closing on it on my birthday!) using your tactics. I paid $44,500 for this one which has a positive cash flow of $410 per month. I bought it about $3,000 below its appraised value. It has another shared mortgage [seller financing of the down payment] just like the first property. In December I bought a real nice duplex for $47,000 with a cash flow of $255 per month. This one I bought where the realtor is letting me make payments to her for her commission on the sale. I do not think I've done badly; I am making about $10,000 a year positive cash flow. Good renters pay me on time every month and I get top dollar rents. Thanks to you we are able to relax a little because my job is seasonal and the real estate gives us a steady income."

—Indiana

Use a "Gift Letter" for Family Loans

As I mentioned earlier, we bankers love to make loans. Why? Because that's the way we earn our money to care for our families. So we try to see a favorable aspect for every loan application.

Thus, when a borrower comes to us for a first mortgage with less cash in a checking or savings account than he/she needs for the down payment, we will often ask: "Can your parents or other relatives lend you the down payment?"

If the borrower answers "Yes," we say: "Then get a 'gift letter' from your relative saying that he/she will give you the down payment for the property." Then:

- **The gift letter goes into our records** for the loan, allowing us to make the loan when the borrower's financial statements do not

show he/she has the needed amount of cash in their savings or checking account (see Figure 3.1).
- **Then, if we're ever examined by the regulatory authorities** and they ask why we made the first mortgage loan when the borrower did not have enough cash on hand, we point to the gift letter. Such a letter is always accepted by the authorities.

(As an aside, the authorities want us to make more loans, too. Why? Because this creates jobs for *them*, giving them more lenders to check on! Get the point?)

Date: ______________

To: Bank of ______________

As parents (grandparents, uncle, aunt, brother, sister, or other relative) we plan to make a gift of $25,000 (or whatever other amount is needed) to our son (daughter, grandchild, nephew, niece, brother, sister, or other relative) to purchase the property at 123 Main Street for which you have agreed to provide the first mortgage. This gift is being made to a family member with no expectation or requirement that it be repaid.

Very truly yours,

Gift Maker

Figure 3.1 Example of a Typical Gift Letter

While I cannot say for certain, it has been mentioned to me that a gift letter has been known to be used when the buyer (called the *mortgagor*) borrowed the down payment for the property being purchased. This, of course, might cause the mortgage applicant to be turned down because all mortgage lenders want the borrower to have some investment in the property.

Many lenders will provide you with the gift letter wording they prefer. Hence, the gift letter above is given only as an example. You should, of course, use the gift letter wording your lender provides to you.

Why? Because it has been proven that when a buyer has no money invested in a property, he/she will often run away when the first serious problem surfaces. I'm sure that none of my BWBs would run—they'd stick it out!

For a gift letter to be acceptable to a lender, it must have these five features:

Requirements for an Acceptable Gift Letter

1. **The gift letter** must be signed by the person making the gift.
2. **The amount** of the gift must be stated exactly in the letter.
3. **The person** giving the gift must give his/her name, address, and telephone number in the letter.
4. **The person** giving the gift must tell what his/her relationship is to the borrower—parent, grandparent, etc.
5. **The person** making the gift must state that the recipient is not expected or required to make repayment of the gift.

While you may not have a wealthy relative who can give you a down payment gift, it is wise to keep in mind this possibility. Your partner, friend, or business acquaintance might be able to obtain such a gift to give to one of your relatives.

Why do I point this out to you, my good friend? Because we bankers want to make more loans to earn more interest so we can buy a bigger boat, play more golf, spend more time on the ski slopes, or other luxuries!

Never Overlook Possible Partners for Your Down Payment Loans

When you're starting your career in real estate, you may need help from a partner for your first few deals. Why? Because your partner can provide you with:

- **Stronger** (called *enhanced*) credit.
- **A cosigner,** co-maker, or guarantor.
- **Real estate experience** you do not now have.
- **Working capital** needed to get started in any real estate investment.
- **A shoulder to cry on** when you run into unexpected problems in real estate ownership.
- **A needed loan** for your income real estate down payment. You do the work and your partner shares in the profit while you repay the loan.

So, although you may be a loner who enjoys working alone, for your first few deals a partner may be just what you need. After all, your entire goal is to get started owning income real estate. So swallow your pride and take on a partner. It can be great! To attract partners:

- **Offer to do all the work** while sharing in the profits generated by your property.
- **Offer an "equity kicker"**—that is a small percentage of ownership in the property. Typically, you'll offer 5 percent of the ownership in the property.
- **Offer a share in the appreciation of the property** when you sell it. Thus, with a 5 percent equity kicker, your partner would receive 5 percent of the profit earned on the sale of the property.

See if You Can Get Some of Your Down Payment Back on Closing

Many of my BWB students are amazed to learn they might be able to *mortgage out*—that is, walk away with Money-in-Fist (MIF) at the closing when they take possession of the real estate they purchased.

Mortgaging Out Successfully

Mortgaging out, as it is called, can help you recover some of your down payment money. Here's an excellent example from a reader's letter:

"Thank you for your advice in your books, newsletters and kits. Last November we purchased an investment home by mortgaging out with zero cash down. The seller's asking price was $36,000. We were approved for a $40,000 loan by the bank. So we proposed that the loan be written for $40,000 and the seller would accept $32,000 for the house, giving us back $8,000, less expenses. At first the seller was reluctant but he finally consented. The bank deducted closing costs, earnest money and points from the $8,000 we would receive.
We received over $6,000 from the bank when the deal closed in December. Currently we are receiving over $1,200 per month from tenants." —Ohio

Your Keys to Real Estate Riches

- ❑ **Zero cash deals** can get you started in income real estate without taking any money out of your bank or other investments.
- ❑ **Focus on your down payment** for your income property because your long-term first mortgage is usually easy to get.
- ❑ **There are seven different types of loans** you can try to get to finance your down payment on income property.
- ❑ **Keep your credit score as high as possible** so you can get any loans needed to start your real estate investment career.
- ❑ **Good sources for your down payment loans** include commercial banks, finance companies, and credit unions.
- ❑ **Secured loans can give you down payment money** quickly so you start your career sooner and with less hassle.
- ❑ **Guarantors can enhance your credit** so it is easier to get the down payment loan you need.
- ❑ **Home equity loans** are an excellent source of down payment loans for your real estate investments.

- ❑ **Property improvement loans** can give you the down payment money you need to buy the income property
- ❑ **Use your credit card lines of credit** for your down payment loans. You never have to explain what you'll use the money for when you tap into your credit card line of credit.
- ❑ **Get the property seller to finance** your down payment. There are many different ways you can use seller financing to start your real estate investment career.
- ❑ **Seek ways to mortgage out** so you get money back at the closing. Also called a windfall, mortgaging out can put money into your pocket!

CHAPTER 4

Bootstrap Your Way to Your Real Estate Cash

WHEN I TELL PEOPLE THAT THEY CAN TAKE OVER INCOME REAL ESTATE and walk away with cash money in their pocket, they look at me as though I'm crazy. By now you may have figured out I'm really not that way! Why? Because, as you'll soon see in this chapter, it IS possible to:

- **Close** (that is, take possession of) a real estate income property and get cash in hand before you walk out the door of the closing office.
- **Take over** income real estate giving you a Positive Cash Flow (PCF) every month without using any of your own money.
- **Pay all your expenses,** including your mortgage and down payment loans, out of the income from the property.
- **Hold the property** for as long as you want while it rises in value and gives you the monthly income you seek, allowing you to sell the property at a profit in the future—should you decide to do so.
- **Shelter** most of your profits with the legitimate depreciation and expenses you are allowed to take on the property by the tax code.
- **Use the equity** (your ownership portion) in the property to get cash loans for other income property you might want to buy.

Several different terms are used to describe and define bootstrapping. Thus you'll see and hear bootstrapping referred to as:

- **Mortgaging out**—that is, you get more money from your mortgage loan than you need to take over an income property.
- **Windfall**—that is, you get cash at the closing represented by the difference in the loans you get and what you have to pay for the property.
- **Overcapitalization**—that is you, again, have more money (capital) than you need to either buy, or build, the income property you want.

No matter what you call this process, it ***does*** put cash in your pocket at the time you close on the property—that is, take ownership of the building. Once you own real estate you are entitled to "enjoy," as an attorney says, the benefits of the real estate. These benefits include both the rental income and the rise in value (appreciation) of the property as time passes.

How to Get in on Good Deals Now

"Now," you ask, "how can I get in on such windfalls and mortgage out?" Here are your hands-on answers that work—again and again. But first, here are two reader letters showing how—in a small way—you can get started mortgaging out:

Good Start at Mortgaging Out in a Small Way

"Many thanks for your outstanding books and newsletters. Because of your books I have a new outlook on life. After being disabled for 16 years I got into real estate. My wife and I now own three properties and intend to buy at least three more for each of our children. I bought one single family home with zero cash down and walked away from the closing with $600 cash in my hand. I also have a net profit of $146 a month on this rental house." —Pennsylvania

On a larger scale, a reader writes:

The Next Step in Mortgaging Out:

"I just bought a 3-bedroom house with an attached garage at 50 percent of its appraised value and cashed out $5,000 at closing. This is my fourth straight zero-cash down deal."

—Virginia

Explore the World of Real Estate Windfalls

A windfall can occur in several different ways. If you know these ways, you can be alert for them when you're considering an income property you want to buy. The ways you can mortgage out in income real estate include:

- **Buy the property** at less than the amount of the long-term mortgage you can get on the property. This can happen when the appraisal value is higher than the selling price of the property. Any excess cash is yours.
- **Get a second mortgage** for more than the required down payment on the property from a lender different from the long-term lender. Again, the excess cash is yours to use as you choose.
- **Use the rent security deposits** to improve your relations with your bank to encourage them to loan you down payment money for this, or other properties you might want to buy for income purposes. You must keep the rent security deposits in an approved savings account. But you can use the money as a powerful negotiating tool with your bank.
- **Negotiate to buy** at a price less than the appraised value of the property so that it supports a loan that allows you to mortgage out. This often happens with motivated sellers who just want to get away from the property for any number of reasons. You can take advantage of this urge and get the property at a price that allows you to receive cash at the closing.
- **Get a Purchase Money (PM) Mortgage** from the seller to cover your down payment plus any other expenses you plan to have.

These expenses can include payment for your work during the time you look for, negotiate, and analyze the property and its potential income for you.

- **Get an equity loan** on other property you own. The amount of your equity loan should be greater than the down payment you need for the property. As before, your excess is your mortgaging out cash to use as you wish. With an equity loan you do not have to tell the lender what you need the money for. Funds from an equity loan can be used for any purpose you choose, including the down payment on other investment real estate.
- **Get the first mortgage approved** and then negotiate a lower sales price. The sale goes through on the approved mortgage amount, with any excess going to you.
- **Get one or more property improvement loans** before you take title (ownership) to the property. Use these loans for your down payment on the property you want to invest in.
- **Restore a neglected property,** getting a loan to cover the restoration (also called *rehabilitation*) based on the value of the property after the work is completed. With such financing, you can often get 25 to 33 percent more than the cost of the property plus the restoration cost. See the example below for full details.
- **Develop a site with a new building on it.** Again, the money you can get can be 25 to 33 percent more than your total costs!

How Mortgaging Out Can Work for You

Mortgaging out can work in many ways for you. Probably the largest amounts of cash for you can come from building or rehabbing real estate. A reader called to tell me:

Burned-Out Building Has Potential

"I bought a burned-out building which I plan to restore. I paid $1.00 for it so you really can't call it zero cash. But it's pretty close to zero cash! Though I've never restored a building in the past, the lender I went to—which I found in your THREE YEAR book—recommended a local builder they approve of. If I use this builder to restore the building, I'll have to pay $350,000 for the property the day restoration work starts. The lender will advance that, plus $400,000 in stages for the rehab work. When the job is done—in about 8 months—the lender will advance me another $100,000, based on the rental value of the building—which will be $17,500 per month, or $210,000 per year. With a Gross Rent Multiplier of 5—low for such a building—the property will be worth 5 × $210,000 = $1,050,000. So the total money advanced will be only 81 percent of the finished value of the building. This is in line with conventional lending of 75 to 80 percent of the property value. And I'll mortgage out with $100,000 in my hand for 8 months' work! Not bad for a beginner." —New Jersey

Though inexperienced, this reader hit upon a perfect mortgaging out formula. This formula is based on the known facts about real estate construction and restoration, namely that:

- **Labor costs** rise 10 to 20 percent during building or rehabbing.
- **Materials costs** rise 3 to 9 percent during building or rehabbing.
- **Land costs** rise 5 to 10 percent during building or rehabbing.

Knowing this to be true from years of experience, lenders are willing to loan on the finished value of a project. This is where your mortgaging out cash can come from.

Use Other Rules of Real Estate for Your Mortgaging Out

There are other rules of real estate that can put money in your pocket if you prefer to deal with rental properties instead of construction or rehabs. These rules are:

- **Gross rent multiplier (GRM)**—for multi-family buildings and for office buildings—the asking price of the structure and the land it is on ranges from 3 to 12 times the gross annual rent. So if a building brings in $50,000 a year in rent, its asking price can range from 3 × $50,000 = $150,000 to 12 × $50,000 = $600,000. You can use the GRM as a negotiating point when dealing with a seller. Lower GRMs are for properties in less desirable neighborhoods or properties in a poor state of repair. Higher GRMs are for newer properties in upscale parts of town.
- **Price per square foot** for existing multi-family residential units is often in the range of $25 to $50 per square foot of net rentable area. Thus, if the multi-family building you're considering has a net rentable area—called NRA by real estate professionals—(which is the sum of the square foot area of all the apartments in the building)—of 15,000 square feet, the asking price of the building could range between $375,000 and $750,000. Again, the lower values apply to the less desirable properties, with the higher values for the newer buildings in the better parts of town.
- **Price per apartment unit** for existing multi-family residential units can range from $25,000 to $40,000 per unit in traditional living areas. (In large cities, the price per unit can go up to $50 million but we're not considering such mega-units here.) The higher values apply to better parts of a city or an area. So if you're looking at a 20-unit apartment building its price could range between 20 × $20,000 = $400,000 and 20 × $40,000 = $800,000.

How to Apply These Powerful, But Simple Rules

"Now how," you ask, "can I use these numbers to mortgage out?" Here are your answers:

- **Use the GRM when looking at multi-family residential properties**—which are of greatest interest to most real estate BWBs. Analyze the GRM to see if the property asking price is too high. In general, an excessively high asking price will make it hard for you to mortgage out. So look for properties priced between 3 and 6 times Gross Rent.

- **Compare the asking price per square foot** with similar buildings in the area in which you're planning to buy properties. Again, a lower price per rentable square foot of NRA will allow you greater leeway in mortgaging out. The key is to get property that can be upgraded at low cost to support a larger mortgage loan to put money into your pocket at the closing.
- **Analyze the price per apartment unit** compared to other buildings in the area. Be certain to compare construction of like buildings—that is, concrete to concrete or wood to wood. The lower the cost per unit, the greater your chances of mortgaging out with money in your pocket.

A reader writes with an interesting chronology of mortgaging out with a single family rental home:

Quick Use of Mortgaging-Out Rules Can Bring Profits

"Five years after emigrating to the United States I came across your book How to Make Big Money in Real Estate. Here's what happened:

Feb. 11: Finished reading your book.

Feb. 13: Made an offer for $62,000 on a single family home for which the asking price was $73,500 with an appraisal of $75,000. I asked the seller to take a Purchase Money Mortgage for 25% of the selling price ($15,500).

Feb. 14: Valentine's Day. My offer was accepted.

Feb. 15: Following your guidelines, I found an offbeat lender who agreed to loan 80% of the appraised value, or $60,000. The same lender also said he did not have any problem with the Purchase Money second mortgage.

Thanks to your books, I have my first Mortgaging Out (I call it Cashing Out) deal. I came away with $11,020 cash in my pocket after the $60,000 First Mortgage, $15,500 PM Second, and closing costs of 4 percent (= $2,480). And I will have a Positive Cash Flow when I rent the property out, after paying BOTH loans! Two highly qualified friends of mine asked me to get real estate loans for them from the same offbeat lender I used. I recommended them to my lender and he paid me a commission on both loans. So I'm now a Financial Broker, also!" —Georgia

Use Every Method You Can to Mortgage Out

The letter above shows how resourceful real estate BWBs can be. You, too, should use every method you can to mortgage out with money in your pocket. Here's another letter showing how BWBs are using real estate today to raise cash for themselves while establishing a steady monthly rental income:

Good Results in Just Three Months of Mortgaging Out

"In the last 3 months I bought 4 properties with zero cash down and received several thousands back at closing on each one. I now have assets totaling over $1 million and a net worth of $360,000. I could not have done it without the information in your books. I no longer work my job. I stay at home with my wife and teach my kids." —Missouri

Another letter says:

More Good Results—in the First Year of Mortgaging Out

"This is my first year of real estate investing and it has been a very profitable one, thanks to God, your books, courses and newsletters. From March to November, I acquired 8 houses and one building lot, all valued at $350,000, with only $650 down. At the same time I mortgaged out with $27,000 of tax-free money. Including my personal home, my real estate assets total $400,000; my net worth is $150,000 and the investment property gives me a Positive Cash Flow of $500 per month. In addition to the acquisitions, I originated and closed $145,000 in first mortgages. Thanks for your creative ideas."

—Virginia

The Powerful Methods You Can Use to Mortgage Out

"So what methods should I use to mortgage out?" you ask. Here are seven practical, hands-on methods to use today:

1. **Offer less than the appraised value of the property.** Why? Because a lender may offer to lend you money based on the appraised value of the property. You then automatically have more money than you need to buy the property. This will be money in your fist—MIF = Money-in-Fist!
2. **Get the seller to give you a Purchase Money Mortgage** for the largest amount possible for the longest term (years) you can negotiate. Why use a PM? Because you may be able to get a Zero Cash deal. With your below-appraisal price offer and your PM second mortgage, you can generate thousands of dollars of MIF on even a small property.
3. **Work with Private Lenders** who believe in creative deals. With such lenders, your credit—my good friend—is less important than your inspirational approach to the deal and your creative ideas for the property. You can call me any time you want and I'll be glad to give you a list of Private Lenders for your real estate deals—if you're a subscriber to one of my newsletters mentioned at the back of this book.
4. **Apply for the largest loan possible** for the property you're considering when contacting first mortgage lenders. Why? The extra money is always useful for your business. Further, the interest you pay is provable and tax-deductible by your real estate business.

5. **Ask for the longest term for your first mortgage loans.** The longer the term of your loan, the lower your monthly payment. With higher Money-in-Fist, you can live a better life. And you can expand your business by buying more properties, mortgaging out on them as you have on earlier properties.
6. **Ignore the negative thinkers in your life** who say "Never borrow money; the interest will "kill" you." Not so when you're in the real estate business! Everyone in real estate borrows money for *business uses* in their real estate activities. And never forget: THE INTEREST YOU PAY ON REAL ESTATE INVESTMENTS IS PROVABLE AND TAX-DEDUCTIBLE BY THE BUSINESS!
7. **Follow the Hicks principle in your real estate life, namely:** *If you can get a loan for your real estate deal that allows you to mortgage out, take the loan, even if the interest rate is high.* Why should you take the loan? See Item 6 above. Further, you can almost always refinance the loan at a later date at a lower interest rate. So the high rate is usually only a temporary condition. In what other business can you get cash in hand plus a monthly income while having fun?

Build Your Mortgaging-Out Wealth Quickly

You don't have to spend years building a mortgaging-out real estate empire. Here's a reader letter showing you what can be done in an area known for its high real estate prices:

Results of Another One-Year Mortgaging-Out Success

"I have been involved in acquiring income producing real estate for approximately one year. I have acquired over one million dollars of property with zero cash down, and have pulled a considerable amount of cash from the transactions. I work part time as a freelance advertising consultant and my wife is a university professor. I have a management company that handles the properties. All the property is currently rented, some with Lease Purchase tenants."

—California

This letter is another example of mortgaging out. As part of his letter, this reader supplied a partial listing of his properties, their value, existing loan balance, current rent, and monthly cash flow from each property.

Table 4.1 shows partial data from his listing of 11 properties that he acquired in just one year. His table lists the actual street address of each property. To protect his privacy, I've given a number to each property, instead of using its street address. I'm sure you would want me to do the same for you if you submitted such a list to me. Besides, the address of the property has little influence on the message this listing has for you.

Thus, you can see this BWB has a monthly cash flow, after paying his mortgages, of $4,518—$54,216 per year. Not bad when he got all this income for zero cash out of his pocket and "a CONSIDERABLE AMOUNT OF CASH FROM THE TRANSACTIONS!" You, too, can do much the same. Just take the steps that your good friend, Ty Hicks, gives you in this book.

Table 4.1
Property List

Property Number	Value ($)	Existing Loan Balance ($)	Rent ($)	Cash Flow ($)
1	75,000	53,600	700	388
2	70,000	53,500	900	608
3	235,000	195,000	1800	821
4	90,000	72,000	750	375
5	75,000	49,000	650	338
6	65,000	40,875	600	329
7	75,000	40,500	760	448
8	65,000	40,500	740	428
9	40,000	24,000	350	183
10	70,000	49,000	550	258
11	80,000	63,750	675	342
Totals	940,000	681,725	8,475	4,518

Know the Other Perks for You from Mortgaging Out

You have many other advantages when you mortgage out. The most important are these three:

1. **You receive a lump sum of cash tax-free.** The money you receive when you mortgage out is tax-free until you sell the property that gave you this delightful windfall. Since most income properties are held anywhere from 7 to 10 years before being sold, you have this long a time to enjoy your tax-free money. When you sell the property your mortgage-out cash may or may not be taxable. Much depends on any upgrades (new roof, new driveway, new windows, etc.) you may have made to the property. You should, of course, have a qualified CPA (Certified Public Accountant) advise you on the tax implications of your mortgaging out when you decide to sell the property. Your main thought here is that you have 7 to 10 years to use your money tax-free. What other investment can give you such an advantage—especially when you can get into it on zero cash?
2. **You get a lump sum of cash plus a monthly income** in just minutes when you close on a mortgage-out deal. *You're being paid to take over an income-generating asset!* Could anyone ask for a better deal? You become a moneyed person and an asset owner with just a few bits of ink on some pieces of paper. Truly, mortgaging out is a dream come true to many people struggling to make ends meet in a tough, downsized, reduced-in-force work world. Not to mention the periodic plunges in the prices of stocks and bonds in the stock market. You can rise above snarling bosses, layoff threats, unrealistic sales goals, for example, by becoming your own boss in the world's best business—income real estate!
3. **You immediately increase your credit score** because you go from a condition of few (or no) assets to one of major assets. Just look at the partial list of real estate assets listed in the previous letter. When you apply for additional *INVESTOR LOANS* for your real estate, the lenders will treat you with respect. And they're much more likely to say YES to your application. Why? Because you have tangible assets!

If these advantages aren't convincing enough, take a look at this reader letter:

> **Take Over an Income Property and Get Cash for Yourself, Too**
>
> "We spoke on the phone recently and I told you that your methods work! I read your books on real estate and using your ideas on no money down I bought my first property a month ago with $8 out-of-pocket expense. The $8 was a bank fee for a cashier's check for the down payment. When I went to closing the owner wrote me a check that paid me back all the money I put down—except the $8 cashier's check. And I have just purchased my second property essentially the same way. By this time next month I will have closed on 4 more properties where the owner (seller) is holding a second mortgage for the down payment. These properties will pay me $600 to $800 per month after all expenses. My goal is to own 30 properties 5 years from now. But who knows? If I can do one a month I'll have more than 60! Thanks for the great information you provide, and just as importantly, the encouragement to put my dreams into action." —Florida

Where and How to Start Getting Mortgaging-Out Cash

To get anywhere in real estate today, you must know the WHERE and HOW of what you want to do. So let's get you started on mortgaging-out cash riches right now!

Where Are the Best Places for You to Start?

"All of this is fine," you say to me. "But where and how do I start mortgaging out?" That's a good question. Here are your answers.

You can mortgage out easily in three distinct areas of real estate. This is your WHERE answer. The three areas, and the degree of difficulty for each, are:

1. **Single-family homes**—relatively easy to mortgage out.
2. **Multi-family dwellings**—much more difficult to mortgage out.
3. **Development and construction**—easy to do but takes experience.

My advice to you with respect to the steps for starting your mortgaging-out career is:

- **Start with single-family homes** when you have little, or no experience in real estate. You'll quickly get to know the ins and outs of the business and then you can move on to larger properties.
- **Consider multi-family dwellings** only after you've successfully mortgaged-out from several single-family home deals. At this stage, you'll have cash to invest and you'll have a much better understanding of how to do big deals.
- **Get one or more partners** for construction and development mortgaging-out deals. Why do I suggest you do this? Because construction and development involve larger sums of money. So you must know what you're doing. With experienced partners you can safely mortgage out with lots of cash in your pocket.

Now That You Know the Where, Go to the HOW

You now have the WHERE of mortgaging out. The HOW is five steps, given to you by your good friend, Ty Hicks:

1. **Look in your local Sunday paper's real estate section for single-family homes for sale.** In highly populated areas you'll see hundreds of single-family homes advertised. Search for ads saying "0 Down. . . ." These houses have real mortgaging-out potential because the seller is highly motivated. Some of my readers find zero-down properties the first week they look. Others have to look for 12 weeks before they find a suitable deal. And some dedicated readers look for 20 weeks before finding the deal they want. ***Remember this:*** in some sections of the country having a high divorce rate, couples who are splitting just want to get out of their monthly mortgage payment. So they'll often be glad to give

you the house or condo for zero down if you'll take over the payments. Many are bitter and "just want out," as they say. You can help them while helping yourself.

2. **Call the advertiser and get the location of the property.** Visit the property. Do what we in real estate call a "Drive By Inspection." Look at the house carefully. Really *see* the house with all its good points and its not-so-good points. Make copious notes on the location of the house, its distance from stores, schools, and houses of religious worship.
3. **Check with your local paper again to see what the typical rents are for 2-bedroom, 3-bedroom, or other houses.** Call local real estate agents to get additional numbers on rents being charged today.
4. **Work out the income you'll have from the house.** If you can't do this yourself, fax the Price, the Income, and the Expenses to your friend Ty Hicks and I'll analyze them free for you. You ***must*** have a positive cash flow from every property!
5. **Talk to the seller.** Explain that you'll have expenses when you take over. Such costs can be clean-up, painting, redecorating, ads for tenants, or other items. Tell the seller you need 3 percent of the price of the house for repairs. Ask for this amount in cash—to be given to you at the closing. Where the house is being sold because of divorce, death, loss of job, or other reason, many people will be happy to pay this amount to get out from under. This will give you your mortgaging-out cash for your single-family home which may be a stand-alone home, condo, or other home.

Try Your Mortgaging-Out Luck on Multi-Family Buildings

Here—quickly—are the five steps you can take to mortgage out with multi-family (apartment houses) buildings:

1. **Consult your local paper's real estate pages,** as given in the previous Step 1. Look for multi-family houses for sale. Don't expect to see "0 Down . . ." ads. Most such building sellers expect to see down

payments of 5 percent to 25 percent of the selling price. But don't let this discourage you! You can always wheel and deal to mortgage out.

2. **Inspect the building.** If you're really interested in the property, check the city or town records at the Building Department. Today—in many large cities—you can check these records on the Internet. For example, New York City has a web site—www.nyc.gov. Go to Services and click on Housing—which allows you to check any violations that may exist on a building.
3. **Contact the seller.** Try to work out a zero-cash deal, using the techniques and approaches given in the letters and text earlier in this chapter. Be alert for anxious or motivated sellers. Estate sellers of property are often in a big rush because the survivors want the money—not the responsibility of running a building. Point out any deficiencies in the building (almost ALL have some!) to the seller. Tell the seller you'll have to spend money to correct these problems. Use these costs as a lever to reduce your down payment and be paid cash at the closing!
4. **Be certain to have a competent real estate attorney** at your side to advise you on every step you take in getting your zero-cash mortgage-out multi-family property. Why? Because you can run into problems with motivated sellers who might want to foist a problem-ridden property on you. I can tell you lots of stories about such deals but I won't bother you with them. Just remember: ALWAYS HAVE THE GUIDANCE OF A COMPETENT REAL ESTATE ATTORNEY!
5. **Work the numbers with the seller** to get the property at the price you know can give you a Positive Cash Flow and at the same time put some money into your bank. Then manage your property carefully to give you the best return possible!

If You Have Time and Experience, Mortgage Out in Development

The way mortgaging out works in construction is based on the completed value of a project. Thus, if you:

- **Buy** land to build on,
- **Have** a building designed by an architect,
- **Develop** the land—that is, put in roads, sidewalks, sewers,
- **Construct** the building on the land, and
- **Ready** the structure for occupancy,

the finished building will be worth 25 to 33 percent more than the cost of the land, its development, and the construction cost of the building. Your mortgaging out comes from the difference between your land and construction cost, and the finished value of the building.

So, to mortgage out in development and construction takes time. The average land development and building construction time will run one year or longer.

Youthful Example of Mortgaging Out in Construction

Kemmons Wilson, the highly respected founder and chief executive of the famous Holiday Inn chain with some 1,700 inns in the United States and many in more than 50 other countries, started in business at the age of 17 with a popcorn selling machine. He then went into the pinball machine business. The profits he earned from that business were used to build a home for his mother. Building the house himself, he saved $1,700; the total cost of the finished house was $2,700. Once he finished construction, he mortgaged the house for $6,500. In essence, he mortgaged out. With the money from the mortgage he purchased a jukebox business—eventually going on to found the popular Holiday Inn chain.

For most people, development and construction require previous experience. So I suggest to you, my good friend, that you start with single- or multi-family residences to mortgage out. Once you have a few years experience you can turn to development and construction.

When that day arrives you can call me and I will gladly help you, as a mentor or advisor, every step of the way. You'll earn enough and be busy enough for several years, just with your single- and multi-family residences.

Your Keys to Real Estate Riches

- ❑ **Mortgaging out** can give you cash in hand when you close on an income property that you buy for zero cash down.
- ❑ **You can start mortgaging out** in a small way and build to greater amounts as you gain experience.
- ❑ **Mortgaging out** also has other names—including windfall and overcapitalization. But all give the same happy results—cash in your pocket on closing.
- ❑ **There are many real estate windfalls** you can enjoy when you mortgage out. It's good to get to know all of them.
- ❑ **Three good rules to use** are:
  - Gross Rent Multiplier.
  - Price Per Square Foot.
  - Price per Apartment Unit.
- ❑ **Quick mortgaging out can bring profits to you** sooner than you think but you must work at building value.
- ❑ **Use every proven method you can to mortgage out** and you'll find success faster than you might imagine.
- ❑ **Know the perks for you in mortgaging out**—they can build a great life for you and for your family.
- ❑ **Get to know the where and how** of mortgaging out. This know-how could make you rich.
- ❑ **Start mortgaging out with single-family homes.** Then go on to multi-family homes. Try development and construction later in your career.

CHAPTER 5

Use Single-Family Homes for Your Quick Real Estate Start-Up

PEOPLE CALL ME—AGAIN AND AGAIN—SAYING: "I JUST FOUND THIS BEAUTIFUL 40-unit apartment building that has an income of $230,000 a year with a cash flow of $150,000. And they're asking only $1,800,000 for it. How can I buy it, even though I have bad credit and I went bankrupt last year? And, by the way, I have only $150 cash at this moment. Please help me, Ty!"

You think I'm exaggerating? No way! Such calls come in at least once a week—sometimes much more often. Gently, I try to tell these ambitious but misinformed BWBs the facts of real estate life. Here are these facts.

Start with the Possible and Grow Bigger

Your future in real estate is better today than ever before. But you must start with the possible and grow bigger with the passage of time. To start with the possible:

- **Look for properties** that can give you a steady and stable income while not requiring a large down payment.
- **Look for properties** having government, state, and city programs that will help you with locating, financing and rehabbing (if needed).

- **Look for properties** having sources of tenants with rents paid by a government organization—national, state, county, or city.

When you look for income properties having the characteristics listed above, you'll find that almost all of them will be single-family homes. Why is this? Because many government programs:

- **Encourage single-family home ownership** because experience shows that real estate ownership is profitable for all.
- **Help first-time home buyers to get easy financing of their homes**—sometimes with zero cash down.
- **Pay the rent for low-income families** to single-family home owners who rent out their property. In several areas of the country there are waiting lists of families needing adequate housing. This means you have a waiting tenant pool to snatch your rental unit.

Know the Numbers of Your Real Estate Opportunities

Let's put this into numbers for you. As an engineer, I constantly go back to the numbers of every real estate deal. You, too, will find that in real estate, the numbers ALWAYS matter! You can't get away from easy and delightful numbers in real estate.

Thus, you should get into single-family home (SFH) real estate because:

- **There are thousands** of lenders nationwide who want to loan money on single-family homes.
- **There are dozens** of government programs for easy, quick, low-cost financing of single-family homes.
- **There are hundreds** of sources of loans for single-family homes for people with poor credit, no credit, and for first-time home buyers with no credit history.
- **There are millions** of single-family homes available for sale throughout the nation and the world.

- **There are thousands** of assumable mortgages for single-family homes with which you can take over an income-producing property with:
  - **No credit checks.**
  - **No job or business check.**
  - **No mortgage application.**
  - **No title check.**
  - **No mortgage closing costs.**
  - **No investigation of your credit history.**
  - **No problems with a previous bankruptcy.**

So you see, good friend of mine, the single-family home is the favorite of real estate lenders. You can buy and rent out dozens of single-family homes to build your real estate wealth in a relatively short time. And I'm here to help you every step of the way.

Always remember that single-family homes can be your "training wheels" for future, bigger, more profitable real estate. Every technique, skill, and ability you acquire with single-family homes can be applied—at a later date—to large multi-family deals, shopping malls, industrial parks, or office complexes. Single-family homes can make you rich enough to be able to buy the biggest price of real estate you might want.

Now Here Are the Numbers of Your Single-Family Home Wealth

"Show me," you say, in a friendly way, "how single-family homes can build my real estate wealth."

"Okay," I reply, "here's a real-life example from one of my readers that shows how you can build your real estate wealth in single-family homes in your spare time, starting on borrowed money. And you can work from your home—be it an apartment, a trailer, a boat—with just a telephone, pen, and a few pieces of paper or a child's school notebook. You do not need a computer, fax, or Internet."

You, we'll say, buy a small, two-bedroom, single-family home in a nearby industrial town where people prefer to rent instead of buying their own home. Here are your money numbers:

Price of house	**$84,000**
Down payment, 10% of house price	**$ 8,400 borrowed money**
30-year mortgage at 8%	**$ 554.75 per month**
5-year down payment loan at 12% interest on $8,400	**$ 186.67 per month**
Monthly real estate taxes	**$ 100**
Monthly maintenance charges	**$ 75**
Monthly insurance cost	**$ 30**
Monthly rental income	**$ 1,400**
Net positive cash flow after all expenses, including loans	**$ 453.58 per month**

Thus, you'll earn $5,442.96 per year (= 12 months × $453.58 positive cash flow per month) from this single-family home. Buy a number of such homes and your income will be impressive. NOTE: Your monthly Net Positive Cash Flow (NPCF) = $1,400 rent – $554.75 first mortgage payment – $186.67 down payment loan – $100 real estate taxes – $75 maintenance charges – $30 insurance cost.

To build your income to the level you need and desire, you buy several of these single-family homes, giving you what I call a "horizontal apartment house." Using this real-life example, your annual income with different numbers of houses will be:

Number of Houses	**Annual Income ($)**
10	**54,429**
20	**108,859**
30	**163,288**

And—of course—when you pay off your down payment loan, your income will rise $186.67 per month per house. This translates to $22,400 per year for 10 houses, $44,801 for 20 houses, and $67,200 for

30 houses. So we're not talking small change here. Your after-payoff income will then be:

Number of Houses	Annual Income ($)
10	76,829
20	153,660
30	230,489

So if you're thinking, "I really want to own multi-family buildings," pause for a moment and remember this:

Ten single-family homes can give you the same rental income as a 10-unit apartment building. And in some areas you may be able to charge a higher rent for your single-family home than for an apartment in a multi-family apartment house.

What Types of Single-Family Homes Can Make Me Rich?

When we talk about single-family homes that can make you rich, we have six types in mind for you, namely:

1. **Detached single-family homes**—that is, a stand-alone building that's a residential unit for one family.
2. **A townhouse** on one or two floors in a two- or multi-unit building with each unit a single-family residence.
3. **A single apartment in a multi-unit building**—usually having 10 or more units in the building.
4. **A condominium single-family unit** in a multi-family condo building designed for long-term living. Such a building may be in either a vacation or a non-vacation area of the country.
5. **A mobile home in a multi-unit mobile-home park** designed for semi-permanent living with electric, plumbing, and parking facilities.
6. **A single-family vacation home** of some type which you rent to others during the vacation season, and also—possibly—during the off-season.

For most of this chapter, we'll get you up to speed on detached, or stand-alone, single-family homes. Once you understand them, the others will be easy for you to acquire and get rich from!

Now Let's Get You Started Getting Rich

"So," you ask, "what's the best way for me to get rich in single-family home real estate today?" My answer to you is: YOUR WAY of getting rich in single-family homes depends on what you like to do, such as:

- **Looking after your detached single-family home,** doing needed maintenance work.
- **Traveling to vacation areas** and doing work related to properties you have in those areas.
- **Buying properties at minimum money down**—say $100—and flipping them after fix-up.
- **Managing properties** by having others take care of the grounds or the structure, for example.

To help you pick your way to single-family home wealth, we'll put you into each of the types of properties listed above and show you the income and expenses you might expect. Then you can make your choice.

Detached Single-Family Home Wealth Building

To start building your real estate wealth in detached single-family homes, take these eight easy steps:

1. **Decide on an area** in which you want to invest. At the start, it is usually best to invest locally, if there are suitable properties available and rentals are a common way of life.
2. **Look for suitable properties.** Do this by looking in the Real Estate Section of your local Sunday newspaper for *Homes for Sale.* Also check any local weekly newspapers. Many of these will list lower-priced houses that are suitable for rental income for you.
3. **Try to find homes** having ads that say: *Zero cash down, No money down, 0 down*, or, *Financing available.* Most such ads are a tip-off to a motivated seller who would be willing to work with you to

help you buy the property with minimum cash outlay—either from your own pocket or borrowed money.

4. **Check the rental situation** in the area. Do this by looking in your Sunday paper under *Houses for Rent.* Make notes of the rent charged for two-, three-, and four-bedroom homes. This is important because it is the rental income that will pay for the home you buy on borrowed money and give you a Positive Cash Flow EVERY MONTH.
5. **Pick one or more homes** you think will make good rental units at the going rent in the area you selected. Visit each home and get full information on it. Thus, you must get the following:
   - **Asking price.**
   - **Down payment wanted.**
   - **Annual real estate taxes.**
   - **Annual fuel cost.**
   - **Annual electric bill.**
   - **Annual water charge—if any.**
   - **All other expenses of the property.**
6. **Set up a *Real Estate Riches Success Book*** with a file, such as that in Figure 5.1, for each house. Enter full data, as shown. Add any remarks concerning the
   - Condition of the house
   - Favorable or unfavorable aspects of its location
   - Rental potential based on your study of the area and the particular property
   - What deals you might make on the down payment
   - Your analysis of whether the seller is anxious to sell, or willing to wait until he/she gets the asking price
   - What the lowest down payment you think you could negotiate to get the property is
   - Your rating, on a scale of 1 to 10, with 10 being the most desirable, of your opinion of the suitability of the house for your wealth-building
   - Your personal thoughts on whether you really do or do not want the property in your portfolio of single-family income real estate.

Date: June 7, 2 – – –

Address of Property: 123 Main Street

Seller's Name, Address, Telephone No.: John Doe, 678 Glenn Av, 654-9876

Asking Price: $65,000

Down Payment Asked: $6,500

Annual Expenses:

- **Real estate taxes:** $1,800
- **Maintenance:** $900
- **Insurance:** $1,068

Total Annual Expenses: $3,768

Condition of Property: Needs some interior painting; exterior needs minor repairs; total estimated cost of both = $1,800.

Favorable Aspects of Property: Good location; near schools, shops, transportation; easily rented since it has 3 bedrooms, 2 baths, 3 parking spaces and nice backyard with room for children's play equipment.

Unfavorable Aspects of Property: Needs some cosmetic repairs.

Rental Potential: $1,125 per month; $13,500 per year.

Negotiable Price: $62,000 vs. $65,000 asking price.

Down Payment Deal Negotiable: $6,200 vs. $6,500 asking.

Seller Attitude Towards Sale: Very, very anxious!

My Rating of This Property: 9, with almost a 10, if I can get it for $62,000 with $6,200 down payment.

Personal Thoughts Re This Property: I like it and think it will fit in well with my future plans for real estate wealth.

Figure 5.1 Real Estate Riches Success Book

7. **Make an offer on the detached single-family home** if it measures up to your requirements in terms of rental potential, down payment requirement, and profit you can earn from the home once you own it. **YOU MUST HAVE A POSITIVE CASH FLOW FROM EVERY SINGLE-FAMILY HOME YOU INVEST IN!** Enter the full details of your offer in your *Real Estate Riches Success Book.*
8. **Acquire the property and rent it to a suitable tenant.** Wait at least three months to get some experience with the property (real estate lenders call this "seasoning.") Then go on to your next single-family home to expand your wealth building.

Work the Numbers for Each Property You Acquire

Once you own your first rental property, you're in business for yourself. And when you're in business, you must "work the numbers"—that is, figure your expenses and your profit.

If you had trouble with numbers in school or on your job, don't worry! When you work the numbers for your income and profit, you'll find them easy. Why? Because when your livelihood is involved, the numbers suddenly have real meaning and they "just seem to add up," as many BWBs tell me.

To work the numbers for any single-family home of any type, take these eight easy steps:

1. **Get the price of the house** from your notebook.
2. **List the down payment** you'll make.
3. **Figure your monthly mortgage payment** using Table 10.1 (on page 210).
4. **Calculate your monthly payment** on your down payment loan using Table 10.2 (on page 211).
5. **List the monthly cost** of your real estate tax, maintenance, insurance, and any other expenses.
6. **Estimate the monthly rental income** you expect to get.
7. **Figure** your monthly Positive Cash Flow.
8. **Compute** your annual Positive Cash Flow.

Now you can perform these steps, quickly and easily. Here's how to figure your Annual Positive Cash Flow (APCF) for a house at 123 Main Street that we're assuming you've decided to buy, after having carefully looked it over, as detailed above.

1. **The Price and Down Payment** come from your *Success Book.*
2. **Figure your monthly mortgage payment** by using Table 1 in Chapter 10, and following the steps shown in the example accompanying the table. This is easy to do. If you have any questions, just call me and I'll do it for you on the telephone once you give me the numbers. Use an interest rate based on the going charge in your area. Just call any bank and ask what their current mortgage fixed interest rate is. Or you can find this in mortgage ads in your local paper.
3. **Figure your monthly down payment loan payment the same way,** getting the current interest rate on your credit card—if you used a credit card line of credit for your down payment. Or use the interest rate for a personal loan you got from a bank, credit union, or finance company.
4. **Enter your info from these steps** in your *Success Book* on a form like that in Figure 5.2, for the home at 123 Main Street.
5. **Next, list the other monthly expenses** associated with 123 Main Street in Figure 5.2. These expenses are: Real estate tax = $150; Maintenance = $75. You get these monthly expenses from the seller or you estimate them, based on data you obtain from the tax authorities. Enter them in your *Success Book. This gives you a complete picture of your costs.*
6. **Compute your monthly positive cash flow** by subtracting the total of your expenses, $805, from your monthly rental income, $1,125, to get your monthly positive cash flow, $320. Your Annual Positive Cash Flow is then = 12 × $320 = $3,840.

Put Your Numbers to Work

"The Annual Income from 123 Main Street really isn't much," you say to me. "I'm a corporate executive and that annual income wouldn't

Income and Expense Statement

For 123 Main Street, Anytown, US 10056

Price of Single-Family Home	$62,000
Down payment at 10%	6,200
Monthly mortgage payment on 30-year mortgage for $55,800 at 6% interest	335
Monthly payment on $6,200 down payment loan at 9% for 5 years	156
Real estate tax, monthly	150
Maintenance, monthly	75
Insurance, monthly	89
Total monthly expense	805
Monthly rental income	1,125
Monthly positive cash flow	320
Annual Positive Cash Flow (PCF)	$3,840

Note: All numbers are rounded to the nearest dollar.

Figure 5.2 Income and Expense Statement

even cover my expense account for one month," you say, laughing. "True," I reply. "But I know a lot of former corporate executives who'd love to have that annual income—especially since their unemployment benefits ran out after they were laid off or downsized. Or after they were passed over at work." Such as this letter from a lady reader saying:

Quick Success in Single-Family Homes

"Last November I was inspired to do something with my life after I was once again passed over for a promotion at work that was dangled in front of me for 6 months and I had truly earned. That same day I went to a meeting of real estate investors with a friend. The next day she gave me a copy of your book, How to Make Big Money in Real Estate, Revised for the 21st Century. I read it in two days and started looking for real estate. By day 30, after about 60 offers to buy, I got my first pieces of real estate. I call them my twins—they are identical homes located next door to one another—for $80,000. I bought them with zero cash down and received cash at the closing. I could not believe it when I closed on January 6. I went to the hotel and just cried. In February I closed on two other properties. In January I got my real estate sales license and started to wholesale (flip) properties. I made $8,000 within 3 weeks with no money out of my pocket for the houses. In summary, it was your book that gave me so many ideas and let me know that it was possible. For non-believers, I say it **can** be done. I had access to about $3,000 and horrible credit, including a bankruptcy. All my properties have positive cash flow. And all I had to do was to let go of my fears!"

—New York

More Modest Beginning

"I called you yesterday about your 3-Year Real Estate Book. I bought my first single-family home rental property from an investor the first week in October with zero cash down on a 30-day note. The seller will also pay the attorney fees and the real estate taxes due."

—Mississippi

See the Numbers of Your Real Estate Fortune

I agree with you, good friend of mine, that the $3,840 per year from 123 Main Street is not too much. But do not depend on just one single-family home for your real estate income. Think in terms of 10, 20, or 30 single-family homes, each with an income similar to 123 Main Street. Thus:

Annual Net Positive Cash Flow ($)	Number of Houses
38,400	10
76,800	20
115,200	30
153,600	40
192,000	50

Now when you remember that depreciation of your houses will shelter most of your income, you may begin to think that single-family homes can make you rich. To verify this, just look at those numbers! No matter how big a corporate executive you might be, $192,000 per year is interesting! To summarize:

You really can't beat the single-family home as a way to build real estate riches in your spare time working from your home. And in this business you need not spend 35 or 40 hours a week at it. Instead, you might spend 30 minutes a week on each house.

Cautions for You When Buying Any Single-Family Home

You MUST have a competent real estate attorney to guide you on the purchase of EVERY single-family home! Do NOT try to avoid this recommendation. Why? Because single-family home real estate:

- **Can present unforeseen problems** if purchased without competent legal guidance to protect you from seller mistakes and neglect.
- **Can lead to ongoing lawsuits** when you're not protected by competently drawn legal documents such as leases, sublet privileges, rental amount, etc.
- **Can lead to state or federal regulation** when environmental rules are not followed by you, or were not obeyed by previous owners or renters.

To help you avoid problems when you buy single-family homes, many states have prepared a Seller Data Information Sheet (SDIS). The SDIS gives you questions you should ask when you buy or rent a single-family home. If you'd like a copy of the SDIS issued by my state (New York), just ask for it when you subscribe for two years or longer to one of my newsletters listed at the back of this book.

How and Where to Get Single-Family Home Financing

I hope that by now you're convinced that single-family homes are right for you to start building your real estate wealth—quickly and easily. And the good news for you, good friend, is that:

> **There are more lenders for single-family homes than for any other type of real estate. Why? Because more than 5 million previously occupied single-family homes are sold in the United States every year! So lending on single-family homes is BIG BUSINESS for real estate lenders everywhere!**

To show you how easy it is to get loans for single-family homes, here's a list of some of the lenders who might finance your single-family home wealth building:

- **Credit unions of almost every type**—state and federally chartered.
- **Commercial banks**—those having the initials N.A. after their name.
- **Government (FHA/HUD/VA)** loan guarantees and loans.
- **Life insurance companies** of many types.
- **Mortgage brokers** who represent many lenders.
- **Pension funds**—both large and small ones.
- **Savings banks** in almost every state.
- **Savings and Loan Associations**—now called Savings Associations.
- **Private lenders** (or investors) from many sections of the country.

Quick Benefits Offered to You by These Lenders

Each of these lenders offers unique features to you as a borrower for almost any kind of single-family home. Here—in quick review—are some of the major features of each type of lender.

For more details, see the specific type of lender you're interested in using for your single-family home wealth building. If you can't decide which type of lender to work with, give me—your good friend—a call and I'll try to help!

Credit Unions

You can join a credit union—free of charge—because credit unions are member-based organizations. Single-family home loans offered by many credit unions include:

- **Low down payment loans.**
- **Less-than-perfect-credit loans.**
- **Really bad credit loans.**
- **No-income verification loans.**
- **Debt-consolidation loans.**
- **Refinance with little or no equity loans.**
- **Fixed, adjustable, and other interest-rate options.**
- **No Doc (no income, no assets verified) loans.**
- **Foreign Nationals Accepted (FNA) loans.**
- **Extended qualifying ratio loans.**
- **Bankruptcy and pending foreclosure OK loans.**
- **Tax-lien and judgments OK loans.**

Enough said? Go see your loan credit union. You'll find it listed in your telephone book *Yellow Pages* under "Credit Unions." Or go on the Internet to *http://www.ncua.gov.*

Commercial Banks

Look in your phone book under the "Banks" listing for commercial banks near you. These banks have the N.A. (National Association) abbreviation after their name. Call the mortgage department and ask for data on their home loans. You'll be sent:

- **A set of loan applications** for you to use.
- **Flyers** on the types of loans they make, interest charged.
- **Full data** on the bank and its history, branches, and other information.

You'll be a lot more welcome at a commercial bank if you have your checking account at the bank. And if you also have your savings account at the bank they'll welcome you with open arms. Get the point, good friend?

Government Loan Guarantees and Loans

There are dozens of government loan programs for single-family homes. Important ones you should look at are:

- **Manufactured home** loan guarantees (Title 1).
- **Single-family home** loan guarantees (Section 203(b)).
- **Low/moderate-income** loan guarantees (Section 221(d)).
- **Rehabilitation housing** loan guarantees (Section 203(k)).
- **Single-family home** guarantees for outlying-area homes (Section 203(i)).

You can find plenty of others by contacting your local FHA/HUD. See their address and phone number in the government section of your local phone book. Or go on the Internet to: *http://www.hud.gov.*

The Veteran's Administration (VA) has a number of loan guarantees to buy or build a single-family home. Other guarantees cover manufactured homes, residential condos, farms containing residences, and the refinancing of an existing mortgage. Loans are made to veterans for no down payment on the property by the buyer. Thus, you get the home for zero cash down. Check your local phone book or the Internet at: *http://www.va.gov.*

Some VA loans can be *assumed*—taken over with no qualifying checks of your credit. These are ideal loans for credit-troubled BWBs. Be sure to look for homes having such mortgages because you can get started with them even if your credit score is 0, or below 300.

The Farm Service Agency (FSA) has a number of useful programs for rural housing you can use to build your single-family home wealth. To buy, build, or repair rural homes, use the FSA 502 program. To repair rural homes, use the FSA 504b program.

Life Insurance Companies

Life insurance companies prefer larger home loans because they can put out more money to earn a higher return on the transaction. And if you have an Ordinary Life Insurance Policy with a life insurance company you can borrow against it. The interest rate you'll pay will probably be the lowest anywhere. Why? Because the insurance company has the collateral (your policy) in its own hands!

Mortgage Brokers

Mortgage brokers have access to numerous single-family home lenders. Some have no other experience but with single-family homes. And some Mortgage Brokers work with government programs and have ready access to a variety of loan guarantees offered to buyers of many types of single-family homes. Working with Mortgage Brokers can be highly beneficial to you because they:

- **Are paid a commission** on each borrower they find who successfully obtains a mortgage loan.
- **Know how to qualify a borrower** whose credit may not be the strongest, helping you get your loan.
- **Work for you at no charge** of any kind because they get their income from the lender when you get your loan.

- **Have inside info** on which lenders are hungry for mortgage loans and help you qualify for one of these loans.

Pension Funds

Pension funds, like insurance companies, prefer to lend on larger, single-family homes. But some smaller pension funds may like single-family home loans of lesser amounts. As they say, "You never know!" So check out smaller—and larger—pension funds. You may get the loan you seek!

Savings Banks

Savings banks just love to make single-family home loans. Some savings banks make *only* single-family home loans. So you can expect an open-arms welcome when you apply. For best results with savings banks:

- **Apply to local savings banks.** They know property values in your area and can give you a quick answer to your loan request.
- **Ask for their special mortgage offers.** Many savings banks have low-interest offers that can save you lots of money. As with commercial banks, it never hurts to have an account at the bank you're asking for a loan!
- **Use the bank's loan application.** The bank knows—and likes—its own loan application. You'll get a faster answer when you use it!

Savings and Loan Associations

Once called "S&Ls" for short, these associations are now called "Savings Associations." And like Savings Banks, the main focus of Savings Associations is single-family homes. Likewise, you'll find these two types of lenders listed in the *Yellow Pages* under "Banks." Keep in mind that Savings Associations:

- **Are "hungry"** to make single-family home mortgage loans because that is their main business.

- **Will welcome** your single-family home mortgage loan application and will do all they can to approve it.
- **Have experienced loan officers** who know single-family home values in your area and can give quick funding decisions.
- **Offer competitive interest rates** that allow you to earn a higher profit on every single-family home you buy.

Private Investors

Private investors are individuals or companies seeking to earn income from loans they make on well-kept, well-located, single-family homes in either their local or a distant area. For example, I have made investments in single-family homes as a private investor. And every deal I've made as a private investor has been profitable.

When you deal with a private investor or lender you have several advantages because such business people:

- **Usually seek less documentation** than most other lenders might require of you.
- **Seldom do a credit check** on a borrower, relying instead on a "gut" feeling about the borrower.
- **Can deliver the money sooner**—in just hours, if necessary—to the borrower.
- **Are easier to deal with** than most other lenders because he/she admires the Beginning Wealth Builder and wants to help.
- **Can be a regular source of money for you**—the BWB—if you make your payments fully, and on time.
- **Will work with you** if you have a sudden and unexpected expense with the property which causes you to be late with your monthly payment on your mortgage.
- **May be willing to make a down payment loan** and a long-term mortgage loan to you, enabling you to get into a moneymaking property for zero cash down.

So seek private investors or lenders for your single-family home deals. You'll find such lenders listed every month in my newsletter,

International Wealth Success, described at the back of this book. Just keep one important fact in mind at all times:

NEVER PAY "FRONT MONEY" OR ADVANCE FEES FOR ANY LOAN! IT IS NOT A NECESSARY PART OF GETTING ANY MORTGAGE LOAN! SO IF A LENDER ASKS FOR MONEY BEFORE YOU GET YOUR LOAN, SAY "NO, I WON'T PAY IT!"

Your Eight Steps to Quick Single-Family Home Financing

Combine the sources given above and you have hundreds—really thousands—of lenders ready to finance your single-family home income property. To get your financing, take these easy eight steps:

1. **Decide what type of financing** you'll seek and use—bank, credit union, insurance company, mortgage broker, or other lender.
2. **Choose a local lender** who makes single-family home loans in the area in which you plan to buy.
3. **Contact your chosen lender** by phone, fax, e-mail, or postal mail and ask for full details on their single-family home loans. This info will be sent to you free.
4. **Study the loan application** you receive. Photocopy it to work on so you can submit the original in typewritten form when you decide to apply for your loan.
5. **Look for a suitable single-family home** to start your wealth-building project. Earlier tips in this chapter show you how to look for suitable properties.
6. **"Work" the numbers** once you find a suitable investment home. Get from the seller the **Price,** the **Down Payment,** and **Expenses** (real estate taxes, insurance, water, etc.) for the property. With these numbers in hand, you'll next estimate the **Rental Income** you believe you can get for the house. Then, figure your **Profit.** (As a reader of this book, or as a subscriber to one of my newsletters, you can contact me and I'll be happy to work these numbers for you when you fax, e-mail, or postal mail them to me. I cannot take them down over the phone.)

7. **Buy the single-family home** that will generate the rental profit you seek. After three months, check into the chances of refinancing this home to pull cash out of it to buy your next single-family home. You may have to wait for 6 to 12 months for what lenders call "seasoning" to get your money. But don't give up! Refinance as soon as you can and get your second house. Do the same with it.
8. **Go on to great riches** in your single-family home business. Once you're successful with several single-family homes, you can go on to build your riches in multi-family homes if you wish!

Now that you know exactly which steps to take to get started in your single-family home wealth building, I want to give you a few real-life examples readers write me about. Then we'll show you how to make money in other types of single-family homes. But first the letters:

Fast Results

"I want to thank you for your book How to Make Millions in Real Estate in Three Years Starting with No Cash. I bought your book last Saturday. On Tuesday I had my first contract on my first single-family rental property and I did it with zero cash down. As soon as I close and this one is rented I will dive right in on No. 2 and keep right on going."

—Florida

Overcoming Adversity with Single-Family Homes

"Thank you very much for the terrific service you provide. I am a single mother of two children trying to get out of the 9-to-5 grind. I am having much success and I've acquired ten rental properties. The first one is the hardest. After that they seem to fall into your lap. My goal is to own 100 to 150 properties and retire by age 47—in the next two years. I have really enjoyed your book How to Make Big Money in Real Estate and it taught me how to prepare a balance sheet. The Loan Officers love such presentations!" —Maryland

Zero-Cash Down Deals

"I bought my first rental house as a repo [repossessed] from the VA [Veteran's Administration]. Two years later I bought my second rental house. The two houses are worth about $110,000. Both are rented out and I have a positive cash flow from them. I am now looking for more single-family houses." —South Carolina

Another Quick Start

"I am a 23-year-old recent college graduate who has read a number of your books. I have to thank you for inspiring me to purchase my first investment property just 10 days after college graduation. I agree with you that real estate is the best way for me to build wealth starting from nothing. Currently I'm working on my second owner-financed zero-cash down deal using the techniques outlined in your books."

—North Dakota

Other Types of Single-Family Home Investments

Earlier in this chapter we showed you five other types of single-family residences you can make money in, starting with no cash. Until now we've been talking about stand-alone single-family homes.

Now we'll give you the advantages and disadvantages of the five other types. NOTE: In general, the financing steps you'll follow are the same as those given previously.

Townhouse Single-Family Home

Advantages:

- **Seldom need major repairs or maintenance** because they usually are of recent construction.
- **Command higher rents** than detached single-family homes because they need less tenant work.
- **Rise in value quickly** when kept in good condition by the owner and tenants.

Disadvantages:

- **May cost more to buy or rent** than a stand-alone single-family home in the area you're investing in.
- **Can be difficult to find** because there often are few in an area in which you want to own rental property.

Apartment in a Multi-Family Building (Apartment House)

Advantages:

- **Can often be taken over** for NO CASH and NO CLOSING COSTS when first offered on the market.
- **Usually require less maintenance** than detached single-family homes because they're better built and have less exposure to the elements—snow, rain, hail, sun, hurricanes, tornados, or others.
- **Are simpler to manage** and easier to rent because there's usually a larger need for apartments than for detached single-family homes.
- **Can be put on the market,** and rented by a Rental Agent for a small fee. This gives you more time for other real estate deals.

Disadvantages:

- **Your rental income may be lower** than for a detached single-family home in the same area.

- **May be hard for you to find** in heavily populated areas because of the great demand for rental apartments.
- **Can take you longer** to assemble a "string" of these units than a group of detached single-family homes.

Condo Single-Family Home Units

Advantages:

- **Simple, easy management for you** that can be done at a distance by yourself or by others.
- **No land or garden care by you or your tenants**—the condo association does it all as part of your monthly fee.
- **You can finance these units easily**—often on zero cash, meaning you have a no-money-down deal!
- **Are usually easy to sell,** if you want to take a profit on your investment and buy other, more attractive income property.
- **You can often buy older units** at low prices if there is new condo construction in the area of your property.

Disadvantages:

- **You may find it hard to locate** a suitable condo in the area in which you want to run your single-family home rental business.
- **Newer units can be more expensive** than a detached single-family home in the same area in which you want to invest.

Mobile Home in a Mobile Home Park

Advantages:

- **Sometimes you can buy them for almost nothing**—just $40 or $50 in some cases our readers have told us about in the warmer areas of the United States.
- **Are often low-maintenance structures** because they are made of long-lasting metals that resist corrosion or decay over the years.
- **Can be rented to the same family** for years, saving you time and money and allowing you to spend more time on other money-making deals you like.

Disadvantages:

- **Tenants may be the less desirable type** because they are restless and don't stay in one location for very long. Such tenants may not treat your property too well.
- **Your mobile home may have to be moved** if the park closes or is sold to a new owner.

Single-Family Detached Vacation Home

Advantages:

- **Can provide you with a high rental income** during the vacation season—often more than a year-round rental pays you in a less desirable area.
- **May provide you with tax-deductible trips** to desirable vacation areas when you travel to inspect your property, check on tenants, or do other work related to your income-producing real estate.
- **Are a "fun" type of business** because your tenants are in a happy mood—they're on vacation!

Disadvantages:

- **May be hard for you to rent** during times of economic downturns or other conditions—war, shortages, stock market debacle, or other economic problem.
- **Can go in and out of style** as the types of vacations or the popular vacation areas change in popularity.

Your Moneymaking Tips for Single-Family Home Success

No matter what type of single-family home you invest in, keep these key needs of your tenants in mind BEFORE YOU BUY ANY PROPERTY:

- **SCHOOLS:** What is the quality of the schools in the area you plan to invest in—good, mediocre, poor? If you plan on renting to young families, look for the BEST school system you can find.

- **HIGHWAY OR FREEWAY ACCESS:** Is the single-family home near a major highway or freeway leading to areas in which jobs are plentiful? The shorter the distance the renter has to drive or use public transportation to go to work, the easier it is for you to rent your unit. And the closer the unit is to major roadway access, the higher the rent you can charge.
- **SHOPPING FACILITIES—MALLS, SUPERMARKETS, CHAIN STORES:** Again, the closer your single-family home is to good shopping facilities, the easier it is for you to rent. And the higher the rent you can charge per unit!
- **POLICE PROTECTION:** A good police force that keeps a lid on crime will help you rent sooner and be able to charge a higher rent. Low-crime areas are highly desirable to all renters—everywhere.
- **SPORTS FACILITIES** rate high with young families today. Soccer fields, basketball courts, swimming pools, baseball fields, hockey, and skating rinks all add to the rentability of your units. And each facility helps you raise the monthly rental by a few dollars.
- **RELIGIOUS ORGANIZATIONS** that are nearby increase your rental chances and the level of rent you can charge. So the closer your single-family home is to various houses of worship the better your business will be!
- **RESTAURANTS, CLUBS, AND BEACH FACILITIES** will all make your single-family home more rentable when they are nearby. So check them BEFORE you buy!
- **TRANSPORTATION FACILITIES** are very important to some renters who do not own or cannot afford an automobile. Closeness to trains, buses, trolley lines, etc., will increase your rental income. Again, check BEFORE you buy!
- **PARKING SPACES:** Don't buy a single-family home that has less than two parking spaces. Why? Because today's families are usually made up of two working spouses. Without parking facilities for two or more cars, renting the property is extremely difficult.
- **BEDROOMS:** Avoid single-family homes with less than two bedrooms. One-bedroom homes are much more difficult to rent than homes with two or more bedrooms.

- **BATHROOMS:** Look for single-family homes with at least one and one-half bathrooms. Single-bathroom homes are hard to rent to tenants today.

Your Keys to Real Estate Riches

- ❑ **Start with the possible** and grow bigger. Small is better at the start. You'll learn your "trade" from single-family homes and can "graduate" to larger properties after you have a few years of experience.
- ❑ **Know the numbers** of your single-family wealth building. No matter how much you might dislike numbers, they become interesting and easy when they're about your money!
- ❑ **Ten single-family homes** can give you the same income as a 10-unit apartment house. But it's much easier to get the 10 homes than the apartment house!
- ❑ **Set up a *Real Estate Riches Success Book*** to keep a record of your activities in searching for, evaluating, and buying your single-family homes.
- ❑ **There are thousands of loans available** for single-family homes. And some First-Time Home Owner Loans offer 100 percent financing to you.
- ❑ **Private lenders** can be helpful to people without credit and to people with low credit scores. So be sure to include such lenders in your financing plans.
- ❑ **NEVER PAY FRONT MONEY** for any loan! It is NOT NECESSARY to pay front money or advance fees to get any loan.
- ❑ **Remember the keys to successful renting.** They include schools, stores, transportation, sports facilities, parking spaces, and number of bedrooms and bathrooms! Provide what renters want and you'll get rich sooner than you think!

- ❑ **Be certain to have every home checked** for lead paint, mold, termites, and plot pollution BEFORE you buy it! Your real estate attorney will remind you of these hazards. But in case he/she doesn't, we DID remind you!
- ❑ **Never buy an income single-family home** until after you have studied the *Seller Questionnaire* required by some 30 states today. It tells you what defects the seller knows of that you might have to spend money on for repairs. ***BUYER BEWARE!***

CHAPTER 6

Where to Find Money for Your Real Estate Wealth Building

REAL ESTATE, AS YOU LEARNED IN EARLIER CHAPTERS, IS A *BORROWED-Money Business.* No one I know who owns real estate for income purposes ever pays all cash for their property. Why? Because real estate is a *Borrowed-Money Business!* Remember, always:

It is a *given* that real estate professionals finance their holdings. And I want you to do the same because that is the way you can build your real estate wealth on OPM—Other People's Money.

In this chapter I'll show you exactly *where* you can get the money you need for all your larger real estate deals—multi-family buildings, business office structures, commercial properties having stores, and—possibly—residential rental units, industrial factories, to mention a few. Many of these funders differ from single-family home lenders.

In our last chapter we focused on single-family home financing for you. This chapter looks at two-, four-, twenty-, forty-, and sixty-unit (or larger) buildings you might want to own to build your real estate fortune on OPM. These buildings might be residential, commercial, or industrial. Your present chapter answers the most common query I get about multi-unit buildings, namely:

"*Where* can I get financing for this beautiful—and profitable—multi-unit real estate project?" The *where* puzzles BWBs again and again, over and over.

Your Money Sources Are Almost Unlimited

Since real estate is a borrowed-money business, there are thousands of funding sources waiting to put money into *your* hands. And this money can take a number of different forms. Here—quickly—are sources of funding for your multi-unit real estate wealth:

- **Loans for your long-term mortgage**s on multi-unit real estate.
- **Loans for your "junior" mortgages**—that is second, third, or more, down payment loans for multi-unit zero-cash deals.
- **Loans for property fix-up**—also called *rehabilitation*—rehab for short—to bring property up to modern standards.
- **Loan guarantees** from government agencies—federal, state, county, city, to help you get quick multi-unit financing.
- **Grants** from both government and private sources to purchase or rehab property for needy families and/or business tenants.
- **Lines of credit**—direct or indirect—to furnish cash for your multi-unit real estate wealth-building.
- **Private sources** for a variety of multi-unit real estate financing with little documentation.
- **Public sources** for large loans for many of your big-money (multi-millions) real estate projects.
- **Investor group**s for large or small sources of money for you where you do the work while your investors receive profits.
- **100 percent financing funders** who will finance your investment properties for every dollar of the property cost.

Now that you know many of the sources available to you, we'll show you exactly where to find such sources in your area. And once you've found suitable sources, we'll show you how to determine if these sources would advance you the money you need. So let's get you the money you need for your wealth-building real estate deals. Such money can turn your life around, as this letter shows:

Building Wealth from Little Cash

"Real estate is the best investment in good or bad times. How do I know? Within the past 5 years I have turned $1,000 into several real estate corporations worth in excess of $12,000,000."

—North Carolina

Getting the Easiest of All Real Estate Money

The easiest real estate money for you to get for any property is the long-term mortgage—called the *First Mortgage.* Why is this? Because the First Mortgage:

- **Is secured by the real estate**—that is, the collateral for the loan is the property you're buying. Since your First Mortgage is anywhere between 75 and 90 percent of the property's appraised value, your lender is protected by the excess property value (25 percent or 10 percent, depending on the Loan to Value Ratio (called *LTV Ratio*) —75 to 90 percent in this case.
- **Can be "called"**—that is ended at any time the borrower does not live up to the payment agreement or violates other terms of the mortgage.
- **Will often be sold** to other groups for almost the full amount of the First Mortgage loan made to you. This means the lender has almost all the money back and can lend it out again while the risk of the loan has been sold to someone else. Meanwhile, you—of course—have the money you need for your real estate!
- **In summary,** your multi-unit First Mortgage loan is a favorite of real estate lenders. Most of them "hunger" to make more multi-unit First Mortgage loans to qualified borrowers. And you can be one of those multi-unit qualified buyers if you use the tips in this book!

Where to Find First Mortgage Lenders

Your best source of First Mortgage Lenders for an investment property in your area is your local telephone book *Yellow Pages* under the

"Mortgages" heading. And if you have access to the Internet through your own computer or a computer in your local library, use the search words "Mortgage Lenders."

If the multi-unit real estate you're investing in is at a significant distance from you—say, more than 50 miles away—check the lists of mortgage lenders at the back of this book. You'll find the *Directory of 2500 Active Real Estate Lenders* especially helpful for out-of-town lenders. And you can always call me—your author, Ty Hicks—for personal help with finding a suitable multi-unit lender, if you're a subscriber to one of my newsletters.

Contact your potential First Mortgage Lenders by phone, fax, e-mail, or postal mail. Ask for:

- **Data on their multi-unit First Mortgage Loans**—amounts, term (that is, 15, 20, 25 years), current interest rate, and points charged, if any. (A point is 1 percent of the loan amount. 1 point = $1,000 on a $100,000 mortgage.)
- **Credit requirements**—your credit score, income status, job, or business history. Some lenders will give you a larger LTV ratio with a higher FICO® score. So, GOOD CREDIT DOES HELP YOU!
- **A copy of their loan application** and other paperwork for getting your multi-unit loan. Study the loan application carefully. Likewise, carefully read their loan requirements. See if you think you can qualify for a loan from each lender. Concentrate on those lenders with whom you think you'll have the best chance of getting a multi-unit loan.

Finding the Second Easiest Real Estate Loan

If your First Mortgage Loan is the easiest to get, than the Second, or Junior Mortgage, must be the next easiest to get. Why? Again, your lender has the best security known to anyone—real estate. "But," you might say, "actively traded stocks and bonds are better security than real estate."

Not so! The stock market can "fall apart" overnight, leading to major capital losses. For instance, a friend of mine bought stock in a "safe" company for $65 per share. A year later her shares had fallen to $1 each. Lenders know this and know that multi-unit real estate rarely shows a loss of this magnitude.

Again, real estate is a borrowed-money business. Lenders know that multi-unit real estate typically rises in value 7 percent per year. So it's the safest kind of collateral around.

That's why you often can get your down payment loan in the form of a second mortgage on the property you're buying—giving you a zero-cash down deal.

Here's a letter from a reader showing how you can get a multi-unit building on zero cash:

Two Apartment Houses on Zero Down

"I'm buying my second apartment building with zero money down. The first was for $185,000 with a $25,000 down payment. I assumed the existing first loan and the owner carried the balance. I got the $25,000 with five $5,000 loans from five different lenders." —California

And another reader writes:

Using Second Mortgages to Buy Apartment Houses

"Four months ago I was beating my brains out trying to make ends meet. Now just the reverse; I'm beating my brains out trying to spend my money wisely. It all started when I read your book and subscribed to your newsletter. I was on my way, following your instructions to the letter. I got leads for second mortgages from the newsletter and then bought my first apartment house. I now own four apartment houses and am in the process of buying a shopping center." —Ohio

Have Others Finance Your Income Property Fix-Up

Lenders are happy to lend you money to fix up (rehab) a multi-unit property. Why? Because the rehabbed property will be worth much more after the work is done than it was before. So—again—your lender has solid collateral that retains its value year after year. You sometimes can:

- **Get a rehab (also called *property improvement*) loan** on a multi-unit property you do not yet own but plan to buy, if you have a neatly prepared rehab proposal to show to your prospective lender.
- **Use part of your rehab loan** for the fix-up and the remainder for the down payment on the multi-unit property, giving you a zero-cash deal.

The best place to obtain small (4 to 20 units) rehab loans is in your local area. Why? ***Because local lenders know values in your area.*** Result? They're ready to lend small multi-unit rehab money to you quickly, with less paperwork than distant lenders. Where can you find such lenders? Again—your telephone book *Yellow Pages.*

Or, if you can't find a multi-unit lender to work with you, ask—as an *IWS Newsletter* subscriber—to have IWS research and generate a personal list of multi-unit real estate lenders in your state that might work with you.

The reader from California whose letter is the first one you read in this chapter continues:

Apartment House Purchase Using a Property Improvement Loan

"My second apartment house is 20 units priced at $90,000, with $9,000 down and a new first mortgage of $60,000. The owner will carry the balance of $26,000, and the loan fee of 1.5 points will be added to the owner's note. On the down payment for this one I'm getting a $5,000 property

improvement loan from the bank, as you recommended. Also, the friendly real estate broker will lend me his 6 percent commission of $5,400."
—California

Get Guaranteed Loans for Your Investment Real Estate

A guaranteed loan for multi-unit real estate is a first mortgage backed by a government agency—such as the Housing and Urban Development Department (HUD) or Federal Housing Administration (FHA). These mortgages, in turn, may be packaged and sold by Fannie Mae or Freddie Mac—short for Federal National Mortgage Administration and Federal Home Mortgage Loan Corporation. Section 203(b) is probably FHA's most popular mortgage insurance program.

To use a guaranteed multi-unit loan, you apply at your local bank or mortgage company for your first mortgage. You'll be told there if your loan can be guaranteed by HUD/FHA or another government agency. If your multi-unit loan can be guaranteed:

- **You must use approved loan forms** because your loan will probably be sold by the lender. To do so, the lender must use approved multi-unit paperwork—namely the application you're given.
- **Type your loan application throughout.** If you can't type, have someone in your family or at a public facility do the typing. A typed application raises your approval chances 30 percent.
- **Give all the data requested.** If some parts of the application do not apply to your situation, mark those parts N.A. (= Not Applicable).
- **Be certain your amount, term, and interest requirements (if any)** come within your lender's guidelines. Don't get turned down for a $1 million loan because the maximum loan made by the lender is $500,000!

On some guaranteed multi-unit loans you may be required by the lender to have Private Mortgage Insurance (PMI). You'll find that PMI is required by lenders when:

- **The first mortgage is 80 percent or more** (typically up to 95 percent) of the value of the property on which the loan is being made.
- **Your credit score is not the highest**—say, less than 600—when you apply for your first mortgage loan. The lender is trying to protect the money being put out on the multi-unit loan.
- **The lender thinks a foreclosure is possible.** The PMI covers any losses the lender may have in a foreclosure with an upper limit of 20 percent of the multi-unit's value.

Where will you use guaranteed loans? Such loans cover a number of different types of properties, including:

- **Single-family homes** (see the previous chapter).
- **Two-, three-, and four-family dwellings.**
- **Multiple-family buildings (apartment houses).**
- **Farms, ranches, and similar agricultural structures.**

You can use guaranteed loans to build your multi-unit real estate wealth. Just see your bigger real estate lenders for larger projects—up to about $5,000,000. Beyond that level of investment, loan guarantees are less important. Loan guarantees are most important for BWBs—Beginning Wealth Builders. And your author is here to help you get any loan guarantees you might need to build your multi-unit real estate riches.

To help you get loans for larger multi-unit projects, you're given a list of such lenders at the end of this chapter. Please be sure to read the *Important Notice* at the start of that list. It will help me be friendlier to you!

Get Grants for Beneficial Real Estate Projects

You can get grants for multi-unit housing you build, rehab, or convert for use by the poor, the handicapped, the needy, the elderly, and others who cannot afford traditional housing. A multi-unit grant never need be repaid, if you do the work for which the grant was made. A loan, by comparison, must ALWAYS be repaid—on time and in full!

You can apply for multi-unit housing grants to the federal government, your local state, city, and county governments. To obtain grant data, contact the following:

Federal Government Grant Data

- **Housing and Urban Development Department:** 451 Seventh Street SW, Washington, DC 20410, *www.hud.gov.*
- **Office of housing:** *www.hud.gov.*
- **Large single-family home construction projects:** *www.hud.gov.*
- **Multi-family homes:** *www.hud.gov.*
- **Public and Indian housing:** *www.hud.gov.*
- **Department of Veterans Affairs,** 810 Vermont Avenue NW, Washington, DC 20420-0001, *www.va.gov.*
- **Loan Guaranty Service** is at 202-273-7331.

State/City/County Government Grant Data

See your telephone book's "Government" pages—they are usually blue and are found at the back of the book. You'll find the names and addresses of government agencies you can call to find housing grants for your work. Such agencies usually have the word "Housing" in their name. Others may use the words "Home" or "Shelter." Check them all. You may find the grant you need! Private, or semi-private agencies may have the words "Housing Commission" associated with them. Some may also appear in the Government sections of your telephone book. If you are a 2-year subscriber to my newsletter, *International Wealth Success,* we will give you a list of agencies that have data on who to contact to learn where to find housing grants in your city or state. This list gives you the name, address, and telephone number of the group to contact.

Apply for and Get Lines of Credit for Your Investments

I get thousands of calls a year saying "I found this great multi-unit income property. It has a wonderful cash flow after all expenses and mortgage payments. But I need the down payment. How and where do I get the down payment?" Your answer is: **Check out the following five forms of a line of credit right now:**

Sources for Your Down Payment Loans

1. **For down payments up to $500,000,** you can use a second mortgage granted by a lender *different from* your first mortgage lender. Or you can ask the seller to take back a mortgage (called a *Purchase Money* or *PM Mortgage*) for part or all of the down payment. Both the second mortgage and PM mortgage are a line of credit extended to you.
2. **For down payments up to $100,000,** you can use a line of credit from your bank. You must establish such a line of credit by visiting your bank and talking to a loan officer. There is a small annual charge for holding your line of credit open until you use it. Once you use your line of credit you will—of course—pay the going rate of interest on the money you borrowed.
3. **For down payments up to $50,000,** you can use your credit card lines of credit. Typically, you can get a credit line of $10,000 per credit card. Five such cards give you a $50,000 line of credit.
4. **For down payments up to $25,000,** you can use a personal loan line of credit from a bank, a credit union, a finance company, a relative, or a business associate.
5. **For down payments up to 20 percent of the price of the property,** you can work with lenders who make both the down payment loan of 20 percent at a higher interest rate (typically 4 to 5 percent higher than the first mortgage rate in your area) and the first mortgage loan at 1.5 to 2.0 percent above the going mortgage rate in your area. Both rates might be termed "hard money rates"—but you do get the money you need! With such combined loans, the lender uses your line of credit to cover the 20 percent down pay-

ment loan. The 80 percent loan is based on the condition of the property you're buying, the appraised value of the property, your credit rating, and your intended use of the property—for income purposes, as opposed to your personal residence.

Thus, your line of credit is a "bridge" that gets you full financing for a zero-cash deal. Without your line of credit, the best loan you could get would be the 80 percent financing.

Private Financing Could Be Your Key to Riches

Private lenders are people—just like you and me—who are interested in real estate and would like to earn money from it. The one difference between the private lender and the BWB real estate entrepreneur is this:

Private lenders have funds of their own or funds from investors who want to invest in multi-unit real estate as silent partners. The private lender is working alone and is not governed by the banking laws, except for the usury limits on the amount of interest that can be charged on the loans they make. And private lenders rarely do a credit check on their borrowers. Instead, the private lender relies on a personal opinion of the borrower and the borrower's real estate project when making a loan decision.

For example, I'm a private lender research specialist. I find private lenders for a variety of real estate projects. This research is in addition to my own real estate activities—which include ownership, investing, consulting, writing, publishing and lecturing on real estate.

The real estate loans I find as a private-lender researcher that have been made have all been repaid in full and on time. My specialty in loan finding is down payment loans with a term of one day to seven years. (Yes, I see a few one-day loans!) These down payment loans help BWBs get started in their multi-unit real estate wealth building.

In our newsletter, *International Wealth Success,* we regularly research and publish lists of private multi-unit lenders for real estate BWBs.

Some readers report good success with private lenders. To get best results with private lenders:

- **Have a specific proposal** with full details of the multi-unit property, its price, income, expenses, and down payment.
- **Provide a short write-up** detailing why the multi-unit property is a good investment for both you and the lender. Project future earnings and profits.
- **Give full details on your personal wealth-building activities.** Private lenders love to hear of the exploits of their borrowers. Such stories are told by the lender to friends—over and over again. Your interesting multi-unit story could get you your loan—even when your credit is shaky.
- **Meet personally with the lender,** if you're requested to do so. Again, the lender wants to "eyeball" the loan applicant (you) to get an idea about your energy, drive, ambition, and future plans. So don't be bashful—your lender is really interested if he/she requests a face-to-face meeting!
- **Try to "sell" your private lender on your deal.** Private lenders often see themselves as "saviors" of BWBs—that is, they are helping beginners get started on an important journey in the BWBs career. As a savior, they love being an important element in your multi-unit success story. Convince your private lender of the soundness of your multi-unit deal and you'll get your money!

Most of the down payment loans I've found have been for readers of my monthly newsletter, *International Wealth Success.* It is *not* necessary that a person be a subscriber to find a loan through me. But I do find that most subscribers think the way I do. So I understand them better than nonsubscribers.

Get Your Real Estate Money from Public Sources

The public—worldwide—loves real estate as an investment vehicle. Why is this? Because:

- **Most families have had good results with their investment in a home.** The home often doubles, triples, or quadruples in value over a period of years. This real-life experience is passed on from parent to child, resulting in a favorable image for real estate. And many kids know that in recent years their parents refinanced their home to pay for the child's education. Could anyone ask for a better result from an investment? (As an aside, I know some parents who lost their kids' college tuition money in the stock market. But I do not know even one parent who lost their children's tuition money in real estate!)
- **People in the workplace, at clubs, at restaurants, and in religious organization meetings** talk about how much money they made from a real estate investment, giving full details. This is great publicity for the advantages of real estate investment. For—as you know—the best form of advertising is WORD OF MOUTH!

Raising Real Estate Money from the Public

Result of all this free advertising? Millions of people will invest in public (and private) real estate organizations. So you can—if you have a unique idea for real estate—raise money for your idea from the public via a *public offering* on a stock exchange.

Or the stock broker who is interested in taking your project public might instead decide to offer it privately to clients. This is called a *private offering*. Such an offering will—in general—get you your real estate money faster than a public offering. It takes about 90 days to do a public offering. A private offering can be done in 90 minutes!

How can you raise the money you need for your real estate idea? Form a *Real Estate Investment Trust* (called a REIT for short—it rhymes with feet.) There all kinds of multi-unit REITs today, such as:

- **Hospital REITs.**
- **Marina REITs.**
- **Apartment house REITs.**
- **Nursing home REITs.**

- **Hotel REITs.**
- **Vacation home REITs.**
- **Mortgage REITS which lend money on real estate.**
- **And other REITs.**

Name a type of real estate and you'll almost certainly find a REIT for it. And a REIT can own real estate or lend on real estate. Or it can do both—own and lend—as a *hybrid REIT*. "So," you ask, "how can I form a REIT?"

"That's easy," I respond. "Just take these nine easy steps:"

Nine Steps to Form Your Own REIT

1. **Decide what kind of REIT you want to form.** Try to develop a unique idea for your multi-unit REIT. For example, there are dozens of apartment house REITS. But an apartment house REIT for handicapped people could be a unique type of REIT. An apartment house REIT for senior citizens could also be unique.
2. **Figure out where your REIT will invest.** Nationwide? East Coast? West Coast? Midwest? The area you select should strongly need the type of multi-unit REIT you plan to start.
3. **Compute how much money you'll need for your REIT.** Most multi-unit REITs need at least $5 million starting capital. And many seek $50 million; some even need $100 million from the public. And most stock brokers who sell REITs to the general public or to their regular clients (called a *private offering*) will not handle a REIT deal that's trying to raise less than $5 million. Why? Because the effort needed to raise $5 million is about the same as for $50 million. Since the commission earned is about 13 percent of the amount raised, the stock broker might as well go for the bigger offering and earn more from about the same amount of effort.
4. **Prepare your Declaration of Trust (called DOT for short.)** Don't let the name DOT frighten you! The DOT is simply a fancy name for an *Executive Summary.* Running 400 to 500 words, your DOT tells what kind of multi-unit REIT you're starting, the types of property or mortgages you'll invest in, the percent return you're aiming at for your investors, the unique features of your

REIT, how much money you'll need for your REIT, the types of properties or mortgages you'll invest in, and the essential benefits of your REIT for investors.

5. **Send your DOT to interested stock brokers who might want to take your multi-unit REIT public or sell it privately to their clients.** Write a short letter outlining the strong points of your REIT and its features for investors. Tell the broker what features make your REIT unique and why these will help your broker sell your REIT to clients.
6. **Wait for a response from your broker.** You can send your DOT to dozens of brokers at the same time. "Won't the brokers be offended if I use multiple submissions of my DOT?" you ask. "No way," I reply. "Brokers want new REITs to take to market—either publicly or privately. So they want your proposal!"
7. **Do what the broker asks when he/she likes your DOT.** One of the users of my REIT Kit, entitled *How to Build Your Real Estate Fortune Today in a Real Estate Investment Trust,* wanted to raise $76 million for his REIT located in California. The brokerage house he sent his DOT to said "You have a great REIT here. We can raise the $76 million you're looking for. But we think you need more real estate management experience in your REIT. So we suggest that you hire an experienced real estate manager." Three months later this BWB found an experienced manager in Texas. In his latest report to me he was ready to have the broker go to market with his REIT to raise the needed $76 million. That's a good start for any BWB!
8. **Go to market with your REIT if a brokerage house agrees to do the work for you.** The brokerage house will not ask you for any money up front for your multi-unit REIT offering. Instead, their income will be taken from the proceeds of either the public or private multi-unit REIT offering they do for you. Their total charge, as noted above, is about 13 percent of the money raised for you. This is a fair—and nominal—charge for their work that you could never do yourself. (NOTE: The percent charge given can vary from one brokerage house to another. Be sure to have your real estate attorney fully review all documents before signing any agreement for a public or private offering.)

9. **Get your money and do what you planned for your multi-unit REIT.** Pay yourself a nice salary and rewards in the form of a portion of ownership of the REIT for the work you do. Build your REIT for the benefit of your investors and yourself! Just ***BE SURE TO FOLLOW ALL REGULATIONS GOVERNING REITs. HIRE A COMPETENT REIT ATTORNEY AND ALWAYS FOLLOW THAT PERSON'S LEGAL GUIDANCE!***

Work with Investor Groups for Your Financing

Investor groups fund billions of dollars of real estate every year. These groups are different from REITs. A REIT is either public or private. Investor groups are almost all private organizations dedicated to investing in multi-unit income real estate. Most investor groups are:

- **Limited partnerships made up of anywhere from 10 to 1,000 investors** seeking real estate profits without the daily management hassles that occur in property operation.
- **Limited partnerships comprised of professionals**—doctors, dentists, attorneys, etc.—with excess cash they want to put to work in safe and sound real estate investments.

You can work with limited partnerships in two ways. These ways are:

1. **Form your own limited partnership** to raise money for your real estate investments. Use the money raised to purchase, rehab, flip, or otherwise earn money in real estate. The steps you'll take in forming your own limited partnership are given in Chapter 8.
2. **Contact limited partnerships** and ask them to invest in your deals after presenting the important features of the real estate deals you're contemplating.

Forming a limited partnership is a creative way to raise money for your real estate. Since the steps needed to form your limited partnership are somewhat detailed, you should have an experienced real estate attorney help you do this. The next chapter covers the steps you and your attorney will take to form your real estate limited partnership.

But if you elect the second method and want to ask other limited partnerships to invest in your real estate, here are the steps you'll take.

How to Raise Real Estate Money from Limited Partnerships

To raise money from limited partnerships you should take these seven easy steps:

1. **Prepare a detailed description of your planned real estate investments with projections of the earnings you expect.** Use color for property photos, charts of expected earnings, and other enclosures. Your computer is ideal for this.
2. **Contact local limited partner investor groups in your area.** Ask if you could present your investment opportunities to them at one of their regular meetings.
3. **Prepare carefully for your presentation.** Or, if you're not good at talking to groups of people, hire someone who is. Give that person a small percentage of the money you raise.
4. **Rehearse the presentation before giving it.** Use slides showing properties you'll invest in. Your audience wants to invest in real estate. If you show them appetizing properties they'll put money into them for you.
5. **Know—in advance—how much money you're looking for.** Ask your investor group for that amount of money. Don't be bashful! The more you ask for, the more you'll get.
6. **Retain a portion of the ownership for yourself.** Thus, if 19 people invest in your properties, you should have one-twentieth of the ownership—that is, 19 + 1 = 20. You earn your portion for the work you do.
7. **Build your income and savings from the property financed by the limited partnership.** Use your savings to buy your next multi-unit property that will be 100 percent yours. The limited partnership allows you to get started by its investment in the property you found!

Use 100 Percent Financing Funders to Get Your Multi-Unit Money

There are lenders who will do 100 percent financing—giving you a zero-cash deal. If you're like some of my readers who say, "That's impossible; I never heard of such a lender," I say, "Read and learn!" And I might add, very politely: "Just because you never heard of it does not make it impossible!"

For example, a West Coast reader called me while I was working on this chapter to say:

Yes, 100 percent financing—zero cash down—is alive and well today. But, like all good things in life, you must search for it!

> **100 Percent Investor Property Financing**
>
> "We're getting 100 percent financing on duplexes and fourplexes in this area for non-owner occupied (investor) properties on these terms: 7.5% for the first 80% of the selling price; 10.5% for the remaining 20% of the selling price. On a duplex costing $520,000, we come away with $700 per month positive cash flow (PCF). Thus, we have a zero down deal and $8,400 PCF per year per duplex. This lender will finance a maximum of 10 properties per investor on these terms. So if we get 10 such properties this year, our gross PCF will be $84,000 (= 10 × $8,400 per duplex.) We found this lender after searching for a suitable one for many months. If you look long enough, you can get what you want! There are such lenders looking for qualified buyers today."
>
> —Washington

Three Steps to Getting 100 Percent Financing

To get 100 percent financing for yourself for multi-unit real estate, take these three easy steps:

1. **Select the type of multi-unit real estate you want to invest in—residential, commercial, industrial.** Why? Because once you choose the type of real estate you'll invest in, your choice will guide your loan search.

2. **Prepare a list of potential lenders for your type of real estate.** You can find such lenders by reading the ads run by real estate lenders in your local newspaper, telephone book *Yellow Pages,* and real estate magazines. Or you can go on the Internet site of such lenders and get this info about the type of loans they make. (As a subscriber to my *International Wealth Success* newsletter, you regularly receive the names of real estate lenders in every issue.)
3. **Write a multi-unit loan proposal to submit to your lender.** You MUST have a written proposal. People call me on the phone and say: "I have a question for you." Without identifying themselves or telling me how they found my phone number, they launch into the details of their project. They rattle off such details as a $17.12 per month trash-removal charge. What they don't realize is that:

   - **It is common business courtesy** to identify oneself at the start of a phone call.
   - **It is common business courtesy** to tell the person you're calling how and where you found their telephone number so the recipient of your call "knows where you're coming from," as people say today.
   - **It is common business courtesy** to submit loan details in writing to a lender before demanding an answer. So put your multi-unit loan request in writing before asking for an answer! Few lenders, including myself, will give an answer to a loan request without having a formal request—IN WRITING!

Lenders That Fund Multi-Unit Real Estate Projects

Here's a list of multi-unit real estate lenders that might fund your real estate project. In using this list, please keep the following in mind:

- **These lenders were all in business offering real estate loans of various kinds at the time of the writing of this book.** I have dated information in my bank safe deposit box showing that each listed lender was actively making loans at the time it was listed. In general, these lenders will expect you to have money invested in the project you seek funding for. This investment will generally be in the form of a down payment on an existing project.

- **Lenders—like other businesses—may merge, downsize, upsize, change focus, or go out of business.** Your author has no control over these events. But I will alter this list as I become aware of such changes, when the next printing of this book is made.
- **Please do not blame, threaten, or try to hold me responsible if a listed lender is not making loans when you apply or has changed its business.** I cannot control this! If you treat me this way I will find it difficult to help you. Again, I have no control over the lenders listed here, nor am I associated with them in any way. Furthermore, none of these lenders—so far as I know—makes 100 percent loans.

That said, here's your multi-unit lender list. In this list the letter T gives the phone number, F the fax number, W the web site, where available:

AFC Realty Capital, Inc., 888 Seventh Ave., New York, NY 10106. T: 212-245-2050; F: 212-245-0025; W: *www.afcrealtycapital.com.*

AMI Capital, Inc., 7255 Woodmont Ave., Bethesda, MD 20814. T: 301-654-0033; F: 301-321-1300; W: *www.amicapital.com.*

ARCS Commercial Mortgage, 26901 Agoura Road, Calabasas Hills, CA 91301. T: 800-ASK-ARCS; F: 818-880-3333; W: *www.askARCS.com.*

Aegon USA Realty Advisors, Inc., 4333 Edgewood Road NE, Cedar Rapids, IA 52499. T: 319-369-2224; F: 319-369-2188; W: *www.aegonrealty.com.*

Allfirst Mortgage Corporation, 25 S Charles St., Baltimore, MD 21202. T: 800-737-2344; F: 410-545-2395; W: *www.allfirstmortgage.com.*

American Property Financing, 6 E 43rd St., New York, NY 10017. T: 212-850-4200; W: *www.apfmultifamily.com.*

AmeriSphere Multifamily Finance LLC, 1 Pacific Pl., Omaha, NE 68124. T: 402-498-9184; F: 402-498-9231.

Apartment Lending Corporation, 10232 S Jill Ave., Highlands Ranch, CO 80130. T: 303-771-1031; F: 303-290-6491; W: *www.1031income.com.*

Arbor Commercial Mortgage LLC, 333 Earle Ovington Blvd., Uniondale, NY 11553. T: 516-832-8002; F: 516-832-8045.

Berkshire Mortgage Finance, 1 Beacon St., Boston, MA, 02108. T: 877-523-7722; F: 617-556-1507; W: *www.berkshiremortgage.com.*

Boston Capital, 1 Boston Pl., Boston, MA, 02108. T: 617-624-8900; F: 617-624-8999; W: *www.bostoncapital.com.*

Business Loan Express, 645 Madison Ave., New York, NY 10022. T: 212-751-5626; F: 212-888-3949; W: *www.businessloanexpress.net.*

CB Richard Ellis, 355 S Grand Ave., Los Angeles, CA 90071. T: 213-613-3333; F: 613-3005; W: *www.cbre.com.*

CTL Capital, 300 Park Ave., New York, NY 10022. T: 212-572-6205; F: 212-572-6424; W: *www.CTLcapital.com.*

CW Capital, 63 Kendrick St., Needham, MA 02494. T: 781-707-9300; F: 781-707-9303; W: *www.cwcapital.com.*

Cambridge Realty Capital, 35 E Wacker Dr., Chicago, IL 60601. T: 312-357-1601; F: 312-357-1611; W: *www.cambridgecap.com.*

CapitalSource, 4445 Willard Ave., Chevy Chase, MD 20815. T: 301-841-2700; F: 301-841-2340; W: *www.capitalsource.com.*

Centennial Mortgage, Inc., 112 W Jefferson Blvd., South Bend, IN. T: 574-233-6773; F: 574-233-6855; W: *www.centennialfhaloans.com.*

Charter Municipal Mortgage Acceptance Company, 625 Madison Ave., New York, NY 10022. T: 212-421-5333; F: 212-751-3550; W: *www.chaRTERMAC.COM.*

Collateral Mortgage Capital LLC, 524 Lorna Sq., Birmingham, AL 35216. T: 205-978-1840; F: 205-9787-1483; W: *www.collateral.com.*

Column Financial, Inc., 3414 Peachtree Road, Atlanta, GA 30326. T: 404-239-5300; F: 404-239-0419; W: *www.columnfinancial.com.*

Courus Bank N.A., 3959 N Lincoln Ave., Chicago, IL 60613. T: 800-890-8837; F: 773-832-3540; W: *www.corusbank.com.*

Country Bank, 200 E 42nd St., New York, NY 10017. T: 212-883-6480; F: 212-883-6450; W: *www.countrybankonline.com.*

Dominion Mortgage Corporation, 11355 W Olympic Blvd., Los Angeles, CA 90064. T: 310-477-3041; 310-477-1601; W: *www.dominfin.com.*

Equity Plus Financial, 9750 Miramar Road, San Diego, CA 92126. T: 858-566-3500; F: 858-566-8785.

FarmandRanchLending.com, 11900 W Olympic Blvd., Los Angeles, CA 90064. T: 310-207-3000; F: 310-207-81943; W: *www.farmandranchlending.com.*

Financial Federal Savings Bank, 6305 Humphreys Blvd., Memphis, TN 38120. T: 901-756-2848; F: 901-756-2155.

First Blackhawk Financial Corporation, 3021 Citrus Circle, Walnut Creek, CA 94598. T: 925-648-3067; F: 925-648-3068.

GE Real Estate, 292 Long Ridge Road, Stamford, CT 06927. T: 800-GE-FIRST; F: 203-357-4475; W: *www.gecapitalrealestate.com.*

Glaser Financial Group, Inc., 2177 Youngman Ave., St Paul, MN 55116. T: 651-644-7694; F: 651-644-0923; W: *www.glaser.com.*

Globe Mortgage, Inc., 2 University Plaza, Hackensack, NJ 07601. T: 201-996-6000; F: 201-489-1865.

Green Park Financial Limited Partnership, 7501 Wisconsin Ave., Bethesda, MD 20814. T: 301-215-5500; F: 301-634-2151; W: *www.greenparkfinancial.com.*

Hall Financial Group, 6801 Gaylord Parkway, Frisco, TX 75034. T: 972-377-1100; F: 972-377-1170; W: *www.hallfinancial.com.*

iCap Realty Advisors, 77 W Wacker Dr., Chicago, IL 60601. T: 312-673-4227; F: 312-553-0767; W: *www.iCapRealty.com.*

Imperial Capital Bank, 888 Prospect St., La Jolla, CA 92037. T: 858-551-0511; F: 858-551-0625; W: *www.imperialcapitalbank.com.*

iStar Financial, 1114 Avenue of the Americas, New York, NY 10036. T: 212-930-9400; F: 212-930-9494; W: *www.istarfinancial.com.*

Kennedy Funding Incorporated, 2 University Plaza, Hackensack, NJ 07601. T: 201-342-8500; F: 201-342-8373; W: *www.kennedyfunding.com.*

Key Commercial Real Estate, 127 Public Sq., Cleveland, OH 44114. T: 888-KEY-2221; W: *www.key/cre.*

Lend Lease Mortgage Capital, 700 N Pearl St., Dallas, TX 75201. T: 214-758-5800; F: 214-953-8400; W: *www.lendleasenei.com.*

Liberty Mortgage Acceptance Corporation, 4980 Hillsdale Circle, El Dorado Hills, CA 95762. T: 916-568-0100; F: 916-568-0110; W: *www.libertymac.com.*

Lichenstein Capital Markets, 5770 Palisades Ave., Riverdale, NY 10471. T: 800-242-9888; F: 212-255-5277; W: *www.doctormortgage.com.*

M&T Bank, 350 Park Ave., New York, NY 10022. F: 212-350-2065; W: *www.mandtbank.com.*

Malone Mortgage Company, 8115 Preston Road, Dallas, TX 75225. T: 214-696-0386; F: 214-696-5162; W: *www.malonemortgage.com.*

Manulife Financial, 200 Bloor St. East, Toronto, Ontario M4W 1E5, Canada. T: 416-926-0100; W: *www.manulife.com.*

Money Realty Capital, Inc., 10475 Park Meadows Dr., Littleton, CO 80124. T: 303-325-1050; F: 303-325-1029; W: *www.mony.com/realestate.*

Mortgage & Investment Corporation, 3001 Cambridge Place NW, Washington, DC 20007. T: 202-944-3001; F: 202-944-8002.

Newman Financial Services, 1801 California St., Denver, CO 80202. T: 303-293-8500; F: 303-294-3280.

NorthMarq Capital, 500 Newport Center Dr., Newport Beach, CA 92660. T: 949-717-5200; F: 949-729-4620; W: *www.northmarq.com.*

Origen Financial LLC, 27777 Franklin Road, Southfield, MI 48034. T: 877-644-8838; F: 248-645-7781; W: *www.origenfinancial.com.*

PMC Capital, Inc., 18111 Preston Road, Dallas, TX 75252. T: 972-349-3200; F: 972-349-3265; W: *www.pmccapital.com.*

Pacific Mortgage Funding Corporation, 11924 E Firestone Blvd., Norwalk, CA 90650. T: 562-864-4006; F: 562-864-6125; W: *www.pacificmortgage.com.*

Principal Real Estate Investors, 801 Grand Ave., Des Moines, IA 50392. T: 800-533-1390; F: 515-235-9700; W: *www.principalglobal.com.*

Prudential Mortgage Capital Company, 100 Mulberry St., Newark, NJ 07102. T: 888-263-6800; F: 873-367-8210; W: *www.prudential.com/prumortgage.*

PW Funding, Inc., 200 Old Country Road, Mineola, NY 11501. T: 800-566-7933; F: 516-873-0080; W: *www.pwfunding.com.*

Quantum First Capital, 8235 Douglas Ave., Dallas, TX 75225. T: 214-346-0200; F: 214-436-0244; W: *www.qfclp.com.*

Reilly Mortgage Group, Inc., 2010 Corporate Ridge, McLean, Va 22102. T: 703-760-4700; F: 703-760-4056; W: *www.reilly.com.*

Related Capital Company, 625 Madison Ave., New York, NY 10022. T: 212-421-5333; F: 212-751-3550; W: *www.relatedcapital.com.*

Sterling Commercial Capital, 53 Unquowa Pl., Fairfield, CT 06824. T: 203-256-9068; F: 203-256-9564; W: *www.sterlingcommercialcapital.com.*

Tremont Realty Capital, 125 Summer St., Boston, MA 02110. T: 617-439-6700; F: 617-951-1477; W: *www.tremontcapital.com.*

USA Capital, 4484 S Pecos Road, Las Vegas, NV 89121. T: 702-734-2400; F: 702-734-0163; W: *www.usacapitallender.com.*

WACHOVIA, 301 S College St., Charlotte, NC 28288. T: 704-383-6315; F: 704-374-6345; W: *www.wachovia.com.*

Webster Bank, 185 Asylum St., Hartford, CT 06103. T: 860-692-1693; F: 860-692-1624.

Your Keys to Real Estate Riches

- ❑ **In income real estate,** you have almost unlimited sources of funding for your projects.
- ❑ **Your First Mortgage** is usually the easiest type of real estate financing to get when your project is in reasonably good condition.
- ❑ **Your Second Mortgage** may be the next easiest type of real estate loan to get.
- ❑ **Guaranteed loans,** with your guarantee coming from a government agency, may be good for you if your credit is not the strongest.
- ❑ **There are some grants available** for real estate projects that benefit large groups of people.
- ❑ **Down payment loans** can be obtained from at least five different sources.
- ❑ **Private lender financing** can be your key to real estate riches.
- ❑ **A REIT** (Real Estate Investment Trust) can be your source of either public or private funding for multi-unit real estate deals.
- ❑ **Investor groups,** such as limited partnerships made up of professionals, can be an excellent source of funding for you. But you must—in general—make a presentation to them to get your money.
- ❑ **There ARE 100 percent funders** in business today. You must look carefully for them in your area. It will usually take time. Or you may find one your first day of looking!
- ❑ **Deal with experienced multi-unit lenders** and you can find the money you seek for your real estate project. Try the lenders given in this chapter for your *larger multi-unit projects.*

CHAPTER 7

Creative Financing of Your Real Estate Fortune

CREATIVE FINANCING BUILDS MORE REAL ESTATE FORTUNES FOR BWBs than any other type of funding known. You, too, can use creative financing to build your wealth. To begin, we'll define what we mean by creative financing:

> **Creative financing is the use of methods that get you investment money you need by recognizing your financial lacks and shortcomings and focusing on them to overcome these negatives in your search for the financing you seek.**

Thus, when you use creative financing you work from your recognized weak points. Focusing on lack helps you build strong results and a fortune in real estate! Here's how.

Quick Proof That Creative Financing Really Works

To show you how viable real estate and creative financing are, here are a few reader letters showing what you can do in the world's best business—real estate:

Getting Started Is Easy—When You Know How

"After reading your books, I found myself getting up and going. I have purchased some apartments and townhouses with your zero-cash ideas and they have worked wonderfully. At present I'm working on buying a private hospital in Europe using your techniques." —Virginia

Quick Start with Good Results

"I thank you. After reading one of your books I went out and bought my first 4-plex. It has made me money every day since. Again, I thank you." —Georgia

Good First Year in Real Estate

"This was my first year in real estate investing, and a very profitable one, thanks to your books, courses and newsletters. From March to November this year I acquired eight houses and one building lot, all valued at $350,000, with only $650 down. At the same time I mortgaged out with $27,000 in tax-free money. Including my personal home, my real estate assets total $400,000. My net worth is $150,000, and the investment property gives me $500 per month positive cash flow." —Virginia

Seven Reasons Why You May Need Financial Help

Your first step in using creative financing for real estate is to analyze your financial lacks and shortcomings. In doing this, we're not criticizing you. Instead, we're showing you how you can help yourself. Here's a list of seven frequently met financial lacks and shortcomings:

1. **No credit history—that is, the person never financed a car, a home, a washing machine, or other large purchases. With no credit history, the borrower can't be "checked out."**

2. **The borrower has a low credit rating on the usual letter credit score of A, B, C, or D. In this rating system "A" credit is the highest or best, while "D" credit is the lowest or worst.**
3. **History of bankruptcy in the last few years. (If your bankruptcy occurred more than 7 years ago, it will usually be off your record.)**
4. **Your FICO® score (see Chapter 3) is less than 600.**
5. **You have court judgments against you for not paying bills in the past.**
6. **You have a record as a convicted felon for earlier indiscretions.**
7. **Any other negative credit history that's on file about you.**

If any of the credit problems above apply to you, take hope! You can still get started and earn big money in income real estate. I have hundreds of letters from people with almost all the above problems who still got started and are earning a big income today in income real estate!

Real Estate Ownership with "No Money"

"I have read several of your books and have used many of your ideas to improve my financial status. Within the last year I purchased two 8-unit apartment buildings at a time when I had no money. I used 100% borrowed money. Both apartment buildings are in my home town—population 1,300. As a result of these two real estate purchases I have increased my net worth from $8,000 to $50,000, after improvements and rent increases." Minnesota

And another reader tells us in a letter:

You Can Overcome Bankruptcy

"After reading your book How to Borrow Your Way to Real Estate Riches we are enthused about becoming Successful Beginning Wealth Builders—SBWBs, as you call them. We thought we would give it a try. So we applied at a local bank for a $6,000 loan to buy real estate. One week later they loaned us $7,000. Tomorrow we are buying our second property with zero cash down. Not bad after having a bankruptcy three years ago!"

—Ohio

How to Overcome Financial Problems

The best answer I've found to financial problems of the type listed previously is *creative financing*. You use your problems to create your solutions. And what do your solutions do for you? They:

- **Give you assets**—that is, ownership of real estate that rises in value as time passes.
- **Give you a regular income** from your rentals, an income that will increase as time passes.
- **Give you the basis** for building a strong credit rating as you pay off your loans.

Yes, *creative financing* can give you a new life—quickly and easily. And while you're building your new life, you're rendering a valuable service to people needing clean, comfortable, and safe housing. So let's overcome any financial problems you may have by using *creative financing!*

NOTE: The first "problem" listed above—having no credit history—is really not of your doing. Some people who start their real estate moneymaking career early haven't had time to establish their credit history. But the "problem" CAN be overcome, as this reader writes:

Youth and Real Estate *DO* Mix

"About a year ago I bought, and read, your book, How to Make Millions in Real Estate in 3 Years Starting with No

> Cash and I began buying real estate even though I was just 21 years old and had no credit. In one year I bought a lovely home, two co-operative apartments, a 5-family and a 6-family apartment house—all for zero cash down. They appraise at just under $800,000. It still amazes me—a year later—that I am able to own real estate, being so young and without a credit rating!"
>
> —New York

You CAN get income real estate for yourself, even with every financial challenge listed before, plus dozens of others you might name! So let's get you started on *your* way to real estate riches using creative financing.

Get Income Property with an Option

No credit history? A bankruptcy last month? Behind in support payments to a former spouse? Out of work, with no prospect of a new job? Yet you want to get into income real estate? No problem!

An option gives you the right to buy or sell a property for a given period of time. Your time allowance can be 30, 60, 90, 120 days, or more. When you take an option on a property, there usually is:

- **No credit investigation.**
- **No income check.**
- **No employment review.**
- **No request for the last three years' tax returns.**

You just pay a small amount for the option—from $1 to $100—for single-family homes. Then you take fast action to:

- **Sell the property** for a profit before the option expires.
- **Get financing** for the property based on the income it will deliver to you.
- **Option the property** to someone else for a much higher fee than you paid.

You can take ALL these steps without ever being asked a single question about your credit, your job, your business, or any other personal matter. Your whole key to success with no-questions-asked options is:

- **You must have a plan** for the optioned property BEFORE you take the option.
- **You must know,** in advance, approximately how much money you can earn from flipping the property after you take your option.
- **You must act quickly** so you get results long before your option runs out.

So consider using an option to control real estate long enough to earn money from it. You can use an option at any age—18 or 80—with any credit rating—A through D—with any financial history! Just follow the easy steps above. A typical real estate option is shown in Figure 7.1.

Don't think that options limit you to small properties. Just read this letter from a reader:

Options Can Give You Great Results

"We received the March issue of your newsletter and thoroughly enjoyed perusing it and examining in detail the vast number of wealth opportunities. We are very active in the Canadian real estate market and just gained control of another piece of property via an option with no expiration date. The property is valued at $5,800,000. Again, we got it with no money down."

—Canada

Buy Properties Having Assumable Mortgages

An assumable mortgage is a loan on a property you take responsibility for when you buy the property and gain title to its income stream. There normally is no credit check when you assume a mortgage. Why? Because the sale is between you and the seller with no financial checking of you by a bank, a credit union, or a mortgage lender.

Option to Purchase Real Estate

Date: ______________

In consideration of the amount of $100.00 (one hundred dollars and no cents), John and Jane Doe (the optioners) hereby grant Mary and Edward Smith (the optionees) the exclusive right to purchase the property at 123 Main Street, Anytown, US 12345 for the next 90 (ninety) days from the date above, at a price of $100,000.00 (one hundred thousand dollars and no cents). During this time the optionees are free to sell the above-named property to anyone of their choice, provided they satisfy the terms of this option in full. This option covers the entire agreement between the above-named parties and no other understandings, written or oral, are in force. In the event of disagreements, this option will be subject to the laws of the State of ______________.

Agreed:
Optioners: ____________________
Optionees: ____________________

Figure 7.1 Example of a Real Estate Option (*Note:* Any option you use MUST be prepared by a competent qualified real estate attorney.)

And most sellers will accept you as you are. They won't "pull a credit report" on you if they feel you're a "good guy or gal." So you're into an income property without a credit check of any kind. Steps to take are:

- **Get the seller to take a Purchase Money (PM) mortgage** for the down payment if you don't have the cash needed for it.

- **The Purchase Money Mortgage becomes your assumable mortgage** because there are no credit checks associated with the takeover loan.
- **Your seller**—in effect—becomes your assumable-loan lender.

A reader writes:

Purchase Money Mortgage for Zero-Cash Takeover

"In three days we are closing a deal on an 11-unit apartment building. We easily got a first mortgage. For the balance we got a Purchase Money Mortgage (from the seller.) So we did not have to put any money into the deal to get the property."

—Michigan

Properties financed by the Veterans Administration (VA) can have assumable first mortgages. So check foreclosures offered by the VA because you can often get into a single-family home with no credit check and no qualifying requirements. You'll find VA foreclosures at *www.va.gov.*

When you combine an assumable first mortgage with a PM mortgage you have a true zero-down deal. In addition, there usually are NO credit checks of any kind with either type of assumable mortgage!

For example, a reader writes:

Sellers Respect Your Experience

"Enclosed is information on the two apartment buildings I mentioned to you on the telephone the other night. The sellers said they would finance the entire sale for someone who has experience in running rental property. Fortunately, I have eight units, thanks to the information I got from reading one of your real estate books. The owners aren't concerned with the terms. They'll work all of that out with a competent buyer."

—Oklahoma

Assumable Mortgage Possibilities for You

When you think of an assumable mortgage, think in terms of two possibilities, namely:

- **An assumable First Mortgage for anywhere from 75 to 90 percent** of the purchase price of the property. With a motivated seller, you might even get a 100 percent mortgage—giving you a zero-cash deal.
- **An assumable Purchase Money Mortgage for anywhere from 10 to 25 percent** of the purchase price of the property.

There's more good news for you on assumable mortgages, namely:

- **The lender cannot raise the interest rate** on any mortgage you assume. Thus, the rate the seller is paying on the mortgage will be the rate ***you*** will pay.
- **The lender cannot refuse to allow you to assume the mortgage,** if the seller wants you to assume it, unless there's a *Due-on-Sale Clause* in the mortgage. Such a clause requires that the mortgage be paid in full if the property is sold by the current mortgage holder—the seller.
- **The lender may omit a Due-on-Sale Clause** from an Adjustable Rate Mortgage (called ARM for short). So look for sellers having an ARM on the property you want to buy. (As an aside, let me say that life insurance companies seldom have a Due-on-Sale Clause in their mortgages for smaller properties. So when you learn that the mortgage on a property you're interested in is held by a life insurance company, rejoice! It probably does not have a Due-on-Sale Clause.)

One final note: FHA and VA loans made prior to December 1, 1986, did not have a Due-on-Sale Clause in the mortgage. So if you're looking at a property having such a mortgage, you know there's no Due-on-Sale Clause to deal with. After December 15, 1989, all FHA mortgages have the Due-on-Sale Clause in them. Keep this in mind when you look at a property to buy.

Find Zero Percent Down and 100 Percent Lenders

Look in your local telephone-book *Yellow Pages* under "Mortgages" for 0 percent down financing. Also look for 100 percent loans in the same place. You'll also find lenders offering "Bankruptcy OK" loans, "No Credit Check" Loans, and "No Income Check" loans among others. Such loans can give you the creative financing you seek.

Also, the IWS publications listed at the back of this book can give you these types of lenders. Many such loans can be yours, even with earlier credit problems. One reader writes:

105 Percent Financing with a Good Net on Closing

"I bought a single-family home with 105% financing which will net me 100% after closing costs and points. I have signed a lease with a tenant that will give me a positive cash flow from the house. And the lease makes the tenant responsible for all maintenance and repairs of the house."

—New Jersey

Use a Lease Option Contract to Control Property

A lease option contract, also called a *lease purchase contract* or a *land contract,* allows you to take possession of a property without a credit check or—in many cases—a down payment. With a lease option contract, you have:

- **Full use of the property for income purposes** for as long as the lease option lasts.

- **Full control of the property** and can rent it out, repair it, expand it, or otherwise make it more livable for your tenants.
- **Part of your monthly lease payment** applied towards making you the eventual owner of the property when you've fulfilled the terms of the lease option.
- **The obligation to pay** the real estate taxes, insurance, water charges, or any other charges on the property, which are included as part of your monthly rent-like payments you make for the duration of the lease contract.

You can use the lease option to get lots of income property to build a monthly positive cash flow without ever having your credit checked out. Why? Because the seller offering a lease option:

- **Wants to get rid of property quickly.**
- **Can be appealed to** and "sold" on your sincerity and dependability.
- **Will rarely run** a credit check on you if he/she believes in you.

And—of course—you can use a lease option contract when you have good credit. In fact, any of the methods you get in this chapter are equally useful to people with good or bad credit, or no credit at all!

Good Financing with a Land Contract

"I just finished How to Borrow Your Way to Real Estate Riches. I am truly excited about the wealth of information in the book. In fact, I just purchased a duplex worth $30,000 paying $13,500 for it with $3,600 down with the remaining $9,900 on a land contract at 10 percent interest with payments of $180 per month. The cash flow from the property is $450 per month. It will be paid off in 5 years. I financed all but $400 of the down payment. It is rented to reliable tenants."

—Michigan

Use Credit Card Lines of Credit

I can just hear some readers saying to me, "Use credit-card lines of credit? I couldn't get a credit card if my life depended on it!" My answer to you is: "That may be true. But what about the credit cards held by the following people?

- **Friends.**
- **Relatives.**
- **Business associates.**

Plenty of my readers temporarily use credit cards from one or more of the sources above. They repay their source quickly and go on to greater wealth. Here are some reader letters showing you the power of using credit card lines of credit to buy income real estate. The credit card line of credit could be yours or that of one of the three sources above:

Credit Card Lines Can Be Your Down Payment

"After reading one of your real estate books I went looking for my first deal. I located a recently rehabbed legal two-unit building whose income would service an 80% mortgage. Since I did not have the remaining 20%, I remembered your suggestions about using credit card lines of credit.

I used my credit cards for part of the down payment and convinced the seller to carry back at 11 percent a second mortgage for 3 years. I bought this property by financing the entire deal with other people's money!" —Rhode Island

Another reader who really uses creative financing to the maximum available to him writes:

Credit Cards as a Way to Real Estate Wealth

"About a year ago I bought one of your real estate books and took the steps you outlined to create a credit line of $70,000 with credit cards and personal loans. That alone was incredible

> to me. Then I recently bought my first property, a townhouse from HUD. I bid below the asking price and won the property. I used credit card lines of credit to pay for the house and received a $600 bonus for a fast closing. I then mortgaged the property and got $3,500 cash more than I paid for it. I ran an ad and will now rent the property for $640 per month, slightly below the market, but I wanted a fast tenant. I have a positive cash flow."
>
> —Georgia

Based on the reports that BWBs give me today, credit card lines of credit are widely used for income real estate down payment money. This source of money is an excellent example of creative financing for BWBs everywhere. So give it some thought for your future wealth building in income real estate!

Flip Real Estate with Creative Financing

When you flip real estate, you buy it at as low a price as you can, fix it up a bit, and then sell it at a profit. Flipping gives you many opportunities to use creative financing to the maximum.

Why? Because when you get real estate to flip, you can use an option, a land contract, credit card lines of credit, or other ways to control the property for the time you need to flip it for a profit. For proof, see these reader letters:

> ### Just Five Months to Positive Earnings
>
> "In January I started full-time buying and selling residential real estate. It has been successful beyond my expectations. During my first 5 months, my financial statement shows I made $46,000. The average length of ownership of my flip properties has been 77 days. Most of the property I buy is distressed, and in need of repairs. It is often vacant and vandalized, with title problems, owners divorcing, and/or being

foreclosed. Mostly, I buy at 50 percent to 70 percent of market value. I won't pay more than 80 percent of market, including any repair costs. I have averaged $5,000 profit on every piece of property sold. I have closed 18 so far this year. I have one crew to do all my work which is guaranteed to pass FHA or VA inspection. With nearly a year of experience, it is getting easier to buy good deals and I am able to earn more profit per house. Next year I expect to handle 25 to 30 houses." —Texas

Youthful Start Gets Good Results

"I started buying rental houses 1.5 years ago. I am 25 years old. In the 1.5 years I've been in business I bought 29 houses. I live and breathe rental houses—I love the business. I just flipped my first house and made $8,000 in two months! I will quit my job at a lumber company as soon as I have a large enough positive cash flow to support myself. I taught my sister how to flip houses and she bought two houses in her first two weeks." —Missouri

How to Start and Be Successful in Flipping Properties

To start buying houses to flip, take these eight easy steps in the area in which you believe there is a good potential for your business:

1. **Look around the area.** Check to see if you have a supply of houses to buy and sell.
2. **See if there is a demand for housing in the area.** Young families need low-priced homes.
3. **Get estimates from HUD, FHA, the VA** on typical housing prices in the area.
4. **Check local papers on Sunday for bargain properties.** Read every classified *For Sale* ad. You'll almost certainly find bargains.

5. **Visit potential bargains;** see how much work they need.
6. **Find a competent contractor** who can help you with needed repairs.
7. **Bid on your first flip house,** after you know how much profit you can make on it.
8. **Do your first flip job.** Go on to more, using creative financing.

You *can* make money using creative financing in flipping. For best results, you should have some experience with home repairs. And you should not be afraid to pick up a hammer and start working!

But if you're "all thumbs"—as some people are—don't give up. Get an experienced house mechanic and arrange to have that person do the work. Offer an incentive—such as a share in the profit on the sale of the property. Then your repair work will be done while you do the financial planning!

Take Lenders Out of Foreclosure Properties

Closely related to flipping is the Foreclosure Specialist who takes lenders out of properties they don't want to own. These properties are often called *REO—Real Estate Owned.* No lender wants REO properties on its books!

Why? Because a lender's business is to accumulate money and then lend it out on safe loans to earn interest. The interest earnings are shared with the suppliers of money. Such suppliers are people who put their excess funds into savings accounts, bonds, and similar holdings.

No lender wants to own property! Every lender wants nothing more than to receive a check on the first of every month for the repayment of a mortgage loan the lender made. That's "lender heaven."

How to Be a Hero with Lenders

You can be a hero to any lender by:

- **Agreeing to take repossessed homes** off the lender's hands.
- **Relieving the lender of an intense problem,** often at zero cash to you.

- **Having all closing costs paid** by the lender because they have an in-house legal staff and the work doesn't cost them much.
- **Flipping the property** for a profit for yourself and making the lender happy because it no longer has REOs on its hands.

With zero cash down for REO properties you have the ultimate in creative financing. And—happily—many lenders will not even check your credit when you take over an REO property.

Why? The lender is so happy to get rid of the REO that a credit check is overlooked. So if you're into fixing up houses and selling them, check out REOs. You'll often find them listed in your Sunday paper real estate section.

You can, of course, work with a house mechanic and have that person do the fix-up. Then you share a small portion of the profit with your mechanic. This allows you to do the financial planning for your future purchases.

Work with the FDIC and VA for Flip Properties

Both the Federal Deposit Insurance Corporation (FDIC) and the Veterans Administration (VA) may have properties for sale at excellent prices for flip BWBs. Thus:

- **The FDIC has a searchable database** of property currently for sale by type, state, city, value range, and other criteria. This list is updated weekly. FDIC properties can vary from single-family homes to some of the largest buildings available anywhere.
- **Properties listed** in the database are sold on an "as-is, where-is" basis, with all faults they may have. So you may be able to get bargains galore!
- **Each listed property** has a contact name and telephone number. The contact name will either be an individual from an FDIC office or an individual associated with the sale of the property. If a property information package (PIP) has been prepared on a property it can be obtained from the listed individual.

- **Property listings are updated** by the close of business each Monday. So you have an ongoing and steady supply of properties to study and consider.
- **Seller financing may be available** on some residential properties with a minimum purchase price of $500,000 or those residential properties sold as affordable housing, and on all commercial and land properties, regardless of price.
- **Go to the Internet site** at *http://www.fdic.gov/buying/owned/index.html* to find FDIC properties that might be excellent flip candidates for you.

Get Section 8 Tenants for Steady Rental Income

Section 8 of the Federal Government Housing Program pays a portion or all of the rent for homeless or low-income families renting homes. In the New York City area, for example, the Emergency Assistance Rehousing Program (EARP) not only pays the Section 8 rent for homeless families, it also pays a one-time rent bonus to the property owner (you) after the family moves in. This bonus is:

Family Size (Number of People)	One-Time Bonus ($)
2	2,000
3	3,000
4	4,500
5	6,000
6	7,000
7	9,000
8	10,000

$1,000 for each additional family member

To make the program more attractive to building owners, the City has added Section 8 subsidies, permitting rent payments up to the Fair Market Rates. Maximum rental fees at the time of this writing were:

Fair-Market Rents	
Studio	$ 845
1 Bedroom	$ 940
2 Bedrooms	$1,069
3 Bedrooms	$1,348
4 Bedrooms	$1,515
5 Bedrooms	$1,753
6 Bedrooms	$1,992

Since rents rarely decline, you can expect these subsidies to rise as time passes. Thus, you have a bright future with such housing.

Other features of Section 8 rent subsidies are:

- **The rent subsidy** does not include the gas and electric for the apartment. The tenant pays these charges.
- **Your bonus is paid** in a single payment once the tenant is approved and signs a lease with you, the building owner.
- **Many areas have waiting lists** of Section 8 tenants. So you can rent your apartment as soon as it becomes available.
- **You choose the tenant** from a pool of eligible homeless families approved for Section 8 vouchers.

Buy and Control Properties in Inner-City Areas

Inner-city areas often offer the lowest-priced properties anywhere. And they also offer the greatest opportunities for creative financing. A reader called to say:

You Never Know When Luck Will Appear

"I saw an ad for a free legal two-family partially burned-out home in the Sunday paper. I called the owner and he said he was fed up with the vandalism in the area and would be happy to give me the property free of any charge. When it came to the transfer of the title my attorney told me that the state required that some money be paid before a title could be transferred. So I paid the seller $1 and the house was mine. I quickly rented the house for $800 a month with an option to buy at a later date. Now, a year later, the person renting the house has repaired it completely and wants to buy it from me for $34,500. My only worry is the capital gain taxes I'll have to pay because my 'cost basis' is just one dollar. But I do know I'll have the money to pay the taxes because I'll be getting all cash."

—Maryland

Now the $1 this reader paid may not be zero cash! But it certainly is very, very close to zero cash. And her willingness to take a chance with a partially burned-out property shows her creative spirit at its best.

Inner-city homes have many advantages for the creative real estate BWB. These advantages include:

- **Low, low prices** in many areas.
- **Plenty of room** for really creative negotiation of price and terms.
- **Lots of local government money** help to rehab the property.
- **An enormous pool of renters** ready to snatch up clean, safe apartments.
- **Local financing,** often available from both the private and public sectors.

So don't turn your back on the creative financing attractions of inner-city housing! You may be overlooking the chance to become a real estate millionaire while providing good housing for needy families. And—of course—Section 8 benefits, described above, are fully available to you.

You should, though, take sensible precautions when traveling in neighborhoods having high crime rates. Consult with police and other informed people concerning the steps you should take to protect yourself and your property.

Search for Low, Low Down Payments

There *are* low, low down payment properties available. All you have to do is look for them! That's where most people fail—they just don't look for long enough. As Ben Franklin said, "Plow deep while sluggards sleep." Low, low down represents the second best type of creative financing. Look at this letter:

> **No-Cash Start and Just $1.00 Down**
>
> "I had no cash when I started this venture of owning income property 19 months ago but I acted on the advice in one of your real estate books. So far I've acquired about $200,000 in income properties and lake-shore raw land. I was able to buy two income properties for $1.00 down on each. I just sold one I didn't want to deal with for a profit of $2,000 after owning it one year. Not bad for a $1.00 investment! I bought another building with eight apartments for $63,000 for a $1.00 investment. With the improvements I've made in it I could sell it for a $10,000 profit. There is no possible way I could put a price on the value your books have been to me during the last 19 months." —Canada

Of course, the lowest low, low down is zero-cash down. Here's a reader who writes:

> **There's No Lower Down Than Zero Down**
>
> "Your advice helped me acquire eight different apartment buildings last year, all with zero-cash down. In addition, they are producing a good positive cash flow." —New York

So how do you find low, low down properties? There's really just one answer to this question. That answer is:

Look in every possible source for low, low down properties. These sources include your large-city Sunday newspapers, your local weekly newspapers, real estate agents, property management magazines, city and state housing agencies, federal housing groups, local real estate investor groups, local building owners associations and *For Sale By Owner* ads.

Keep looking until you find what you want. Looking costs little. But it can deliver big results! Why? Because there are few people willing to invest the time and energy it takes to look widely and deeply.

Borrow to the Hilt for Income Real Estate

While you were growing up you might have been warned: "Never a borrower be." While that's good advice for your personal life, it's not accurate for business. And income real estate—remember—IS a business!

So for income real estate, the advice often is: Borrow to the hilt to get the income properties you want. A reader writes:

Fast Growth in Three Years

"For the last three years I have used your methods. I now have four apartment buildings worth $450,000. Three years ago I had only a triplex. By using your wonderful methods of borrowing to the hilt, I have been able to acquire these four larger buildings." —California

When you borrow to the hilt you use the value of the properties you own to collateralize (back up) your loans. So:

- **The property you've bought on borrowed money backs up new loans for more property**—which you buy using borrowed money!
- **The property you bought with borrowed money pays off the debt** you incurred to buy the property.

- ***Money Makes Money; and the Money Money Makes Makes Money!***

So don't be afraid to borrow money for income real estate. Just be sure you have a positive cash flow from *every* property—after paying on *all* loans associated with that property!

Use Home Equity and Personal Loans to Build Your Wealth

If you own real estate now you can borrow against your equity in it and use the money to buy income real estate. This technique of creative financing is used again and again by real estate BWBs. Here's a letter from a reader showing this method at work:

> **100 Percent Financing with a Home Equity Loan**
>
> "I currently own a 4-unit apartment building bought with 100% financing using a home equity loan for the down payment and settlement costs. I am using your principles which you give in How to Make Big Money in Real Estate."
>
> —Delaware

Yet another reader is using a personal loan:

> **Getting Started with a Personal Loan**
>
> "I just wanted to let you know I bought an income condo with zero cash down by borrowing from my pension, using a personal loan. I got a good interest rate because its in a new condo development. Since its a first mortgage I don't have a balloon payment to worry about later. It may not be the biggest deal ever reported to you. But I did get started. I put

> thought into action! I feel your newsletter helped me with an article you had on condos that sparked me to do something ASAP to get the ball rolling."
>
> —Illinois

There is good news for you about home equity loans and creative financing. When you apply for a home equity loan you never need tell the lender what you plan to use the loan money for. So you can buy as many properties as you can afford using a home equity loan.

With a personal loan you must tell what you intend to use the money for. Acceptable uses include: education, vacation, home improvement, debt consolidation, medical, dental, miscellaneous, and others. Unacceptable uses include—for certain lenders—home or real estate down payment. Other lenders make personal loans for these uses. You are not allowed to borrow personal funds to buy stocks or bonds, unless you're using a stock broker's margin account.

Places where you can get personal and home equity loans include:

- **Commercial banks.**
- **Savings banks.**
- **Credit unions.**
- **Finance companies.**

To get a loan from any of these lenders, be sure you type your application throughout. And if your FICO® score is less than 600, or your Debt to Income is more than 35 percent, have a cosigner handy to help you get your loan. And be certain to use some of your loan for the stated purpose given on your loan application!

Mortgage Out to Get Paid for Creative Financing

Earlier we said that low, low down payments were the second best type of creative financing. So what, you ask, is the BEST type of creative financing? It is *Mortgaging Out* where you:

- **Are paid to take out a loan** to buy income-producing property.
- **Pay off your loan with income from the property** you bought with the loan money.
- **Receive tax-free cash** at the closing to use for whatever purpose you choose. If would be wise to use your mortgaging-out cash to buy more income property!)

So you really can't beat Mortgaging Out as a way to real estate wealth. Just take a look at these letters from readers:

Mortgaging Out in Country Property

"I bought 30 acres of land plus house, barn, equipment shed, cattle shed, silos and smokehouse at auction for $60,000 and got a loan from the bank for $65,000. The assessed value at the courthouse at the time of the purchase was $114,000. So I mortgaged out with $5,000 cash plus the property!" —Virginia

Mortgaging Out with Development Land

"I opened a company and bought—with 107 percent financing—my first investment real estate. It is a piece of land zoned for apartment buildings." —Canada

Yes, mortgaging out *can* be *your* way to real estate riches. But to mortgage out you must plan each step of the way. You must:

- **Pick property** that has a market value higher than the purchase price.
- **Arrange for secondary financing** that's based on the market value, not the selling price.
- **Have good legal advice** from a competent attorney every step of your way.

- **Be completely honest** in all your dealings with lenders.
- **Give accurate, checkable facts** on every loan application you fill out.
- **Work your numbers on every property.** If you're not good at numbers, I'll work them for you, if you subscribe to my *International Wealth Success* newsletter or to my *Money Watch Bulletin* newsletter for two years or more.

Other Ways to Creative Financing

Real estate—the world's best business—has hundreds—if not thousands—of ways to use creative financing to acquire income property. We've touched on just a few in this chapter. Later in this book you'll find many more creative approaches to financing income property.

To get some of this creative financing for your deals, keep alert to the many opportunities that come your way. And if you ever have any questions, give me a call. You'll find my business phone and fax numbers at the end of this book.

Your Keys to Real Estate Riches

- ❑ **Creative financing** can get you started in real estate on little or no money sooner than you think.
- ❑ **When you use creative financing,** you capitalize on your financial lacks or drawbacks to build strength into your borrowing skills.
- ❑ **Your first step to creative financing** is to analyze your financial lacks and shortcomings.
- ❑ **Creative financing can give you** *Assets, Income,* and a *Base* on which to build a solid future.
- ❑ **Options allow you to get real estate**—in many cases, with no credit check.
- ❑ **Look for assumable mortgages;** they can be your key to creative financing.

- ❑ **Government loan guarantees** can mean the difference between approval and rejection.
- ❑ **Flipping real estate** can give you an income with little credit investigation.
- ❑ **Section 8 tenants** can keep your income property 100 percent filled.
- ❑ **Always try to mortgage out**—it's the premier creative financing technique.

CHAPTER 8

Find and Use Unique and Unusual Funding Sources

YOUR WHOLE KEY TO GETTING RICH ON BORROWED MONEY (OPM) IN real estate is finding suitable lenders. In this chapter, you'll learn how and where you can find suitable lenders for your real estate projects.

Sure Steps to Finding *Your* Suitable Lenders

You can get better results—sooner—in your search for real estate money—if you follow a proven procedure. "And what's that procedure?" you ask. Here it is, in seven simple—and lucky—steps for you:

1. **Decide what type of real estate you want to own.** At the start, it is best to specialize in just one type of real estate. Why? Because then you don't scatter your efforts or energy.
2. **Search in your area for the type of real estate you want to own.** Earlier chapters tell you where to conduct your search. If you can't decide, give me a call and I'll help you on the phone.
3. **Get full data on projects that interest you.** You'll need the *Price*, the *Income*, the *Expenses*, and the *Down Payment*.
4. **Focus on one project that appeals to you.** Don't try to juggle three or four at once. It will boggle your mind and you'll give up—confused. (And please don't send me four or six projects to evaluate at one time! I'm just one skinny little guy and I can only think of one project at a time!)

5. **Determine how much money you need to take over the project.** Remember: *Your first mortgage is usually easier to get than your down payment money.* Buy if your credit isn't the strongest, your first mortgage may be harder to get than you expect at the start.
6. **Look for your money in two places:** long-term lenders for your first mortgage; short-term lenders for your down payment money.
7. **Take the action needed to get each loan so you can close on the property and start earning money from it.** That—remember—is the whole idea of your work—to earn money for yourself and your loved ones!

Pick the Type of Real Estate You Want to Own

You must know what kind of real estate you want to own. "Why?" you ask. Because for each type of real estate:

- **There are specialized** and unique lenders.
- **Who know and specialize in** one type of real estate.
- **Making loans** on that kind of real estate almost daily.
- **Giving advice and help** to borrowers who come to them.
- **Understanding the ins and outs** of that type of real estate.
- **Being more willing to make loans** on "their" type of property.

So if you know what type of real estate you want to own to build your fortune, you can approach a lender who specializes in that type of real estate. There are four basic types of real estate you can own for income purposes:

1. **Land** for development or leasing to others.
2. **Residential properties**—single- or multi-family.
3. **Commercial properties**—stores (strip malls and shopping malls), offices, recreational facilities.
4. **Industrial properties**—factories, storage buildings, and yards.

Most of my readers already know what type of real estate they want to own when they call or write me. I'm sure that right now you have a good idea of what type of real estate you'd like to own. So let's get you your lenders!

Find the Unique Lender for Your Kind of Real Estate

For every kind of real estate, there's a group of lenders that specialize in handling loans for that kind of property. And—also—for every kind of real estate, there are a few unique and unusual lenders.

Your job is to find both types of lenders. And I'm here to help you every step of the way in finding those lenders. For example:

If you want to own raw land for development or leasing purposes, you'll find there are fewer lenders who'll work with you than with other types of real estate. Why is this? Because raw land—in general—does not produce income. So lenders rate raw land as a non-income producing asset. Hence, they're less likely to lend you money for it. Yet there are some lenders that like raw land as a loan asset.

Finding suitable lenders can be highly rewarding for you. Why? Because once you find a suitable lender and do a deal, the next deal becomes much easier. So, too, for follow-up deals with that lender. Thus, your efforts are rewarded—again and again.

How to Find Unique Lenders for Land Deals

Few lenders specialize in land deals. So you have a real challenge in finding such lenders. When you want to buy raw land, look at these loan sources:

- **The seller**—many sellers will finance their land sale, asking for little down payment-sometimes as little as just $100.
- **Government sellers**—state and federal governments sometimes offer land for as little as $1 per acre—with no financing charges. And if you buy large amounts of this land—several thousand

acres—the government may extend credit to you to pay for your land over a period of years.

- **Farm Service Agency**—offers loans to beginning farmers and ranchers for up to $200,000 for purchase of land, construction of buildings, purchase of equipment, or other needs. These loans are under the Direct Farm Ownership, Beginning Farmer Down Payment Farm Ownership, and other programs.
- **Area development agencies**—private groups interested in developing a town, city, or state offer financing for land purchase to individuals and firms seeking to build single- or multi-family housing, shopping malls, or industrial facilities. To be eligible for such financing you should have previous experience in the field. However, if you do not have this experience, you can join with a partner who does have a suitable background and get the financing you seek.

Raw land can be highly profitable to you in your real estate wealth building. But you *must* buy raw land wisely, using the most leverage you can. *Leverage* allows you to control something of great worth with little money.

So try to borrow as much of your purchase price for land as you can. When you use *double leverage*—that is, borrow the down payment and the long-term money—your percent return on your investment is infinite, or nearly so. Key ideas on making money from raw land are given in some of the specialized land books listed at the back of this book.

Search for Unique Residential Lenders

Everyone has to live somewhere. Thus, the single-family home and the multi-family apartment house are popular throughout the world. And you can finance such properties using money from unique lenders. Here are such lenders for you:

- **Private real estate lenders** that do their entire business in residential properties. These lenders do long-term first mortgages, second mortgages, bridge loans, and other funding for residential properties. No upfront fees are charged for such loans.

- **REO—Real Estate Owned-lenders** often offer 100 percent (zero-cash) financing on repossessed single-family and multi-family homes. Such lenders are banks, mortgage companies, and government agencies. The whole key to getting such unique 100 percent financing is your willingness to take over foreclosed property. To do so, you should get as much experience as you can in managing properties before you agree to take over a foreclosed building.
- **"Reverse-flip" seller-credit lenders** can be used for your down payment money. How? By having the seller use credit to obtain a loan for your down payment. You agree to repay this loan over a term of—typically—three or five years. The "reverse-flip" would occur any time you are unable to repay the down payment loan. Then the property would revert (reverse flip) to the seller and all payments you make are credited to the seller who still owns the property and can sell it to someone else for full price. Once you pay off your down payment loan for the seller, you will own the property—its title will be in your name. Your real estate attorney arranges the paperwork for the reverse-flip unique financing.
- **Installment sale of property** can reduce the seller's tax burden on the gain he/she has on the property since the purchase. With an ordinary sale, the seller gets the full price of the property, less any money owed on it—such as first or second mortgages. The gain in value of the property is fully taxable in the year received. You offer an installment sale to the seller so he/she receives the same amount of money, plus interest, over a period of years—5, 10, 15, or more. Then the money received in any given year is less, making the overall tax much less than if the seller received the full price in one year. Have your attorney and accountant explain the advantages of an installment sale to the seller.
- **Get Chamber of Commerce help in finding lenders;** this can be crucial to you. Why? Because members of the Chamber usually know local lenders who can help you get funding—especially for neat, clean, safe residential units—either single-family or multi-

family units. All you need to do is ask—you'll be amazed at how much free help you'll be given.

- **Work with multi-family lenders lending nationwide.** Such lenders understand multi-family housing financing needs and can give you lots of help as part of their funding package. Six outstanding lenders in the multi-family field are:
  1. **AMI Capital, Inc.,** offices nationwide. 800-800-1871; *www.amicapital.com.*
  2. **American Property Financing,** Atlanta, GA, 404-252-5960; Washington, DC, 301-654-6400; New York, NY, 212-850-4200; Seattle, WA, 206-505-8900.
  3. **Corus Bank,** Chicago, IL, 800-890-8837; *www.corusbank.com.*
  4. **GE Real Estate,** offices nationwide. Stamford, CT, 888-GE-FIRST; *www.gerealestate.com.*
  5. **Inland Mortgage Corporation,** Walnut Creek, CA, 925-952-3900; *www.inlandmtg.com.*
  6. **L. J. Melody & Company,** offices nationwide. 713-787-1900; *www.ljmelody.com.*

Start Small in Commercial Properties

Commercial properties include stores, strip malls, shopping malls, offices, recreational buildings, or others. Each type is served by a group of specialty lenders you can work with. Let's see how you can get rich in commercial types of property using unique lenders.

Know the Range of Commercial Properties

To give you an idea of the range of commercial properties you can own, and earn money from, here's a quick summary of a number of types:

- **Amusement and recreation**—such as bowling alleys, indoor and outdoor tennis courts, billiard rooms, dance halls, theatres, or other recreations.
- **Churches and other religious structures**—such as synagogues, mosques, temples, cathedrals, or other religious structures.

- **Schools and other educational structures.** Private schools offer good potential earnings for you in many areas of the country today.
- **Hospitals and nursing homes.** Private hospitals and nursing homes offer substantial income chances for real estate BWBs. Ownership is best for people who are health professionals.
- **Hotels and motels.** Room rental income is your main source of revenue in these properties. Restaurant and lounge income can also be significant in larger hotels and motels. Likewise, casino income can exceed room and restaurant income where such establishments are permitted by local law.
- **Parking garages.** Such structures are confined mostly to large cities where safe and adequate parking are scarce.
- **Private and professional offices.** These can be highly profitable for you when you own and rent to professionals. Why? Because your tenants are reliable and need their space for income. So they pay their rent on time and in full every month!
- **Public and administrative buildings.** For BWBs, these include post offices and similar small buildings. Rental is the big income source from such buildings.
- **Service stations.** Gas stations are the most common example of combined income (fuel sales and repair of vehicles) and ownership for BWBs.
- **Stores, shopping malls, and other retail buildings.** BWBs often start with one store as part of a residential property and expand from there as they acquire a liking for the business.
- **Utilities buildings.** Such buildings are for EWBs—Experienced Wealth Builders—with years of real estate experience. Examples of these buildings are electric and gas power company facilities.
- **Other nonresidential buildings.** Any other type of nonresidential property comes under this category. What you do with it depends on the type of property and the function it fulfills. Hence, what you can do with it varies widely with your interests and skills!

So start thinking what you could do with one of these properties to build your wealth in real estate today! I will help you every step of the way. Just be sure to pick a property type you like!

Now we'll look at a few specific commercial properties to see how you could finance, own, and profit from them. We'll start with an amusement and recreational property.

Earn Your Real Estate Wealth in Tennis Courts

Tennis is one of the most popular sports in the world today. And the people who actively play tennis are:

- **Usually in the middle class** and above income level, own their own home, two cars, several credit cards, for example.
- **Highly enthusiastic about their sport** and are willing to spend generously to enjoy it year-round on a nearby court.
- **Enthusiastic for life;** many tennis players enjoy playing into their nineties—playing almost every day of the week.
- **Always looking for places to play** year-round, summer and winter, indoors or outdoors.
- **Willing to finance a good facility** with membership dues, initiation fees, monthly minimum fees, time purchases, or other fees. Hence, you can tap your membership for various financing needs of the facility.

You can build wealth as a real estate BWB (Beginning Wealth Builder) by buying and owning one or more, tennis facilities—either indoor or outdoor. Your keys to success as a tennis real estate BWB are:

- **Own the tennis facility,** namely the ground and building, if any. (Outdoor tennis courts may not have a building.)
- **Rent the land** for your facility from a land owner for a stated number of years—usually five, with a five-year renewal option in the rental agreement.
- **Lease your facility to a tennis expert** (if you're not one yourself) to operate for five years, or a longer time.
- **Have your attorney write a *Net Net Net* lease.** This means your tennis expert lessee will pay you a monthly rental and will also pay the real estate taxes, insurance, and maintenance on the facility

rented from you. Thus, your monthly rent check is net net net—free of these costs.

- **Include rental increases in your lease**—have your attorney prepare your lease with 3 percent or 5 percent annual rent rises for your tenant. Then your income will keep pace with inflation.
- **Use your tennis pro's lease as collateral** for a loan for your facility for your first or second mortgage.

You do not need a permanent building on the land you own or lease for your tennis business. And you can still lease your facility on a year-round basis by:

- **Having an inflatable "air bubble" building** on the land that you own. The air bubble will allow winter play. And for year-round play, you can have your air bubble building air conditioned to allow both summer and winter usage.
- **Being prepared to pay $6 to $11 per square foot for your air bubble building.** This compares to $36 and up per square foot for a light-steel prefabricated building. An air compressor keeps your air bubble building inflated year-round.
- **Knowing that your air bubble building can last for as long as 20 years,** depending on the fabric used in it. And your building can withstand sustained winds of 80 miles per hour and wind gusts of 100 miles per hour.
- **Earning your real estate income from:** your monthly rental payment to you from your tennis expert; the constant rise in value of your property with the passage of time. (You can use this value rise as collateral to get loans to buy other income real estate to build your wealth.)

So if tennis ownership appeals to you, look around your area for properties that might be for sale or lease. You can have fun while building riches for yourself!

You can also finance your facility yourself using a Limited Partnership. This form of financing is covered later in this chapter.

Build Your Real Estate Fortune in Office Buildings

Dozens of real estate BWBs call or write me to tell me about their real estate holdings in a small city somewhere in the United States. Their story usually goes like this:

> "I own a small office building in __________. It has one major tenant—a small local bank. Also, I have a real estate broker, an attorney, and an insurance agent as tenants. My total Positive Cash Flow is $1,000 per month. I bought the building for almost zero down because it was half vacant. But the bank that's now my main tenant loaned me the long-term mortgage. So things are going rather well for me and the building."

Most BWBs I meet want to invest in residential properties. While such properties have built and are building thousands of real estate fortunes, I suggest you also look at small office buildings as your potential source of real estate wealth. Why? Because:

- **Office properties can be bought by you** with better financing than residential properties because there are fewer buyers for office buildings. Hence, sellers are more creative in the unique financing options they offer buyers—namely you.
- **Office properties usually give owners fewer problems** than residential properties. Why? Because office properties normally have only adult tenants. There are no children or pets to cause a variety of nuisance complaints and woes.
- **Office properties can have leases written** such that the first $1,000 (or any other agreed-on amount) in repairs are the responsibility of the tenant. This reduces the number of small-repair calls you get, allowing you to have a quiet life with your office-building real estate holding.
- **Office properties may be the only type of real estate to invest in** when you want to own real estate in an area where there are few residential properties. Hence, offices become "the only game in town." Yet they can be just as profitable and more hassle-free than residential properties.

How to Find Financing for Office Properties

To find suitable financing for office properties, you must first have a property you want to buy. Take these three easy and quick steps to find suitable office properties:

1. **Look around your area** to see if there are office structures rented to businesses. In most urban (non-city) areas, such structures will be one- or two-story buildings with a parking area in front or on one side and a tiny backyard for tenant services—trash removal, minor storage, or others.
2. **Contact local real estate brokers,** asking for listings of office properties in your area. Such listings will be sent to you free. Be sure each listing gives the *Asking Price, Down Payment, Income,* and *Expenses.* You must have these numbers.
3. **"Work the numbers" for each property.** You MUST have a Positive Cash Flow from each property! As a starting guide, look for at least $500 per month PCF for each office building you buy, depending on the size and location of the property. A larger monthly PCF is—of course—welcome and desirable.

To find financing for your office building, see the listing in Chapter 6. Many of the lenders listed there lend on office buildings. And if you can get a bank as a tenant in your office building, ask the bank to finance the long-term mortgage. Many banks are willing to finance well-run office buildings.

Remember: Banks prefer to lend on real estate rather than to own it—except, perhaps, for their headquarters building. Knowing this, getting your long-term first-mortgage is easy!

Consider Making Your Fortune in Stores and Malls

Many stores today are in small groups—formerly called *strip malls.* Today such malls are called *mini-malls.* A mini-mall might have as few as four small stores—or as many as 20. If you're interested in owning stores as your way to real estate wealth, the mini-mall is the best starter property. Why? Because:

- **There are many lenders** that will finance mini-malls.
- **You can begin** with little experience and learn fast.
- **If you run into trouble,** your losses won't be great.

Some commercial lenders will consider financing mini-malls. Why? Because the mini-mall is usually on well-located land in a city or town. Such land rises in value over time. So it is a valuable asset that is good collateral for a loan.

Mini-malls usually cater to smaller stores than larger shopping malls. While your *anchor tenant*—your largest tenant—may be a big company, its store will usually be smaller than in a large shopping mall.

With smaller and fewer stores, your operating challenges are simpler. So if you want to own this type of real estate, start with a mini-mall. After a few years you can "graduate" to a full-blown shopping mall with large parking fields and a major anchor tenant.

Who Funds Mini- and Shopping Malls?

Shopping malls require experience for their financing, purchase, and operation. You'll get this either as an owner of mini-malls or as an employee of a large shopping mall. Just be sure you *know* what you're doing before you buy a large shopping mall.

Funding for mini-malls and shopping malls often comes from local banks near the facility. Why is this? Because local banks:

- **Feel safer** with property near their own.
- **Understand** nearby property values better than distant ones.
- **Have personnel** who shop locally and want to see the area grow.

So your best opportunity for mini- and shopping mall financing is often at your local commercial bank. Check your local *Yellow Pages* under "Mortgages" and "Loans" for banks that might want to work with you. You will also find lenders for mini- and shopping malls in the lender list in Chapter 6.

Wait Before Investing in Industrial Properties

Industrial properties—factories, storage buildings, warehouses, or others —are not for beginners. It takes experience and know-how to make it big on zero cash in these properties. So for now, I suggest that you get experience in other types of properties before investing in industrial projects.

When you're ready to take on industrial properties, you can call me and we'll meet for lunch to discuss your plans. And I'll pay for lunch—that I guarantee!

Unique Funding You Can Do Yourself

Today is the age of the do-it-yourselfer. Thousands of people rebuild houses, construct their own home, build walls, or other projects. So why not expand this to do-it-yourself financing? Thousands of BWBs are doing just that. You, too, can do the same. Let's see how—right now.

Two Quick Unique Ways to Raise Money Yourself

There are two quick unique ways you can raise money for real estate yourself at low cost. These ways are:

1. **Limited partnership to raise $500,000 to $50 million.**
2. **Real Estate Investment Trust (REIT) for $5 million to $100+ million.**

Of these two methods, the Limited Partnership (LP) is the easiest for BWBs and has been used much more often than the REIT. However, we do have REITs being formed almost every day of the year to raise big money for real estate investment. Let's look at each unique funding method to see how you might use it today.

Use a Limited Partnership to Raise the Money You Need

In Chapter 6, you learned how to raise money from a Limited Partnership. Now you'll learn how to form your own Limited Partnership to raise money directly from investors in *your* partnership.

A Limited Partnership (can raise money for real estate investment at little cost. In a typical real estate limited partnership, you, as the *general partner*, work with limited partners who invest their money in some aspect of income real estate.

As general partner, you invite *limited partners* to put money into the partnership in the form of *participations*. Each participation can be priced at anywhere from $5,000 to $50,000 or more. Thus, if you get 20 limited partners to invest, say $50,000 each, you'll raise 20 × $50,000 = $1,000,000 to invest in income real estate.

As general partner, you have control of the investment funds. You can use them in any way you believe will earn a profit for the Limited Partners. And your Limited Partners are limited in their liability in the partnership to the amount of money they originally put into the partnership.

Thus, if a Limited Partner put $15,000 into your real estate LP, that partner is limited to no more than the $15,000 if an outsider sues the LP and is awarded money for damages or other charges.

Six Steps to Setting Up Your Limited Partnership

To set up your Limited Partnership, take these six easy and direct steps:

1. **Write a brief description of your LP, telling what you'll do with the funds you raise.** You can do any of several things, namely:
   a. **Buy income properties** and manage them for income.
   b. **Lend money** to real estate investors to buy, and manage, income properties.
   c. **Find and buy** properties to flip for short-term profits.
2. **Contact a competent real estate attorney familiar with Limited Partnerships.** Have this person evaluate your proposed Limited Partnership and your plans for it.
3. **Decide on how much money you want to raise and how many limited partners you'll need.** Today, most advisors will suggest that you have no more than 35 limited partners who are "qualified investors"—that is, have assets of a certain amount, as defined by the Securities Exchange Commission (SEC). Your attorney will advise you on this, using the latest requirements.
4. **Prepare your offering for your Limited Partners.** This is a one- or two-page document covering the amount of money they put

into the LP and how they will share in the profits earned by the LP. (When preparing the offering and the description of the LP, most people use, as a guide, previously written offering circulars that have successfully raised money. You'll find one such document described at the back of this book.)

5. **Sell your participations to your Limited Partners.** You can do this personally, or you can have a stock brokerage house do it for you. Their charge is about 12 percent of the amount of money raised.
6. **Get your money and start your real estate work—depending on what your LP is organized to do.** You—as general partner—will normally own one participation in the LP. This ownership is based on the work you do to conceive the partnership, raise the money, and run it on a day-to-day basis.

Typical real estate LP raise anywhere from $5 million to $50 million. Today, most new LP fundings are in the $5 million to $10 million range. Your ownership cash holding might be $100,000 to $500,000, depending on the number of limited partners in the organization. You will—of course—use these funds for investment purposes to build the LP.

While forming a LP may seem complex, it is really very simple. And the LP can be your unique way to raise money for the income real estate you want to acquire. A reader writes:

Try a Real Estate Investment Trust to Raise Your Money

Limited Partnership Helps BWB Get Started

"My first real estate purchase was from a bank. I formed a limited partnership to fund the down payment. The bank provided very favorable terms and even upgraded the property to the tune of $23,000. All this and a positive cash flow, too."

—Illinois

While writing this book I had a call from a reader saying:

Quick Results for a REIT Applicant

"I just had a call from the __________ stock brokerage house and they want to raise $80 million for our REIT. We sent them our Declaration of Trust [DOT for short] and they loved it. In fact, they apologized for taking 3 weeks to call us back. But the broker calling said he had been away on business. And all they need from us now is our Business Plan for the REIT. We're working on it and we'll send you a copy as soon as we finish it. The DOT [a 400-word Executive Summary] did wonders for us." —California

This reader used our "Real Estate Investment Trust Kit" described at the back of this book to guide her and her husband in planning their REIT. You can, however, go to any large public library and get the information you need to write your own DOT. And at the same library you'll find the names and addresses of stock brokers who might take your REIT public or private to raise the money you seek.

You can form your own REIT following the nine steps given in Chapter 6—with the guidance of a competent and experienced real estate attorney. Then you can submit your plan in the form of a DOT to a stock broker to see if it can be funded, either publicly or privately.

If a stock broker wants to take your REIT public or private, the brokerage house will help you with the legal and other compliance work that has to be done. To form your own REIT, take the steps given in Chapter 6. Meanwhile, here's an example of a potentially profitable REIT DOT you might write, or have someone write for you:

Golden Age Real Estate Investment Trust

The Golden Age Real Estate Investment Trust (the Trust) is being formed to invest in housing for the elderly in the state of ________, where there is a scarcity of such housing and a growing need for it. Thus, it is estimated that 10,000 new seniors (over age 65) seek affordable housing in ________, every year. Few such facilities exist today in the state of ________.

The Trust seeks $75 million to acquire land and build eight hundred new apartments for seniors in the ________ City area. These apartments will be handicapped-friendly with special walkways, elevators, bathing facilities, kitchen access, etc. Construction will be high-quality throughout, with emphasis on low-maintenance and environmentally acceptable materials. The Trust will operate the apartments after construction, renting to qualified seniors. Rents charged will be competitive with other rents in the area. Where possible, the rent charged will be keyed to the income the senior has from pensions and Social Security.

A return of 8 percent will be sought for Trust investors. As required by law, 95 percent of earnings will be distributed to investors in the Trust.

A full Business Plan is available for potential investors in the Trust. The management team assembled for the Trust has experience in both real estate and senior counseling and care. Additional information on this new Trust can be obtained from John Doe, 123 Main St, Anytown XC 00000. Telephone: 123-456-7890.

You now have many unique and unusual ways to raise money for your real estate wealth building. If you have any questions, you can call me day or night. I'll be happy to try to answer all your questions. Where numbers are involved, I prefer to have you fax or mail me your questions because it is difficult to follow a long series of numbers on the telephone. As I've mentioned before, I try to answer questions from my newsletter subscribers first.

Your Keys to Real Estate Riches

- ❑ **Your whole key to getting the money** you need for your real estate investments is finding suitable lenders for the properties you want to work with.
- ❑ **There are seven simple steps** you can take to find the real estate money you need—*decide, search, get full data, focus, determine, look,* and *take action.*
- ❑ **Pick the type of real estate** you want to own. Doing so will focus your efforts and help you get faster results in your search for financing.
- ❑ **There are four types of real estate you can own**—raw land, residential, commercial, and industrial. The best type for you is the kind of real estate you enjoy working with.
- ❑ **Look for and find lender**s for raw land starting with the seller and moving on to government and area agencies.
- ❑ **There are many residential lenders** you can work with. And it's wise to give them all a try to see if they want to work with you.
- ❑ **Commercial properties range widely** in their diversity. Finding lenders for such properties can be easy if you approach specialty funders.
- ❑ **Office buildings offer many ownership advantages** to real estate BWBs. And office buildings may be the "only game in town" in some areas.
- ❑ **Mini-malls and shopping malls can be highly profitable.** BWBs should get experience with mini-malls before taking on large shopping malls.
- ❑ **Limited partnerships and Real Estate Investment Trusts** are two unique sources for large real estate funds that BWBs should consider using.

CHAPTER 9

Use Sellers Having Built-In Funding for Your Deals

THERE ARE MANY DEALS YOU CAN FIND WHERE THE SELLER HAS FUNDING ready for you—the buyer. When you find such a deal, half your challenge has already been solved for you. "And what's that challenge?" you ask.

It can be summarized in one word—*FINANCING!* Getting financing for income properties is the BWB's universal challenge. So when you find a deal with financing in place, rejoice! Then go and close the deal—if the numbers—Chapter 10—allow you to earn a profitable Positive Cash Flow (PCF).

Eight Real Estate Deals with Financing in Place

Deals in which you will find the financing worked out in advance for you include these eight ways:

1. **Government foreclosures** from a variety of agencies in your local area funded by housing authorities, state, county, or city government.
2. **Internet searches** for government foreclosures that you can access quickly and easily from a small computer.
3. **New property construction financing** for residential units; some commercial units may also have prearranged financing for buyers.
4. **"Financing Available" Ads** will usually have seller financing or an assumable mortgage ready for the buyer—hopefully—you.

5. **Zero-down property ads** in which the seller states that the property is available for sale for zero cash down.
6. **For Sale By Owner (FSBO) properties** often have financing available because the seller is anxious to get rid of the property and move on.
7. **Private lender financing** for a variety of properties that will be suitable for building your riches in real estate.
8. **Unusual offers** made by sellers seeking to get out of property quickly can give you many new opportunities to build riches.

Let's look at each of these financing-in-place scenarios and see how you might use it in your real estate wealth building. I hope—in just days—to get you started on becoming a real estate millionaire!

Government Foreclosures Often Come with Financing

In earlier chapters, we mentioned the U.S. Department of Housing and Urban Development (HUD) and the Veterans Administration (VA). Both these agencies often have foreclosure properties for sale with financing in place. Here's a letter telling of one BWB's experience:

Where to Get 100 Percent Fixed-Rate Financing

"As an avid reader of your books and a subscriber to your newsletter, I, like many others, can attest to the fact that your methods work, and work very well indeed.

"Thus, during the past year I acquired six properties—five single-family homes and one 4-unit building from lists of HUD and VA foreclosures. I took over each property with at least a 25% discount off the market price. In two cases, the VA sold to me at over 30% discount and provided 100 percent fixed-rate financing for 30 years. By best estimate these properties are valued at about $435,000 with combined equities of $126,000.

> "Though this effort required some work, I'm amazed at how easy it has been. I am 56 years old and I recently retired. I am really pleased with the results of my real estate investing."
>
> —Virginia

This letter shows that—on occasion—the VA and also HUD have built-in financing available for 100 percent-financed foreclosure properties. So how do you get such financing for your foreclosure deals? Here are the steps for you to take.

Seven Steps to Getting 100 Percent Financed Properties

1. **Contact HUD and the VA** by mail, phone, Internet, or by visiting the local office of each agency.
2. **Ask for lists of foreclosure properties** being offered to the public. At the HUD web site you'll find the properties listed under "HUD homes/REO."
3. **Study each list you receive** to determine if any of the properties interest you based on the location, potential income generation, or other criteria.
4. **Ask if any of the properties** that interest you have in-place financing. If the answer is YES, ask what the amount of the financing available is.
5. **Also ask if there is 100 percent financing available for any properties.** If there is, request a list of those properties. Study the list carefully when you get it to see if there are any properties on it which might be good investments for you.
6. **Bid on those properties** you believe will make money for you on either a rental or flip basis. Just be sure to work your numbers carefully before you bid!
7. **Take over your property** and start your wealth building steps immediately. You'll find—I'm sure—that the whole process is faster and easier than you might think. To confirm this, just read the last letter again!

Do Internet Searches for Your Properties

The Internet is here to stay—no doubt about that. And government sales of foreclosed properties are based—more than ever before—on property data furnished to you on the Internet. So you must learn how to use the Internet.

I can hear some readers saying, "But I don't have a computer. And I don't think I'll ever be able to afford a computer."

"Not to worry," as the British say. You can easily get to a computer free of charge at:

- **Your local public library.**
- **A Boy Scout or Girl Scout organization in your area.**
- **An American Legion or VFW Hall, if you're a veteran.**
- **IWS, if you're in our area in New York.**
- **At your local religious organization headquarters building.**
- **In labor union offices, if you're a union member.**

In many of these facilities, people will teach you free of charge how to use the computer and get started finding suitable properties on the Internet.

Never resist free instructions! You can learn a lot in a short time! And what you learn can put lots of real estate money into your pocket.

Internet sites worth checking for government foreclosures include the following:

- ***www.hud.gov***
- ***www.irs.gov***
- ***www.hud.gov/offices/hsg/hsgabout.cfm***
- ***www.sba.gov***
- ***www.gsa.gov***

Check Your State, County, and City Web Sites for Foreclosures

Nearly every state, county, and city has a Web site. Log onto the site for your area and go to the foreclosure section of it. You'll find information on how and where to obtain data on foreclosure sales in your area.

Attend a few of these foreclosure sales or auctions to get the "feel" of what goes on. Then make a bid on a property that you believe has business potential for you. Just be certain to "work the numbers" BEFORE making your bid. And—if you wish—I'll be happy to do this for you, if you're a subscriber to one of my newsletters. But I must have at least one day to do so!

Don't Overlook New Property Financing

Many new properties have 100 percent, or near 100 percent built-in financing as part of their offer to sell single-family homes, condo apartments, or industrial suites. These are often called "Pre-Sale Buys." *You* can take advantage of such built-in offers. How? By using the generous offers made by sellers who:

- **Have negotiated with local (or distant) lenders** to provide built-in financing for their newly built single-family homes, townhouses, multi-family apartment-house condo units, or industrial spaces.
- **Often offer 100 percent financing** on a pre-sale basis for their brand-new units that are nearly maintenance-free for about five years from the time you acquire them with built-in financing.
- **Allow you to get started** in income real estate for a nominal earnest-money deposit of typically \$100 to \$500. The built-in financing saves you tons of time and energy.
- **Permit you to buy** as many as five units in one large multi-unit building, getting you off to a fast start when you rent these units to tenants at a price level giving you a positive cash flow every month so the units are self-sustaining, paying their built-in financing charges.

"This sounds good, " you say. "But where do I find such offers with built-in financing?" The answer is simple. You look:

- **In your local large-city Sunday newspaper real estate *For Sale* section.**

- **National real estate magazines advertising newly built properties.**
- **Local real estate magazines and newspapers.**

Five Ways to Find Fully Financed New Properties

"But," you say, "it's hard to find such offers." That may be true if you're in an area where little or no new construction is taking place. But if you're in an area of rapid home or industrial expansion you may be able to find dozens of pre-sale offers with built-in financing every week.

So what can you do if you're in an area of slow or no new construction? You can:

1. **Buy out-of-town Sunday newspapers** and look in the real estate *For Sale* section for pre-sale built-in financing ads for new properties.
2. **Contact nationwide real estate agents** and tell them you're interested in pre-sale properties with built-in financing in selected areas in which you'd like to own income units. Realtors earn commissions on such sales—even with the built-in financing.
3. **Go on the Internet** to real estate sites covering new construction and look for properties in areas you like. Download full data on properties that interest you and find out if you can get a pre-sale built-in financing deal for yourself.
4. **For residential units,** look for apartments or condos near universities or hospitals. Why? Because you'll always have a steady flow of tenants for your units from both types of institutions. Such tenants are reliable and can afford to pay a substantial rent. With university students, be sure to have the parents sign your lease—not the students. The parents have the money—not the students! Today, you should look for a monthly PCF of at least $200 for each residential rental unit of any type you own which you bought on a pre-sale built-in financing basis.
5. **For industrial units,** look for spaces or suites in areas having lots of light manufacturing, sales reps, and other non-storefront businesses. Why? Because such units are widely needed and rent quickly to reliable tenants. Seek at least $300 per month PCF from every industrial unit you own.

Yes, pre-sale buys with built-in financing can make you rich in real estate. Your main challenge is finding such units in the area you want to invest in. Just keep looking. *Never give up*!

Take Advantage of "Financing Available" Offers

Sellers use "*Financing Available*" offers when they're anxious to sell a property quickly. Or these offers may be used when:

- **The seller is an estate**—called an *estate sale*—that is, the owner died and the survivors want a quick sale so they can get their money and do what *they* enjoy in life.
- **The seller has had the property on the market for a long time**—often one year or longer—and is worried about selling it to an acceptable buyer.
- **The seller has a time deadline to meet** and must get rid of the property. To encourage a quick sale, financing is provided to the buyer.
- **The seller knows the property needs a lot of repairs,** and wants "out" to let someone else do the rehab work.
- **The seller is on in years**—often the late seventies or early eighties—and wants out because retirement beckons more strongly than ever.

You may encounter other reasons for a seller to offer financing to a buyer. If you do, good! Work the numbers and grab the property quickly, if you can show a positive cash flow. Here's a letter showing how zero-cash buying with seller financing can work:

Zero Cash Builds Strong Equity Growth

"I bought your 3 Year book and I think I am doing what you advise in Chapter 14 of that book. Then I called your business phone number and, to my surprise, you answered. You asked me to fax you details of our investments. Here they are:

"In May of a recent year, my husband and I bought our first property—a two-story, two-bedroom, 2.5-bath condo with zero money down for $136,000. Recently, it was appraised—34 months after we bought it—at $230,000. Thus, our equity in the condo rose $94,000 in 34 months, or $2,765 per month while we had it rented out.

"After we rented our condo out, we bought another home, our primary residence, with zero money down, for $276,000. It was recently appraised for $400,000. Thus, our equity rose by $124,000 in 35 months, or $3,543 per month.

"Hence, our total equity rose by $2,765 + $3,543 = $6,308 per month. Now we're refinancing both properties to buy other properties and pay off our student loans. We would love to continue buying properties with no money down. Having your equity rise by $218,000 while you sleep is very impressive!" —California

This letter is a good example of how financing available from a seller can improve your net worth quickly. Never overlook a chance to get zero-cash financing for properties whose numbers work!

Look for and Find Zero-Down Properties

If you read the real estate ads carefully every Sunday in a large-city newspaper, sooner or later you see an ad saying:

0 DOWN 3 br/2 bath beauty in ______________.
Call 123-4567 for full info. Own your own home!

Now you may not find such ads in your hometown paper. Instead, you may have to look at ads for properties in nearby towns. This is okay for most people because the travel between towns is tax-deductible when you're checking on your income property. Zero-down properties may be for sale by:

- **Banks.**
- **Mortgage companies.**
- **Credit unions.**
- **Governments—federal, state, county, city.**
- **Private sellers wanting "out" in a big hurry.**

And when a sale is offered at zero down by such sellers, it often means you get the property:

- **With no closing costs to pay.**
- **With no down payment to pay.**
- **With no legal fees to pay if the seller's attorney represents both sides.**

Are there any negatives for you with zero-down seller-financing deals? In general: no, there aren't any negatives. However, take my advice and take these four precautions when buying seller-financed property.

1. **Hire a real estate attorney** to represent you; it's the safe step to take for every property you buy and you will never regret it!
2. **Figure—in advance**—if you can make money from the property renting it out to reliable tenants.
3. **Buy—for zero down**—only properties giving you a positive cash flow (PCF) every month of the year.
4. **Be certain to have the property inspected** BEFORE you buy so you know what repairs, if any, you'll have to make before you can rent it out.

Over time, I've collected zero-down ads from papers around the country. Why? To show to "doubting Thomases" that such properties really do exist.

I'll be glad to show you copies of such actual ads to subscribers of my newsletter, *International Wealth Success.* The ads—of course—will show properties that most likely will have been sold. But the ads will give you the flavor of actual, real-life offers you could have looked at. Both the name and date of the paper are given.

Other facts about zero-down properties you should keep in mind are these interesting ones, namely:

Zero-Down Property Facts to Keep in Mind

- **You must be very cautious** about zero-down properties you select. Look at several before making your choice.
- **Look for properties** having at least 2 bedrooms and at least 1.5 baths. Why? Any houses with fewer bedrooms or baths will be hard to rent.
- **Never accept a substandard property** because it is selling for zero-down. You could be getting into an endless drain on your income because such properties may be hard to rent to top-quality tenants.
- **Seek properties** having at least two parking spaces for autos. Why? Because with today's two-worker families, both people have cars and need space to park.

Look for and Buy FSBO Properties

FSBO—*For Sale By Owner*—properties offer many opportunities to you to get built-in financing. Why can FSBO properties be your path to wealth? Because FSBO sellers are often:

- **"Stressed out"** by having their property on the market so long that they're worried it won't sell.
- **Ready to wheel and deal** so they can unburden themselves of the property and go on with the rest of their life.
- **Ready to accept a sincere and honest person** like you and make a deal with you that includes built-in financing giving you the property for zero or very little cash.
- **Independent thinkers** who believe they can do everything themselves, including arranging financing with someone they like. So if you work on getting the FSBO person to like you, you'll probably get a dream deal.
- **Likely to overlook your credit score** if they feel you're the ideal person to take over their property and relieve them of the burden of it.

Private Lenders Could Be Your Money Source

As mentioned in Chapter 6, private lenders are individuals, companies, or groups of people seeking to lend money on real estate. You can tap into these sources for the loans you need for:

- **First mortgages** for income properties of all kinds.
- **Second mortgages** for larger income properties—commercial, residential, or other.
- **Bridge loans** for the purpose of buying new properties using an existing property as collateral for your loan.
- **Construction loans** for both new and existing properties of all kinds.
- **Equity loans** for well-kept income properties of almost any kind.
- **Purchase of mortgage notes** at a discount (called *mortgage cash-out*) to give quick cash to the seller, eliminating years of waiting to be paid a small amount each month.
- **Foreclosure-purchase loans** helping the borrower to buy properties at 60 to 75 percent of their market value for flipping or rehabbing and rental.
- **Government-guaranteed loans** for all types of residential income real estate in which the lender is protected by the government guarantee.
- **Investor loans** for real estate wealth builders who might not be able to get a loan from traditional lenders who think investor loans are too risky for them.
- **Many other types of real estate loans** are made by private lenders to real estate investors. Later in this chapter we'll show you how and where to find private lenders for your deals.

Why You Should Use Private Lenders

When thinking about getting a loan from a specific type of lender, you should consider the pros and cons of each type of lender. When using private lenders, the advantages to you are many, including these four:

1. **Quick service**—some private lenders give an answer in just one hour, after you apply for your loan. Other non-private lenders

may take days or weeks to give you the answer you seek—a YES on your loan application.

2. **Less stringent paperwork** is required by the usual private lender. Why? Because the usual private lender makes more "aggressive" loans. This means that the average borrower does not have to prepare loads of paperwork to get the loan. So you're not spending hours doing boring work to get your loan.
3. **A more understanding relationship** between you and your lender usually occurs when you use private sources. Why? Because private lenders are often in the real estate business themselves. So they understand your challenges and often sympathize with them. Result? You're more likely to get the loan you request—sooner!
4. **Professional help on your loan request** from the private lender's staff can often save you money and time. Most private lenders have a staff of accountants, attorneys, and engineers on call. These professionals can help you with your paperwork, loan application, income calculations, or other matters.

Yes, private lenders can give you the effect of built-in funding for your deal. They can be your powerful tool in building your wealth in real estate. So look to private lenders as one strong source of your real estate funding.

To find private lenders, look at the "Money and Funds Available" page in my monthly newsletter *International Wealth Success.* A number of such lenders are regularly listed there. You may be able to work with one or more of them.

Also, I'm a private lender specialist. "What's that?" you ask. It's someone whose eyes light up with delight whenever the words "Private Lender" appear in an advertisement, brochure, online page, or elsewhere. The result? My company, IWS, Inc., has lists of many excellent private lenders interested in making real estate loans of various kinds.

Look for the Unusual Offer

A reader sent me the information below. What does it show? It shows that this reader in Missouri was offered an excellent 12-family property that he was able to mortgage-out on. Then he bought a condo apartment building for zero-cash down because the seller had the financing in place.

So, you might say, there's built-in funding of $320,000 on the condo apartment and $10,000 on the 12-family property. Both these deals contain the "unusual offer." Here's this reader's letter:

Busy Successful EWB Does Well in Real Estate

"Just finished reading 'How to Make Big Money in Real Estate.' I own two businesses. Am active in one as manager/accountant/owner. I manage the following real estate, which I also own:

Commercial building	Value = $375,000
12-family apartment house	Value = $175,000
Luxury duplex	Value = $186,000
Luxury home	Value = $400,000
Total	Value = $1,136,000

"You will be pleased to know I bought the 12-family by over-mortgaging—bought for $200,000 with a $210,000 loan. No repairs were needed. Just closed on an 8-unit condo apartment house listed at $395,000; bought for $320,000 with zero-cash down! Current net income = $35,000. Many thanks for your help!"

—Missouri

This Experienced Wealth Builder (EWB) is building his holdings by doing smart deals through unusual offers. And you, too, can find such offers. It just takes a bit of looking. But it *really* is worth it! Why? Because:

Once you become known as the "Unusual Offer" wealth builder, people will bring deals to you almost every day of the week. Why? Because most people are so frightened by the unusual offer that they shy away from it—losing a great opportunity.

But if you seek such deals you will soon find they come flooding your way!

To show you what I mean by being flooded with offers, here's a letter from a reader telling of his experiences:

People Are Calling Me a Lot Trying to Sell Me Deals

"I want to share my success story with you: I bought 10 houses (one is a 4-plex). I did this with $1,000 down on each one—a total outlay of $10,000 for 10 very nice houses, all under their appraised value. The seller took back second mortgages on each (zero cash for me) and I still have a nice positive cash flow after all payments for all loans and expenses. I used to think this couldn't be done without 20% or 30% down. Now people are calling me a lot, trying to sell me deals!"

—South Carolina

Don't Let Built-In Funding Pass You By

So far this chapter has given you eight ways you can use built-in financing to get zero-cash income real estate deals. There are plenty of other ways for you to find built-in financing. Here—quickly—are six more.

1. **A family squabble can produce "I want out!" sellers** who will finance your quick takeover of a good income property. Such squabbles may arise in an estate settlement, giving you built-in funding.
2. **Divorce—though sad and disappointing**—can deliver zero-cash properties to you. Couples often say "I just want to get this over with—give the place away—if you have to!" You're the lucky recipient of a desirable income property with built-in funding arranged for you ahead of time.
3. **Partially burned-out income properties** sometimes sell for as little as $1.00. While not quite zero-cash or built-in funding, $1.00 is

fairly close to it! And if you don't have the $1.00 for the actual deal, I'll contribute it to you. Then you'll have a true zero-cash deal!

4. **Flood-damaged houses also sell for almost nothing**—sometimes $1.00 to $100. Again, not zero-cash or built-in funding, but very close to it.
5. **Bankruptcy situations can produce built-in funding** with "take it off our hands" requests with the financing essentially in place. You'll find such offers at banks and mortgage lenders.
6. **Tax-lien sales can sometimes get you high-value income property** with built-in funding, with as little as $10 to $500 down. Check your local sheriff's office for data on where these sales are held in your area. Then take action to see what's available for you with built-in funding!

In this chapter you learned of fourteen sources of built-in financing. Search for one or more of them in your next real estate deal and then use the built-in funding available to you. You'll be delighted with the results of having your own "private bank." And you'll be a lot richer than you ever thought possible!

Your Keys to Real Estate Riches

- ❑ **Built-in funding** can solve your real estate financing needs quickly and easily. Look for it in every deal.
- ❑ **Government foreclosures** may come with built-in funding. So be sure to check it out in advance to save time and money.
- ❑ **Internet searches** for government and private foreclosures can show you many different properties for sale that you can consider buying and earning money from.
- ❑ **New property construction financing** can get you the money you need for spanking clean residential units you can rent for a profit.
- ❑ **"Financing Available"** ads usually have seller financing or an assumable mortgage ready for you—the buyer.

- **Zero-down property** ads say that the seller has a property available for you for zero dollars down. This means you can get into business nearly free.
- **For Sale By Owner (FSBO) properties** may have financing available because the seller is anxious to get rid of the property and move on.
- **Private lender financing** may be available for a variety of properties you can use to build your real estate riches.
- **Unusual offers** made by sellers seeking to get out of property quickly can give you many new opportunities to build riches.

CHAPTER 10

Count Your Way to Your Real Estate Wealth

IF YOU HAD TROUBLE WITH NUMBERS IN SCHOOL, YOU'LL FIND YOUR REAL estate will make you a numbers lover! Why?

Because the four simple numbers you deal with in real estate concern *your* money! And your money is lots of fun to figure and count. Further, the bigger your numbers, the larger—in general—will be the income from your real estate.

Know the Numbers You Must Know

Here are the four easy, fun numbers you should know if you want to build riches in real estate on zero cash:

1. **Positive Cash Flow (PCF).**
2. **Monthly Debt Service.**
3. **Debt Coverage Ratio.**
4. **Capitalization Rate.**

We'll look at each of these numbers in terms of an income property you might buy. You'll see how you can use the numbers to figure the income you'll earn from one of your own properties. That way the numbers will have importance to you—personally.

Positive Cash Flow

Positive Cash Flow (PCF) is just what the words say, that is:

> **Your monthly cash income after paying all costs of your income property, including your monthly loan payments for all mortgages you have on the building.**

There's no magic about PCF—you either have a monthly positive cash flow or you do not.

Figure 10.1 and Figure. 5.2 (see page 103 in Chapter 5) show Income and Expense statements for two types of income properties.

Figure 10.1 shows an Income and Expense Statement for a large income property—namely an 8-Unit Multi-Family Building. This property has an $816 per month PCF, rounded to the nearest dollar.

Figure 5.2 shows a Single-Family rental unit having a monthly PCF of $320.00. Such a PCF number is common for Single-Family rental units.

Note that your PCF with each property includes your having paid for all these expenses BEFORE your PCF is figured:

- **First mortgage**—your long-term loan on the property.
- **Second mortgage**—your short-term (3 to 5 years) down payment loan for your zero-cash deal.
- **Real estate, water, sewage,** and all other property taxes.
- **Maintenance of the property**—repairs, cleaning, updating, expansion, painting, carpet replacement, or other.
- **Any management fees to collect rents,** find new tenants, or other fees.
- **Heating,** air conditioning, other climate control.
- **Vacancy allowance—usually 5 percent** of your annual rental income—but actually often much less or zero!
- **Electric, gas, and other utilities** for the building not paid by your tenants or an agency if they're on a rent payment program from the city, state, or national government.
- **All other operational expenses** of your building.

Date: April 20, 2---

Property Name: 8-Unit Multi-Family Garden Apartment

Address: 2312 Pacific Avenue

Annual Rental Income with 5% Vacancy Factor: $59,000

Miscellaneous Annual (Laundry) Income: $440

Total Annual Income Before Expenses: $59,440

Annual Expenses:	
Real estate taxes	$ 6,200
Trash removal	480
Water charge	600
Electricity	840
Ads and telephone	420
Insurance on property	1,200
Maintenance & cleaning	1,800
Salaries for building employees	4,000
Accounting & legal	2,500
Other expenses	2,000
Total Annual Expenses	$20,040
Annual Mortgage Costs:	
First mortgage of $190,000 for 25 years @ 8.00%	$17,598
Second mortgage of $45,000 for 5 Years @ 12%	12,012
Total Mortgage Costs	$29,610
Annual Positive Cash Flow	$ 9,790

Figure 10.1 Income and Expense Statement

Thus, your PCF is true Money-in-Fist (MIF)—money you can spend for improving your property, deposit into a savings account, buy another income property, use to take a vacation, or another wish. You can use your PCF for any purpose you choose.

Remember—always—the Hicks rule of getting rich from zero-down income property, namely:

You must ALWAYS have a monthly PCF from every income property. Never buy an income property unless you can see it giving you a monthly PCF from the first day you buy it! Violate this rule and you'll regret it when you must pay from personal funds to keep the building in operation.

Monthly Debt Service

In every normal real estate project, you will make one or more monthly debt payments. To determine if you have a positive cash flow you must know the amount you'll pay each month on every loan you have on the building. Such loans might be:

- **First mortgage**—15-, 20-, 25-, or 30-year loan.
- **Second mortgage**—3- or 5-year loan for your down payment.

First Mortgage Payment Strategies for You

When applying for your long-term (15, 20, 25 years) First Mortgage, keep these three key facts about your monthly payments in mind at all times:

1. **Apply for and get a *fixed rate* long-term First Mortgage.** Why? Because with an *adjustable-rate* mortgage, your loan payments representing Principal and Interest (P&I) can increase if the measure on which the rate is based changes. You do not want to be faced with rising First Mortgage payments. **REMEMBER:** Never accept an adjustable-rate First Mortgage. Demand and get a fixed-rate First Mortgage for every investment property you buy.

2. **Choose monthly P&I payments for your First Mortgage.** Why? Because by doing so you pay down your debt, increasing your equity (ownership) in the property every month. Every dollar of equity you gain becomes a dollar (or possibly even $1.25) that you can borrow to buy another income property or improve your present building. **REMEMBER:** Pay P&I monthly. Doing so builds your real riches (your assets) in real estate!
3. **Keep your First Mortgage for its full term—15, 20, 25 years.** Why? Because partial, early repayment only takes cash out of your pocket without getting you much relief from your regular P&I payments. The only time you benefit from early repayment of your First Mortgage is when you can pay it off in full. Then you gain relief from your P&I payment, giving you an instant increase in your PCF. **REMEMBER:** Don't make partial advance payments on your income-property First Mortgage. Instead, save your extra cash and wait until you can pay off your First Mortgage in full!

Second Mortgage Payment Strategies

Your Second Mortgage—usually your down payment loan—has different financial implications for you. So you'll treat your Second Mortgage differently from your First Mortgage, namely:

- **Pay off your Second Mortgage in full** as soon as you can. Why? Because paying off your Second Mortgage in full early requires less cash than doing the same for your First Mortgage. Further, you get an instantaneous PCF increase for yourself—the most important person in this entire deal! Thus, if you're paying $600 per month on your Second Mortgage and you pay it off in full, your PCF immediately rises by $600 per month. **REMEMBER:** Pay off your Second Mortgage in full as soon as you can to increase your PCF.
- **Don't fret or worry about the interest rate you pay on your Second Mortgage.** Why? Because the interest you pay is provable and legitimately tax-deductible. Your main concern is to *get* your Second Mortgage loan because this loan opens the door to

the world of real estate wealth for you. Without your Second Mortgage you could not get the property you own unless you dipped into your savings. *With* your Second Mortgage you're on your way to real estate wealth! So look for and get the Second Mortgage you want and need. Never get discouraged when looking for your Second Mortgage. Keep applying at suitable lenders. **REMEMBER:** Your Second Mortgage is your key to wealth when you're just starting your journey to your real estate fortune. Use every legitimate means you can to get your Second Mortgage loan!

Figuring Your Monthly Debt Service Cost

It's easy—and fun—to figure your monthly debt payments using Tables 10.1 and 10.2 in this chapter. What I've done is this:

> **To simplify your calculations, I've listed your costs in terms of each $1,000 you owe on either your First or Second Mortgage. This speeds your figuring because it reduces to simple multiplication. You just use numbers from the tables below.**

Table 10.1
Monthly Principal and Interest Payment Per $1,000 for Real Estate Loans

Interest Rate (%)	Term of Loan (Years)			
	15	20	25	30
5	7.91	6.60	5.85	5.37
6	8.44	7.16	6.44	6.00
7	8.99	7.75	7.07	6.65
8	9.56	8.36	7.72	7.34
9	10.14	9.00	8.39	8.05
10	10.75	9.65	9.09	8.78
11	11.37	10.32	9.80	9.52
12	12.00	11.01	10.53	10.29
14	13.32	12.44	12.04	11.85

Table 10.2
Second Mortgage Monthly Principal and Interest Payment Per $1,000

Interest Rate (%)	Term of Loan (Years) 2	3	4	5
6	44.32	30.42	23.49	19.33
8	45.23	31.34	24.41	20.28
10	46.15	32.27	25.36	21.25
12	47.07	33.21	26.33	22.24
14	48.01	34.18	27.33	23.27
16	48.96	35.16	28.34	24.32

Now Do the Simple Numbers

Let's say you're buying an income property priced at $100,000 with a 25-year first mortgage for $90,000 at 8 percent, and a 5-year second mortgage for $10,000 at 12 percent. What will your total mortgage payments be?

Here are the five easy steps you take to figure your monthly payment:

1. **Go into Table 10.1** and enter on the left at 8 percent and project across to 25 years and read $7.72 per $1,000 in mortgage loan.
2. **Write these numbers:** ($90,000 mortgage/$1,000)($7.72) = $694.80. This is your monthly debt service payment on your first mortgage.
3. **Next, go into Table 10.2,** entering at the left at 12 percent and project across to 5 years to read $22.24.
4. **Write these numbers:** ($10,000/$1,000)($22.24) = $222.40. This is your second mortgage monthly principal and interest payment.
5. **Add the amount** from Step 2 to the amount from Step 4. Thus, $694.80 + $222.40 = $917.20. This is your monthly debt service for the first 5 years you own this property.

The good news for you is that after 5 years, your monthly P&I payment drops to $694.80. Why? Because you will have paid off your second mortgage which gave you your down payment. You'll then be "in clover," as people say, because your payment drops by about 25 percent.

Know What Your Debt Coverage Is

As I mentioned to you earlier, good friend of mine, I'm the director of a large, multi-faceted lender in the New York area. When we make any loan we have a simple human desire. "What's that?" you ask. It is:

Every lender wants to have every loan repaid in full, on time, and in accordance with the promissory note signed by the borrower.

That's all a lender seeks. So when we make an income real estate loan, we look for the ability of the property to repay the loan. To get a quick reading on this we look at the *Debt Coverage Ratio.*

"And what's that?" you ask. The Debt Coverage Ratio is a number based on your income from the property that tells a lender whether you can easily make the monthly first mortgage payment.

To figure your Debt Coverage Ratio for a specific property, take these five steps:

1. **Figure your Annual Income** from the property. We'll say it is $80,000.
2. **Figure your Annual Expenses** for the property BEFORE your P&I mortgage payments. We'll say it is $41,000.
3. **Figure your Net Operating Income** BEFORE debt service by subtracting from your Annual Income (= $80,000 for this building) the Annual Expenses (= $41,000 for this property). Thus, $80,000 – $41,000 = $39,000.
4. **Figure your Annual P&I Debt Service Cost.** For this building, it is $28,000 per year.
5. **Figure your Debt Coverage Ratio** by dividing your Net Operating Income by your Annual Debt Service Cost. Or, $39,000/$28,000 = 1.39. This is your Debt Coverage Ratio.

As lenders, we look for a Debt Coverage Ratio of 1.3 or more. So this property, with its 1.39 Ratio, would be attractive to us as a loan candidate.

That's all there is to the ***Debt Coverage Ratio.*** When you approach a lender for your mortgage loan, you will always point out the ratio for your debt coverage, if it's 1.3 or higher. Your lender will be delighted that you took the time to figure this out in advance.

Quickly Figure Your Capitalization Rate

Your last easy number for your real estate millions is the *Capitalization Rate.* This number tells you your percent return on your income BEFORE your P&I debt payments, based on the price you paid for the property.

As a lender we always look at the Capitalization Rate. Why? Because it tells us, in just seconds, whether the real estate is a good business deal for you—and for us!

To figure your Capitalization Rate, divide your Annual Operating Income BEFORE Debt Service by what you pay for the property. Thus, if you paid $480,000 for the property discussed above, your Capitalization Rate = $39,000/$480,000 = 0.08. Or, multiplying by 100, your Cap Rate = 8 percent.

Typical cap rates range between 6 percent and 20 percent. Hence, this property is an attractive loan candidate for any lender—including the lender for which I am director.

Now Put Your Numbers to Work

You now have and know the four numbers we lenders look for. "So how do I use these numbers?" you ask. That's easy. You:

- **Include each of these numbers** when you write your "Cover Letter" which accompanies your Loan Application that you should send to every lender when applying for your investor income real estate first mortgage.
- **Point out in your Cover Letter** that the numbers show that the property is a good investment for both the lender and the investor.
- **Are ready to answer any questions** about the numbers that the lender may ask. Being able to do this will impress your loan offi-

cer. Why? Because—in my experience, at least—most loan officers have secret ambitions to be real estate investors. So when you have a ready and accurate answer to their questions about your numbers, their admiration for you quadruples! And, by the way, many of the questions will come from the loan officer's supervisor, not directly from the person you're talking to.

So there you have your four easy and simple numbers. Now get to work using them. Your good friend—me—will be happy to help you if you have any questions about them.

Your Keys to Real Estate Riches

- ❑ **There are four easy, key numbers** you must know about every income real estate project.
- ❑ **Your four easy, key numbers are:** Positive Cash Flow (PCF), Monthly Debt Service, Debt Coverage Ratio, and Capitalization Rate.
- ❑ **Get to know your key numbers** so you can easily explain them if a lender asks you to do so. "Knowing your numbers" will make you a hero to every lender and your chances of getting your loan increase enormously.
- ❑ **Include your key numbers in every Cover Letter** you write to a lender. You'll impress the lender most favorably.

CHAPTER 11

Turn Your Real Estate Holdings into Your Private Bank

ONCE YOU OWN SOME REAL ESTATE—EVEN JUST ONE SINGLE-FAMILY home—you can turn it into your private bank! And this bank can be:

- **Your ready source** for one or more loans.
- **Your base** for buying more income property.
- **Your asset** for improving your credit profile, making you eligible for more investor loans.
- **Your key** to building greater wealth in real estate—sooner.

Truly, good friend of mine, income real estate can be your "magic carpet" to wealth. Starting with your first small house, you can build a portfolio of income real estate that can make you a millionaire in a few years or less. Here's how.

Use Your Real Estate Equity to Build Wealth

"Equity" *is your ownership portion of a real estate property*. Consider this four-step example:

1. **You buy a two-family income property** for $100,000, putting down $10,000 of borrowed money.

2. **You hold the property** for two years, making regular monthly mortgage payments, while collecting rental income that pays all your costs, plus giving you a profitable positive cash flow (PCF) every month. And you make many improvements to the important parts of each rental unit—namely the bathroom, kitchen, windows, doors, or other improvements.
3. **You decide,** after two years, that you'd like to refinance this income property to take cash out of it to use for other real estate investments.
4. **You analyze** the property, finding that the market value of your investment today is $180,000. An appraisal by a local real estate broker verifies your analysis. The broker says your property is worth $184,000! But you decide to use your own more conservative estimate of value: $180,000.

You have paid off your mortgage to the point where you owe only $88,000. So your equity in the property is: $180,000 – $88,000 = $92,000.

"But," you say, "I put $10,000 of borrowed money into the property. How do I get my borrowed money back?"

The answer is easy. Just deduct it from your equity. So your equity becomes $92,000 – $10,000 = $82,000. Your next challenge is to use your equity. Here's how.

Tapping Your Equity for Profit or Fun

You can borrow against your equity—that is, take money out of it in the form of a loan against your equity—to do any of several profitable or fun things, such as use the money:

1. **To buy more income real estate.** This is called "double leverage" by real estate wealth builders.
2. **To fix up or rehab other real estate you own.** Then raise the rents in that property to increase your monthly income and pay off your equity loan.

3. **To buy tax-free bonds that finance worthwhile real estate projects.** (I regularly do this and have built a significant "nest egg" of tax-free real estate income, while helping provide better housing and medical facilities, for example.)
4. **To pay for your dream vacation, buy a boat, an airplane, a sport utility vehicle, or other dream.**

Note that all of the profitable investments, Numbers 1 through 3, will earn you money you can use to repay your equity loan. Of the three steps you can take, the first will probably earn the most money for you and enable you to repay your equity loan in the shortest time. Here's an example of using an equity loan to buy more income property, as given in a reader letter:

Equity Allows Buying More Income Property

"We're off and running. Borrowed $407,000 to buy the $390,000 income property this way: $100,000 equity loan, $231,000 land acquisition loan, $76,000 signature loan—total = $407,000. You said it could be done and we did it! All the money was borrowed from an S & L bank. When we found the right lender they sold us on our own project!"

—New Jersey

Another reader writes about building up equity for additional loans using minimum cash input with an assumable mortgage:

Smart Real Estate Deals in Paradise

"Here in Hawaii we use an 'Agreement of Sale' which allows us to easily get into good property without the costly six percent sales commission. We can close with the original seller within one year. All the properties I've bought have

> assumable mortgages and I've refinanced them where the cash flow makes sense. You can get these properties in just weeks. I'm really excited about these opportunities because they give people a chance to get a piece of 'Paradise' without the typical down payment, making it great for investors." —Hawaii

And another reader writes to tell how his equity is increasing in his real estate holdings:

> **Monthly Equity Buildup**
>
> "I currently own five 4-unit buildings and a 3-bedroom house. And I'm looking to buy more in the future. The properties are gaining about $1,500 per month in equity, plus $1,500 per month positive cash flow." —Kentucky

In effect, these readers have another hidden source of income from their equity buildup. Since increases in your equity occur while you're awake and asleep, you can say you have another "job" which is paying you tax-free income. And you're really not doing any work for this income. That's why I say you're a smart person to be in the world's best business!

Taking Steps to Repay Your Equity Loan Quickly

Here are steps you can take to repay your equity loan in the fastest way possible:

- **You buy,** with $50,000 of your equity money (from the $82,000 in the example above), an income property that pays you a PCF of $800 per month.
- **Your monthly loan payment** on your equity loan is $500 per month. This leaves you with a net PCF of $800 – $500 = $300 per month.

- **You have increased your real estate holdings in dollars,** while not taking any money out of your pocket to do so!
- **You repay** $500 a month to your equity lender to "retire" (that is, pay off) your equity loan that you used to buy an asset that repays its own cost! Such a strategy on your part verifies the famous statement that ***"The money money makes makes money!"***

How Much Can I Borrow on My Equity?

Equity loans seem to get more generous every day of the week. Typical loans you can get with your $82,000 equity are:

- **75% of equity = $61,500**
- **100% of equity = $82,000**
- **125% of equity = $102,500**

Today, the 125 percent equity loan is now a very popular type. Why? Because you get more cash in hand. Meanwhile, as you pay off your equity loan, your property rises in value with the passage of time. And when your property value exceeds what you owe on your equity loan, you can go back and get another equity loan!

So, good friend of mine, in just two years, you—as a "Beginning Private Banker"—multiplied $10,000 of borrowed money from a credit card line of credit or a personal loan into cash ranging from $62,500 to $102,500!

Doesn't this show you—very quickly—the enormous power of real estate? I almost feel like shouting, "I told you so!" You, while earning a monthly Positive Cash Flow from your property, which rose in value while you slept, also:

Multiplied a borrowed $10,000 by a factor of 6.25 to $62,500, or by a factor of 10.25 to $102,500!

Where else could you do this? Not in the risky stock market. Not in some unknown business of your own! Only in real estate.

That's why it's the world's best business! And if you use your equity money to buy another income property, the positive cash flow from that property will repay your equity loan!

How Is the Value of Your Equity Figured?

The property you bought for $100,000 was worth $188,000 two years later. How was the value of $188,000 determined?

Here, good friend of mine, is how the value of real estate you own is determined in today's real world of real estate investment. Read on for info on what really happens.

As you learned earlier, I'm director of a large general loan and real estate lender. When someone comes to us for a real estate loan, we ask for a financial statement listing what the prospective borrower (such as yourself) owns—their ***assets***—and what they owe—their ***liabilities.*** This is called their ***balance sheet.***

To prepare your balance sheet for your property that you paid $100,000 for, you:

Quick Steps to Prepare Your Balance Sheet

- **Contact your bank** by phone and ask for the amount you currently owe on your mortgage—and they tell you it is $88,000, as listed above.
- **Walk out in front** of your beautiful income building and, thinking about the improvements you plan, and those you've already made, along with rent increases you've made and plan to make, decide the building is now worth $190,000.
- **Look in your local newspaper** for similar buildings and see that they're priced from $175,000 to $210,000. This makes your price—$190,000—look right.
- **Contact a local real estate agent** and ask that person for a price quote, after giving full details about your property. That person says, after checking "comparables" (prices of similar properties sold in the area), "$188,000." So you settle on that number and

enter it as an asset on your balance sheet when you apply for your equity loan.

And do you know what, good friend of mine? As lenders, we:

- **And all other lenders I know** accept your estimate of the current value of your property.
- **And some other lenders I know** rarely go out to your property and make a physical inspection of it. We accept your word as to its condition and value. If we doubt your word, we will have a "drive-by" inspection in which an inspector drives by the property in an auto and estimates its value from the external appearance of the building and land.
- **And all other lenders I know** use your listing of assets as a critical element in our loan decision. In brief, the more assets a borrower has, the easier it is for that person to get an equity loan.

So, good friend of mine, hear what I say—namely that:

High-asset borrowers get more loans than low-asset borrowers because lenders believe that people with larger assets are more reliable and better loan risks. So hear the word and build your assets to the highest level possible. You'll get more loans and reach your millionaire status sooner!

How to Increase the Value of Your Equity

The clear message for you in the last several paragraphs is:

Increase your equity in your present real estate holdings as quickly and as much as you can. Then your equity borrowing power will rise enormously.

"Yes, that's a good tactic," you say. "But how can I increase my equity to raise my assets and borrowing power?" Here are six lucky ways to raise your equity in any income real estate:

Six Steps to Increase Your Equity in Real Estate

1. **Raise rents as quickly as possible once you buy a property.** Why? Because the higher your rents, the larger the mortgage payments you can make on a property, reducing your mortgage on the property, increasing your equity.
2. **Make needed repairs on the property.** You can do these yourself, or you can have the repairs done by an outside contractor. Just remember that every dollar you spend on repairs raises your property's value by at least $1.33. So repairs increase your equity in your property.
3. **Get every unit in the property rented.** Being fully rented raises your monthly income and allows you to project a higher annual income. Lenders will apply a "5 Percent Vacancy Factor" to your Projected Annual Income when you apply for an equity loan. But the fact that you're 100 percent rented will impress every lender and give your property a higher rating in their opinion—which helps you get a loan!
4. **Give your property an upscale name.** Use this name on all your loan applications. Names you might use could be "Regency Arms," "Excellency Apartments," or "Golden Shores Tower." An upscale name for your building makes it a better loan project in the eyes of loan officers.
5. **Take attractive photographs of your property.** Use these photos in your equity loan application. Today you can easily and quickly take attractive photos of your property with a digital camera. These photos can be printed out on your computer and sent to the lender along with your loan application.
6. **"Dress up" the front of your building** so it looks more attractive. This can usually be done for little money but it can give great results when you apply for your equity loan. You can do this work yourself, or you can have an outside contractor do the work. Either way, the cost will not be excessive. But the results can be enormous when you apply for your equity loan.

Use Your Increased Equity to Build Your Wealth

The six steps just listed for increasing your equity can really work—if you work them. Just take a look at this letter from a reader:

Starting on Zero Cash and Getting Equity Loans to Expand

"I recently finished reading your book How to Make Big Money in Real Estate for the second time. The first time I read your book it led me to begin buying income property in my hometown. I now own seven units, all of which were bought with zero money down.

"My first property, a triplex, was bought with a 100% FHA loan. I paid $220,000 for it, and it appraised at $385,000. After one year I had the property reappraised and I gained about $165,000 in value. I made some improvements myself—new fence, tile, paint, doors, etc., which cost about $5,000. I did a cash-out refinance and received about $20,000 in cash, while lowering the interest rate. I then got a second equity loan for $60,000. This is the money I used for the down payment and closing costs on my next deal—a fourplex. Because I had made some minor improvements on the triplex myself, I was able to raise the rents on the triplex enough to cover the two new mortgages while giving me a positive cash flow of $200 per month.

"On my second deal, for the fourplex, the price was $505,000. I put 10% down. This was the money I received on the second loan on the triplex. I was able to raise the rent on one of the units in the fourplex, giving a positive cash flow of $300 per month.

"And though I bought the fourplex just 3 months ago, I found a lender who will accept a new appraisal. So I am refinancing the fourplex at $560,000 with an Adjustable Rate Mortgage (ARM) at 5%. The existing loan is at 7.25%. The projected positive cash flow from the fourplex when the refinancing is finished is $1,000 per month.

"Since real estate has been so good to me, I'm planning on buying units until I can quit my teaching position. In less

than one year I got properties worth $950,000 with a PCF of $1,300 per month on zero cash. I look forward to greater success."
—California

How to Get around "Seasoning" Requirements

Lenders will sometimes tell you when you apply for an equity loan that "more seasoning is needed before we can make the loan to you." What does a lender mean by this and how can you answer their statement?

Seasoning is a repayment record on a property. When a lender asks for seasoning, they usually mean a satisfactory payment record of 12 months or longer on a given building. "Satisfactory" means you made your monthly mortgage P&I (Principal and Interest) payments in full and on time.

What often happens is that the BWB in real estate seeks to get an equity loan before the required seasoning has been put in. Can you get around seasoning requirements? Yes, you can. Here are three ways how:

How to Get a Loan with No Seasoning

1. **Show the lender that your income from the property** is more than enough for your P&I payments needed on the building.
2. **Show the lender that you have an excellent payment record** for loans you've had in the past, such as auto, home, boat, or other income real estate.
3. **Show the lender your future plans for the property** and how your income will rise as time passes, guaranteeing that the payments will be made on time, and in full.

There is a five-step approach to qualifying for your loan when your seasoning is shorter than requested:

Five Ways to Get a Loan with Short Seasoning

1. **Apply to lenders** who have a shorter seasoning requirement.
2. **Call one lender after another,** asking what their seasoning requirements are.

3. **Tell each lender** about the property on which you're seeking an equity loan. Have your request in writing, ready at your telephone.
4. **Continue calling lenders** until you find one that's willing to work with you. Again, your cost is small compared to the size of the loan you can get!
5. **Get a new appraisal** as the BWB above did and find a lender who will accept that appraisal. You will use your new appraisal to get around the lender's seasoning requirements. Your calling cost will usually be small compared to the loan you can get.

Build Your Own "Bank" with Your Properties

There are many ways you can turn your income properties into your personal "bank." And each of these methods will put tax-free cash into your pocket. Five important ways to take cash out of your properties are:

Smart Ways to Get Cash from Your Properties

1. **Borrow on your equity.** You learned how to do this in the sections above. The methods you read about there really *do* work! Try them and see for yourself.
2. **Get rehab (fix-up) loans on your property.** Use part of the money for rehab and part for other moneymaking projects. Be sure your cash flow can repay your loans.
3. **Refinance your property**—that is, get a new long-term first mortgage at a lower interest rate while putting cash into your pocket. Your monthly mortgage payments will be lower if your new interest rate is less than what you were formerly paying. And you will probably pocket cash from the growth in value of your property. Here's a letter on refinancing:

Refinancing Helps BWB Expand

"I've refinanced two of my single-family homes to get cash to buy other income homes." —Virginia

4. **Convert your property into a Limited Partnership** with yourself as the General Partner. Have your Limited Partners put cash into the partnership to buy more income property. You manage all the properties and receive a portion of the ownership of the new properties for your work. Your total ownership share of the partnership is based on the original properties you put into the partnership, plus the work you do. You MUST have a competent attorney guide you and the partnership. See Chapters 6 and 8 for more data on limited partnerships.
5. **Put your property into a Real Estate Corporation.** Sell shares in your corporation to raise more money to buy additional income properties. You'll own controlling interest in the corporation. Again, you MUST have a competent attorney to form and guide your real estate corporation.

Yes, real estate can be your personal "bank." Use the methods given in this chapter and you can be your own "banker." And if you have any questions you can always call me—day or night. Just use the telephone number at the end of this book.

When you call, please tell me if you're a subscriber to one of my newsletters. Why? I try to help them first.

Your Keys to Real Estate Riches

- ❑ **You can use your real estate equity** to build wealth in income properties of all kinds.
- ❑ **It's easy to tap into your real estate equity** for profit or for fun.
- ❑ **Your real estate equity** can help you buy more income properties, becoming your private "bank" for loans.
- ❑ **Monthly equity increases in your properties** become another source of income for you. You have a "no-show job" that pays you while you sleep!

- ❑ **Borrowing on your equity buildup makes sense**—especially when you reinvest the money in other income real estate.
- ❑ **Your equity buildup** can improve your business and personal balance sheets enormously.
- ❑ **High-asset borrowers get more loans** than low-asset borrowers because lenders like the former.
- ❑ **You can take positive steps** to increase your equity quickly to improve your business balance sheet.
- ❑ **Seasoning is required by many lenders** before they'll make a loan to you. But you can take steps to show the lender why you're deserving of a loan.
- ❑ **Build your own "bank"** with your income properties and your success in real estate investing is assured!

CHAPTER 12

Save Time and Build Your Real Estate Fortune Faster

YOU LIVE IN A TIME OF NO PATIENCE. AS I TELL PEOPLE, "PATIENCE FELL out of the dictionary!"

Today, nearly everyone seems to want everything yesterday. So you'll find that many BWBs want to earn their real estate fortune faster. Result?

Some BWBs seek ways to get into fast-track real estate. This chapter gives you a number of ways to earn your real estate fortune faster.

Learn the Fast Track to Real Estate Wealth

There are a number of quick ways to earn money faster in real estate today. Good ways to fast money in real estate include:

- Flipping properties.
- Subletting for a profit.
- Using options to control real estate.
- Be a real estate loan finder.
- Build self-storage wealth.
- Earn big profits in off-campus housing.
- Use "liquid" real estate for your wealth source.
- Become a Loan Correspondent for a local lender.
- Plus many more.

To show you how you can make money from these ways, we'll take a fast look at each. You'll quickly see if the suggested method appeals to you.

Flip Real Estate for a Quick Profit

You briefly learned about flipping in Chapter 7. Here is more detailed data that will allow you to make money faster today. When you ***flip*** real estate you:

- ***Buy at a price*** below the going market value of the property.
- ***Sell quickly*** at a higher price than you paid, earning a profit on the sale.

There are two ways BWBs approach flipping:

1. ***Do little or nothing*** to the property before you sell it.
2. ***Do moderate or major*** cosmetic or structural work to the property before selling it.

Method 2 will usually give you a higher profit, but it:

- ***Takes you more time*** to do the work.
- ***Costs you more*** in fix-up fees and materials.
- ***Can be riskier*** to you because a higher profit isn't guaranteed.

You get best results by flipping single-family homes (SFH). Why? Because:

- ***There are more*** SFH available to work with.
- ***You have more*** potential buyers for SFH.
- ***SFH offer greater*** price flexibility than any other type of property.

So look to SFH as your flipping "training wheels." Start with REO foreclosed homes (see Chapter 7) and build from there. For SFH flipping, here are your estimated time inputs:

Estimated time for your project: Looking for suitable SFH to flip: 8 hours; Purchase of SFH: 6 hours; Property checkup, preparation for sale: 7 hours; Qualifying prospective buyer: 4 hours; Sale closing: 5 hours; *Total estimated time: 30 hours. Profit potential: $50 to $500 per hour, based on a profit of $1,000 to $15,000 per sale.* And—of course—your profit might be higher—or lower—than given here!

Special Notice on Flipping

In May 2003, the U.S. Department of Housing and Urban Development (HUD) adopted a rule intended to curb misleading practices in flipping that sometimes occur. Homes that are sold within 90 days or less of their date of purchase will not be eligible for mortgage insurance issued by the Federal Housing Administration. The FHA is said to insure about one million mortgages per year—some 15 percent of the total number of mortgages issued annually.

Sublet Properties for Non-Ownership Profits

You can rent an apartment, office space, warehouse facilities, etc., and sublet them to a tenant for a higher fee than you're paying. Thus:

- ***You rent*** a 3-bedroom apartment in a desirable area for $1,000 per month.
- ***You furnish*** it with basic items—couch, armchairs, beds, tables, and so on, which you buy at auction or remainder sales for $750.
- ***You sublet*** the semi-furnished apartment for $1,600 per month, with two months' security deposit, or $3,200.

"Can this really work?" you ask. It certainly *can,* and it *does,* work in many highly populated areas. The whole key to your sublet success is:

You MUST have a sublet clause in your lease allowing you to sublet the apartment. Don't try this method without a sublet clause!

"Why does this method work," you ask, "when my tenant could rent the apartment for $1,000 per month just like I have?" It works because, by putting in a few pieces of furniture, you change the whole offer—you're renting a furnished apartment—not an unfurnished apartment!

> ***Estimated time for your project:*** Find suitable apartment with sublet clause: 6 hours; Sign lease: 1 hour; Buy and install furniture: 4 hours; Find suitable tenant: 8 hours. *Total estimated time: 19 hours.*

Use Options to Control Real Estate

You learned a brief amount about options in Chapter 7. As you saw there, you can take an *option* on a piece of property to buy it at a stated price within a specified number of days. During this time you will have the sole right to resell the property. Your option period can be 30, 60, 90, or 120 days. Or you can negotiate a longer schedule—180 days, 270 days, or more. Most options are based on 30-day intervals. With an option on real estate:

- ***You pay an option price***—$100, $500, $1,000—depending on what you (the optionee)—work out with the seller (the optioner).
- ***During the period of the option*** you can sell the property for whatever price above the option price you can get.
- ***When you sell the property*** you earn a profit based on the difference between your cost and your sales price. For example:
  - ***You take*** a 90-day option for $1,000 to buy a 20-unit multifamily apartment house for $800,000.
  - ***You advertise*** your optioned property for sale for $890,000, knowing that you'll accept a low of $850,000. But you hope to get at least $860,000.
  - ***To convince buyers*** of the desirability of the property you prepare a Profit and Loss (P&L) statement for the property showing a Positive Cash Flow (PCF) of $3,000 per month, or $36,000 per year after all expenses and mortgage payments. You show the P&L to every prospective buyer.
  - ***After 63 days*** of advertising and meeting with prospects you get an offer of $855,000 for the property. You're not too pleased

because your acceptable "floor" price is $860,000. You negotiate with the buyer and finally get him to a price of $862,000.

- ***You sell*** at the $862,000 price and have a simultaneous closing at which time you buy the multiunit property for $800,000 and sell it for $862,000 within minutes. Your net profit after all fees and charges is $18,900. You figure that you earned $18,900 profit/63 days = $300 per day. Not bad when you spent only a few minutes a day on the deal!

Estimated time for your project: Looking for suitable multi-unit building you can buy on an option: 6 hours; Option negotiation: 2 hours; Advertising (ad preparation, selection of places to advertise, etc.): 3 hours; Meeting with potential buyers: 7 hours; Negotiation with actual buyer: 3 hours; Closing for purchase and sale: 4 hours. *Total estimated time: 25 hours. Profit potential: $15,000 to $60,000, depending on the size of the property.*

Be a Real Estate Loan Finder

"What's the most needed service in real estate?" is an often-asked question. The answer is a simple five-letter word—***MONEY!***

Finding investment money is—always has been, and always will be—the toughest task for BWBs in income real estate. You can help solve this problem for yourself and others by acting as a Real Estate Loan Finder.

"And what does a Real Estate Loan Finder do?" you ask. A Loan Finder:

- ***Finds loans*** for BWBs wanting to buy income real estate.
- ***Brings*** a borrower and a lender together and steps back.
- ***Earns a fee*** from the borrower for finding the needed money.
- ***Is paid the fee*** AFTER the loan is completed and the borrower has the funds.

During the process of finding money for others for a fee, you—as the finder—will learn a lot, such as:

- ***Which lending organizations*** (banks, mortgage companies, private individuals, or others) are making real estate loans.
- ***What types of loans*** each lender prefers, including loan amount, term, purpose, and so forth.
- ***Where a prospective borrower*** will most likely get the loan he/she seeks for their income real estate.
- ***Why a borrower*** will be accepted for a specific loan type, and why a borrower will be rejected for another type of loan.
- ***How to best present*** a real estate loan application to each lender you deal with.

To set yourself up as a real estate loan finder you take these five simple steps:.

1. ***Choose a name*** for your business. If you operate under your own name, you—in general—do not need to register your business with your County Clerk. However, you MUST check with that person or a competent local attorney to learn what the local rules are so you can comply with them.
2. ***Learn as much as you can*** about the finding business. In essence, you act as a middle person to bring a borrower and lender together. You then step back and let them negotiate and handle the paperwork.
3. ***Advertise your services*** as a loan finder in local papers, after you have complied with local business registration rules and have had the advice of a qualified business attorney.
4. ***Watch for responses*** from local banks or mortgage companies. Many times they will offer to make you their local Loan Correspondent to find mortgage applicants for the bank or mortgage company. You serve as an Independent Contractor working under the lender's real estate license.
5. ***Find clients.*** Negotiate loans for them. Collect your fee on completion and go on to the next deal. Meanwhile—of course—you'll get to know who's lending locally, and for what types of deals. You can then structure your deals to comply with the going lending

practices. When you serve as a Loan Correspondent, the lender typically pays you 40 percent of the fee earned for the loan. The lender keeps the remainder of the fee earned.

Estimated time for your project: Getting your business started: 12 hours; Advertising for clients: 3 hours; Choosing qualified clients from among the responses you get: 2 hours; Filling out and submitting the loan application: 4 hours; Loan approval time: 8 hours. *Total estimated time: 29 hours per early project; 14 hours per project after you're established.*

Build Self-Storage Wealth Today

When you own residential income real estate you must be a "people person." That is, you must learn how to deal with cranky tenants, spoiled children who damage your property, and pets that irritate tenants who do not like animals.

But with mini- or maxi-self-storage real estate:

- **You rarely** see your "tenants."
- **Your tenants** can do little to damage your property.
- **You normally** have no children or live-in tenants to contend with.
- **Your monthly** "rent" can be much higher in dollars per square foot of space you rent than in almost any other type of real estate.
- **If a tenant fails** to pay rent for a stated period of time (which varies from one state to another), you can auction whatever is in the rental space for additional income for your business.

You'll find self-storage warehouses for sale in the columns of real estate magazines and your local large-city newspaper. The Consulting Services Group of National Self Storage Management Inc., 17 W. Wetmore Rd, Suite 302, Tucson, AZ 85705, T: 520-577-9777, can be helpful in showing you how to turn weak-earning self-storage warehouses into outstanding profit makers.

Your self-storage warehouse will provide many amenities, including:

- ***Storage*** for residential, commercial, and professional items and belongings.
- ***Monthly,*** yearly, and seasonal rentals.
- ***Locked*** storage area with a personal key for the tenant.
- ***Camera*** surveillance of the storage and parking areas.
- ***7-day*** storage access for customers.
- ***Plus*** many other convenient features for tenants.

Estimated time for your project: Find suitable self-storage property: 3 months; Negotiate sale: 1 month; Closing: 1 day; Convert it to profitable operation: 6 months. *Total estimated time: 10+ months.*

Build Big Profits in Off-Campus Housing

One of the biggest lacks of housing around the world today is for college and university students. Why is this? Because:

- ***Most colleges and universities*** are in a budget squeeze, so there's no money available to construct additional student housing on-campus.
- ***Many students*** think it's "childish" to live on campus; they want to live in housing away from the school but close enough to walk to it—this is called *off-campus housing.*
- ***Living off campus*** broadens a student's life experiences, preparing them more effectively for life after school.
- ***Off-campus living*** is relatively unsupervised, giving students a greater feeling of freedom—which they love.
- ***Colleges and universities*** are glad to recommend off-campus housing to students at NO cost to the student or property owner (you)—your advertising costs nothing!
- ***Property owners*** (you) can have a student's lease guaranteed by the parents, meaning there's much less risk of not being paid.
- ***Giving parents*** a small discount (5 percent) on the rent often results in the owner (you) being paid in advance for the rent, removing any worries of not being paid.

- ***With Internet access*** needed by all students today, you, as owner, have other revenue sources which can increase your income enormously.
- ***Many colleges and universities*** are located in small towns where housing prices have not yet "gone through the roof," as people say; your acquisition (buying) cost is low.
- ***With more students*** staying in college longer, you will have a year-round demand for your housing because summer sessions are often almost as crowded as regular classes. (You can get a good idea of this stay-in-school mentality by remembering the modern definition of a "dropout." It is: ***He or she only got their bachelor's degree!***) This definition tells you that today's college graduate has to get at least a Master's degree to get a good job. Anything less and you've dropped out!
- ***Older single-family homes*** suitable for off-campus student housing are often available at bargain prices in many college towns all over the world. This means you can get started quickly on little or no money. One reason why older single-family homes are available at bargain prices in small towns is because few people recognize the high income potential in student housing.
- ***Student room rents*** are higher than ever before. The actual rent you'll receive depends on the section of the country you're in. Rents of $800 per month per student are typical in some areas. With 10 such rooms you'll have an income of $96,000 per year, before expenses. In other areas the rent may be as high as $2,500 per month per student. Figure the income you'll have with several such units!
- ***You don't provide*** any personal services to students. They do their own laundry, make their beds, may supply their own furniture, and definitely buy their own food, which they cook. You're just supplying a comfortable room!

"This all sounds good," you say. "But what are the negatives of off-campus student housing?" Here are the negatives:

- ***Unless you live in a college or university town,*** you will have to buy housing at a distance from where you reside.

- ***All student housing requires some kind of supervision.*** So, if you buy out-of-town houses, you won't be a local resident. You'll then have to hire a local manager to look after your properties and watch that the students behave while in the housing you own.
- ***Some students may have wild parties*** in your building unless you strictly enforce safety rules at all times.

Despite these few negatives, student housing can start to make you rich in real estate in just months. Here's how to decide if off-campus student housing is for you:

- ***Look around the area*** in which you live to see if there are any colleges or universities. Don't overlook junior colleges and technical institutes.
- ***List your local colleges and universities*** and their driving distance from where you reside.
- ***Visit each campus*** that interests you. Call on the *Student Services* or *Student Housing Department* and ask about the housing situation for students. In most schools, you'll be told there's an intense shortage of suitable (neat, clean, and within walking distance) housing.
- ***Look at local real estate*** near the schools where housing shortages exist. Get prices for multi-room—usually two- or three-story—single-family homes. You'll often find that prices are in the $65,000 to $95,000 range for beautiful, turn-of-the-century, colonial-style homes. Students love older homes because such houses provide a home-like atmosphere with familiar rooms and other facilities.
- ***Make a drawing*** of the single-family home layout. See how many individual rooms you start with and can later create. Only one kitchen is needed because the students share the kitchen area. Try to find houses with as many bathrooms as possible—the more the better.
- ***Seek an architect*** to help you determine if the building could be conveniently converted to student housing. Such advice will usually cost you about $500, along with some basic sketch plans of the redesigned building. Your results will be well worth such help.
- ***Work out a price*** for the property based on going rents in the area. The college or university will provide you with this data. Compute your cash flow based on price, typical rent, and number of stu-

dents you can house. (If you can't do this, fax me the info and I'll do it free of charge if you're a subscriber to one of my newsletters.)

- ***Open your off-campus housing*** and get student renters, after hiring a local competent part-time manager. Some owners use a student to manage the building. Pay is in the form of reduced rent on the room the student occupies. Have your manager collect your rents regularly; you can then use the cash flow to buy more student housing in the same area.
- ***Get your house wired*** for the Internet in each room you rent. You can charge students $10 or $15 per month for each Internet connection. Your cost might be $30 per month for the entire house. You collect $100 to $150 per month extra income when you have 10 rooms in your house and a charge of $10 or $15 per month per room.

So if you want to earn $100,000+ per year in real estate, consider off-campus student housing. All you do is buy your first house and use the equity in it for your down payment on the second one. Soon you'll be a student-housing wealth builder! Just keep expanding the number of houses you own as time passes.

Estimated time for your project: Find suitable house for student housing: 1 month; Negotiate sale: 2 weeks; Closing: 1 day; Home rehab to suit students: 1 month. *Total estimated time: 3 months.*

Use "Liquid" Real Estate for Your Wealth Building

"Liquid" real estate is the ownership of one or more swimming-pool facilities—either indoor or outdoor, or a combination of the two, to earn a profit for yourself. In swimming pool ownership you:

- **Own a property** containing a pool that will be used for recreational swimming and diving by adults and children.
- **May also have** competitive swimming contests at your pool for local schools, Boy Scouts, Girl Scouts, clubs, and other organizations that have swimming teams.
- **Can also rent** your pool for scuba diving training lessons to organizations training individuals, police and fire departments, Coast Guard personnel, or other organizations.

How much can you earn from your swimming pool real estate? Much depends on where your pool is located, the population in the area, and whether you sublet your pool to an operator. Remember:

- **In swimming pool real estate,** your income comes from people who "rent" your water space for a few hours. You may, however, have organizations that rent for a month at a time to hold in-the-water scuba instruction, swimming lessons, competitive meets, Boy/Girl Scout contests, or other events.
- **In swimming pool real estate,** you also have the annual rise in value of your property. This will run between 3 percent and 5 percent per year for typical pools. Indoor pools tend to rise more in value annually because they are a year-round business, compared to outdoor pools that are seasonal.
- **In swimming pool real estate,** you can expect to earn from $50,000 to $75,000 per year, not counting the rise in value of your property. Yes, "liquid" real estate can give you both fun and a decent income!

To find a swimming pool that you can buy—because it's best to start in this business with an existing pool—take these five steps:

1. ***Look in your local telephone*** *Yellow Pages* for a listing of swimming pools in your area and in surrounding cities and towns.
2. ***Call or write each pool;*** ask if the facility is for sale. Get full data on the asking price, down payment, income, and expenses.
3. ***Look in your Sunday newspaper*** under the heading "Miscellaneous Real Estate for Sale." When you see a pool listed, contact the seller; ask for an Income and Expense statement, price, down payment, type of swimmers, and other details.
4. ***Figure if you can pay*** for your pool out of earnings and still show a Positive Cash Flow (PCF) each month. You MUST have a PCF before you buy any swimming pool!
5. ***Make an offer to buy*** the swimming pool if you can see you'll have a PCF large enough every month to pay for the work you'll do running the pool.

Estimated time for your project: Finding suitable pool for sale: 1 month to 6 months; Negotiate sale: 1 month; Closing: 1 day; Get the pool organized the way you want it: 1 month; Finding team-type clients, 6 months. *Total estimated time: 1 year.*

Be a Loan Correspondent for a Real Estate Lender

Earlier we saw how you could be a finder for people seeking real estate loans. As a loan finder:

- **You work** with many different lenders, none of whom you represent on an exclusive basis.
- **You get** your fee from the borrower, not from the lender.
- **You may not**—in general—have an ongoing relationship with specific lenders.

As a Loan Correspondent, you have a different set of working conditions, namely:

- **You represent** one lender—either local or national—and work exclusively with that lender.
- **Your fee is paid** to you by the lender—not the borrower.
- **You are often** provided leads by the lender, or you can generate them yourself.
- **You are associated** with a known-name lender and that lender's good reputation is shared by you, to your benefit.

As a Loan Correspondent, the work you do is to:

- **Find people** seeking a mortgage loan for a home they're buying, offering them an attractive interest rate.
- **Find people** who want to refinance their home at a lower interest rate than they're currently paying.
- **Find people** seeking a home equity loan to take cash out of a house that's nearly paid off, or has enough equity to provide a loan of $10,000 or more.
- **Find people** who want to get cash now for a mortgage they received when they sold a property a few years ago—called a ***mortgage cash-out.***

As a Loan Correspondent, you'll:

- **Meet many people in your area** who seek loans for real estate of several different types, both locally and nationally.
- **Hear lots of actual real estate loan requests** from people with details of how they were treated by various lenders.
- **Learn why real estate loan applications** were rejected and how. The reasons for rejection will be highly educational for you in your work of qualifying people for real estate loans.

"So how do I become a Loan Correspondent for real estate loans?" you ask. The answer is:

- **Look in** your local telephone book *Yellow Pages* under "Mortgages" and "Loans" and list all the banks and mortgage lenders advertising loans.
- **See if any** of the lenders have a line in their ad saying "Loan correspondents sought." If so, contact that lender immediately.
- **Call or write** each lender, saying, "I'd like to become a Loan Correspondent for NAME OF LENDER on a commission basis. What must I do to get started?"
- **Wait for an answer.** You will get it in a few days if the lender is looking for Loan Correspondents.

What will your working conditions be as a Loan Correspondent? You will:

- **Be typically paid a commission** by the lender of 40 percent of the lender's loan fee, though this amount can vary between lenders.
- **Be an "Independent Contractor"** for the lender. This means you will ***not*** be on the lender's payroll. And you will pay your own expenses—telephone, auto mileage, medical and dental insurance, and other expenses.
- **Be working** under the lender's real estate license. You do NOT need a separate real estate license for yourself.
- **Be earning** anywhere from $12,000 to $50,000 per year, depending on how many home loans you close each year.

You can also be a Loan Correspondent for commercial real estate loans. The difference between being a Loan Correspondent for home loans and commercial loans is:

- **Commercial loans are fewer in number** than home loans.
- **Commercial loans usually take longer to close** than home loans because the amount borrowed is usually larger and the deal more complex.
- **Commercial loans pay a higher commission** than home loans but there is usually more competition from lenders for these loans.
- **Commercial loans take experience to close.** It's best for you to gain skills and know-how with home loans before trying commercial loans.

Estimated time for your project: Find lender to be a Loan Correspondent for: 1 month; Be trained by lender: 1 month; Get your first loan applicant approved: 1 month. *Total estimated time: 3 months.*

Get Loans and Grants from Little-Known Sources

If you plan to invest in rural real estate in lightly populated areas of the United States, you should know about the United States Department of Agriculture Rural Housing Service (RHS) which offers:

- **Rural Housing Guaranteed Loan Program (Section 502)** for loans up to 38 years (at this writing), depending on the borrower's income, with no down payment required. But the family must be able to afford the monthly mortgage payment, including interest and taxes. Interest rates may be subsidized to as low as 1 percent. Under the terms of the program, an individual or family may borrow up to 100 percent of the appraised value of the home, eliminating the down payment.
- **Rural Housing Site Loans (Sections 523 and 524)** are loans made to provide housing for the purchase and development of affordable housing sites in rural areas for low- and moderate-income families. Eligible groups include nonprofit organizations, public bodies, and federally recognized Indian groups.
- **Multi-Family Housing Development (Sections 515 and 538)** provide loans and grants to finance rental and cooperatively owned housing of modest size, design, and cost for very low, low- and

moderate-income households. Under Section 515, RHS makes direct loans to developers of affordable multi-family rural rental housing. Funds can be used to build new rental housing complexes or to repair and rehab existing units. Loans are for up to 50 years at a very low interest rate.

- **Multi-Family Section 538 Direct Loans** are intended to fund construction of multi-family housing units to be occupied by low-income families.

Other programs you might wish to look into include the Farm Labor Housing Program, Housing Preservation Grant Program (Section 533), and Housing Application Packaging Grants. To learn more about these and other programs, call the Program Support Staff at 202-720-9619. Or write Rural Housing Services, 1400 Independence Avenue SW, Washington, DC 20250.

Estimated time for your project: Finding suitable property for one of these programs: 6 months; Negotiate loan or grant: 4 months. *Total estimated time: 10 months.*

Make an Excellent Income Upgrading Older Rental Units

Many older rental units don't have the amenities that today's tenants want, namely:

- **Fiber optic lines for speedy communications.**
- **High-speed copper wiring for fast services.**
- **Coaxial cables for TV access.**
- **Internet access at high speed.**

We all live in a wired and wireless world today. So today's tenant wants access to these services as part of the rental agreement. What's more, most tenants are willing to pay extra for these services. So you can increase your income as a real estate owner by offering wired services. Or, as a contractor, you can install these services and earn a good fee for doing so.

Here's how you can earn extra income from your properties as an owner by giving older rental units a new life: Decide to offer wired and wireless services for today's information age using your roof and other unoccupied spaces for:

Cable television	**Fax machines**
Internet access	**Computers—desktop, laptops**
Telephones—all types	**Entertainment systems**
Satellite television	**High-speed data transmission**

Conceal your wiring behind baseboards, attractive enclosures, ceiling moldings, in mail chutes, elevator shafts, trash tunnels, or any other unused space. Your tenants will love you because they don't have a tangle of wires in their apartments or offices.

But how can you pay for installing such information-ready wiring? You can:

- **Contact** local communications companies—see your *Yellow Pages.*
- **Offer** your roof area to communications companies needing space.
- **Provide** space for satellite dishes, microwave antennas, and other communications devices used by these firms.
- **Work out** an annual rental fee for each firm, with three months' advance rent from every firm using your roof space.
- **Use the money advance** from your roof rentals to pay for the internal wiring in your building. Or use a swap deal to have the communication firm(s) install the wiring in place of 3 months' rent.
- **Estimate your costs** for data transmission, video, and voice wiring at $2,000 to $7,000 per apartment, depending on how many outlets you have per apartment, type of concealment, and other factors. Work can be done by outside contractors or by you.
- **Plan your wiring** so it provides the services your tenants seek and need—see the list above for typical wiring needs. Be certain your wiring is reliable, that outlets are easily reachable, and that new developments in information services and technology can be handled. Then your rental income will boom, with no vacancies.

You may be able to get multi-family apartment houses for zero cash down—with no credit investigation—if you can show the seller you'll be able to increase the property's income. With the right wiring and roof rentals you may be able to double—or even triple—the income of some older buildings. And some of these are available at zero down for you—the hard-working real estate BWB!

Estimated time for your project: Contact companies needing rooftop space for equipment placement: 1 month; Negotiate with companies for space and placement: 2 months; Close deals: 1 month. *Total estimated time: 4 months.*

Finance Your Real Estate Down Payments at 0 Percent Interest

Do you presently hold one or more unsecured credit cards on which you owe some money? Good!

You can use this situation to get 0 percent interest down payment loans for income real estate you want to buy. Here's how:

- **Recognize**—here and now—that you ***can*** get 0 percent interest "Introductory Rates" on some credit cards for 6 months, or longer, when you turn in your present cards for new credit cards.
- **With this 0 percent interest rate** good for Cash Advances, Purchases and Balance Transfers (what you owe) on your new credit cards.
- **Allowing you** to get interest-free money for as long as 9 months. You can use this money for any purpose—including down payment on income real estate. You do NOT have to disclose what you're using your Cash Advance for when you access it on your new credit cards!
- **Being free of** any Cash Advance or Balance Transfer Fees of any kind, while having a Line of Credit up to $20,000 or more with some credit cards.

So how can *you* get in on such deals? It's easy. Just take these three quick steps:

1. **Check your local newspapers** every day for ads run by banks and other credit card issuers, offering credit cards with special 0 percent interest rates, free balance transfers, larger lines of credit, and other inducements for you to swap cards.

2. **Call or visit the bank or go on its Web site.** When you contact the bank, describe your credit situation, giving your FICO® score, if you know it. Ask the bank employee if you'd be approved for the bank's special offer. Tell this person you don't want to have your credit checked; you just want an opinion.
3. **Apply for your new credit card** if you get a YES answer! Why? Because you'll be able to get the cash you need for your real estate down payments for up to 6 months—sometimes even longer, like 9 months!

Once you get your new credit card, decide how you'll use your Line of Credit. Many real estate BWBs today:

- **Use their Line of Credit** to get cash needed for the down payment on an investment property. The income from the property pays off the credit card Line of Credit used to buy the property.
- **Wait until the day of the closing** on their new property before using their Line of Credit. Why? Because the usage does not show up until one month later, long after they are earning money from their investment property.

I hear you saying loudly—"But isn't the interest rate on credit card debt too high? Why pay such exorbitant rates when you can get a down payment loan at a much lower rate?"

The answer, my good friend, is this: "Few lenders will loan you money for real estate down payment. All lenders want you to have some money in the real estate you buy. Why? Because then you won't walk away from the property the first time a problem pops up! This principle of lending has been true for more than a century!

"Further," good friend of mine, "the interest you pay on your down payment loan is provable and tax-deductible because the money is being used for business purposes! So forget the interest cost. Get the loan you need and start building your real estate fortune!"

Your Real Estate Wealth Schedule

You ***can*** get rich in income real estate! How do I have the right to say this to you—my good friend? I have the right to say this to *you* because thousands of readers call me on the phone, write letters to me, e-mail me, and fax me to tell me they ***are*** getting rich using the methods I suggest to you in this book.

Put succinctly, I have proof, voluntarily supplied, that people—just like you and me—***are*** getting rich in income real estate today.

But to get rich in income real estate today you ***must*** plan, and ***schedule*** your future. Here's a suggested Real Estate Wealth Schedule for you. Use this schedule:

- **As given, with no changes.**
- **With changes to suit *your* needs.**
- **Or throw it away, after using it as a guide to prepare *your* own unique schedule.**

But no matter what you do, use it—for your own benefit!

Your Real Estate Wealth Schedule

Your Starting Date ________________

Action You Will Take	**Timing of Your Action**
1. Learn all you can about income real estate.	Next three months.
2. Start looking for money for your future income real estate.	One month from now.
3. Look for suitable income property to buy.	Two months from now.
4. Find my first acceptable income property to buy.	Three months from now.
5. Make a bid on my first income property to buy.	Three and a half months from now.
6. Buy and own my first income real estate to earn money from.	Four months from now.
7. "Get comfortable" with my first income property from a business standpoint—rents, maintenance, etc.	Six months from now—allow two months to "get to know" my buy.

8.	Report your success to your author by any means you choose.	Six months and one week from now.
9.	Start looking for my second income property to buy.	Seven months from now.
10.	Buy and own my second income property.	Eight months from now.
11.	"Get comfortable" with your second income property.	Ten months from now.
12.	Sit back, relax and enjoy your first year in income real estate while you look ahead to your future in the real estate business.	Twelve months from now.

So here we are at the end of your journey, with me to put you on the road to real estate riches in income property. And to give you one final proof that ***you really can get rich in real estate today,*** here's a faxed letter I received while writing this chapter. It summarizes for you, I think, everything I've been trying to tell you throughout this book, and serves as the basis for your Key Ideas for this chapter:

From Borrowed Down Payment to Millions in Real Estate

"This letter is a follow-up to the telephone conversation I had with you this morning regarding property/real estate investing. I want to give you (and your readers) a background of how I started in real estate with no money.

"My parents divorced when I was 12 years old, which was not a good situation, but it happened. I started working at the age of 14, mostly after school, and held two jobs. The harder I worked, the more money I made. But the more money I made, the more often my car broke down and my school bills grew. It was never-ending!

"When I got to college I worked as a waiter at two to three restaurants each week. At the age of 24, still working as a waiter, my step-grandfather, with whom I was living, became ill and his family sold the house. So I had to find a place to live.

"I had less than $500 in my checking account, and one credit card with a $5,000 line of credit on it. I was working as a waiter at a large hotel in the morning and at night as a waiter at a fine dining restaurant. I was making about $3,000 a month between both jobs, working 80 hours a week.

"My mom suggested I buy a condo to live in. I thought 'I can take a cash advance on my credit card and make payments from my income.' So I called my credit card bank and asked what the payment would be if I took the entire $5,000 advance. After I explained what I wanted to do, the operator put me on hold. After a few minutes of waiting (which was well worth it) she said 'Because you've been with us for 4 years and have a good payment record, I can raise your credit and cash advance limit to $10,000 and I can also reduce your interest payment by 4%!'

"At the time real estate prices were low in my area. I looked at condos for $120,000 but nothing struck me as a 'nice place to live.' After 3 days of looking the realtor took me to see a home (not a condo) that was a Bank Repo for $167,000. It was a wreck. It had a hole the size of a basketball in the garage, insect infestation, overgrown landscaping, broken windows, etc. I told the realtor I wanted that old house on the corner lot and that I could learn to fix it up on my own. He laughed and said 'You don't want that house. I just wanted to show you what you'd pay for the cheapest house in the neighborhood vs. a condo in the same area.'

"But I did **not** want a condo. And with my $10,000 of borrowed money I could afford an FHA loan at 3% down plus closing costs. That day we made an offer and within 30 days I owned my first home for a purchase price of $158,000.

I spent the next six months fixing up that old house, including living in the garage for two months. I took in a roommate for $350 a month rent.

"At the end of six months, in December, a mortgage broker called me and asked if I'd be interested in refinancing my home. I said 'I don't have money for that.' He told me I could do it for free and pull out $50,000 in cash on a second loan and that my current interest of 8.5% would be reduced to 6.75%. The saving would almost cover the cost of the larger loan! I was so excited. Within a week my house appraised at $225,000. It was now one of the nicest homes in the neighborhood and all my neighbors thanked me for cleaning it up because it was such an eyesore before.

"During the next few weeks I searched for other homes to buy. I found my 'dream' home, a Bank Repo that went on the market an hour before I saw the sign. It was on almost an acre of land, a huge house (3,000 sq ft) with 4 bedrooms and 3 baths. The one drawback was there was no landscaping. I did not mind this as I was into landscaping and gardening. I got this house for $475,000 and it was a steal (about $50,000 under market).

"I rented my first house for the monthly payment I was making on it and moved into the new home. I fixed it up like the first one with new paint, carpets, landscaping—all with no money out of my pocket. It all came from the refinance money from the first house and I only had to put a portion of the money down on the second home.

"Within 10 months, in October, I sold the second home for $735,000 to a cash buyer who needed a one-level home (an elderly lady). I made $260,000, less realtor fees, commissions and approximately $40,000 in supplies to fix up the home.

"I took my profit and moved up to a new home near the beach. I bought it for $780,000 and within 2 years sold it for $1,400,000. I kept repeating this process of buying, fixing and refinancing, pulling out my equity to leverage myself. And it does work!

"Last June I bought my current home for $2.5 million which was in a distressed situation. The home was being sold 'as is' by a couple getting a divorce. They just wanted out. The home on the left of my home just closed escrow for $2.6 million, without an ocean view. Two doors down, the house on the right sold for $2.8 million in one day!

"I feel my house is a good deal because two other houses that just sold were old but all three (including mine) are one street above the Pacific Ocean in a very highly demanded neighborhood which commands top dollar.

"So I am adding 4 bathrooms and 2 bedrooms and a large master closet. I've already cleaned up the yard and upgraded the interior. I will list my house for $5 million in July of this year when it is done and get close to the asking price as this is what 'newly remodeled homes' go for in this neighborhood.

"With my approximate $2 million in profit I will do a 1031* exchange and buy income properties of the type we discussed on the phone this morning. I have always said: **'If you always do what you have always done, you will always get what you have always gotten!'**

"I am **not** a waiter any more. I am a National Sales Manager for a financial firm. I started from nothing and I am now making 7 figures a year from real estate—**not** my job! I am still frugal and plan on retiring from my job in 3 years to work full time in real estate. I only wish I could have read your book sooner! But at only 31 I cannot complain. I DID IT and will continue to DO IT! I hope we can meet someday so I can say 'Thank you' in person. Until then, please accept my deep gratitude for sharing your knowledge." —California

*A 1031 exchange is a tax-free trade of income-producing property under provisions of Section 1031 of the IRS Tax Code. It is used by experienced real estate investors.

I sincerely hope that when you write me a letter sometime in the future that your results will be as good as this reader's. You ***can*** make it happen! Just start taking your first step ***NOW.***

To ensure that you will—someday—write me such a letter, here are some rules to keep in mind during your real estate deals. I call them my "Best Rules."

Best Rules for Your Success in Income Real Estate

YOU CAN BE SUCCESSFUL IN INCOME REAL ESTATE, if you follow proven rules. Here a number of these rules you can use:

1. **NEVER PAY "Front Money"** or advance fees for loans. A fee is fair AFTER you receive your loan money, NOT BEFORE!
2. **DON'T BASE YOUR FINANCIAL OPINION** of an income property on whether or not you would live in it. The only valid measure is if the property earns a Positive Cash Flow for you and rises in value as time passes.
3. **HAVE STRICT RULES FOR YOUR TENANTS**—and enforce the rules. Demand that rent be paid on time. Get a three-month security deposit. Do not waste time with dead beats. Get them out of your property quickly.
4. **TRY TO BUY EVERY PROPERTY** with zero cash out of your pocket. Using this approach will make you more much successful—faster—in income real estate today.
5. **NEVER PAY ASKING PRICE** for a property unless the seller is helping you finance it. Then consider paying the asking price to make the seller more generous in the terms you are offered.
6. **KEEP ACCURATE RECORDS** for all your income properties. Your records will help you support your tax deductions and give you exact profit numbers.
7. **START WITH SMALL LOCAL INCOME PROPERTY.** Keep it neat and clean and your vacancies will be low. Make repairs as soon as they are needed—don't let them hang on.

8. **USE A COMPETENT ATTORNEY** and accountant for every real estate purchase. Never buy without legal advice.
9. **LEARN ALL YOU CAN ABOUT FINANCING** your real estate. Since you're in a "borrowed-money business" the more you know, the easier it is to get the money you need.
10. **KEEP YOUR CREDIT SCORE** as high as possible. This makes it easier for you to get any loan you need for real estate.
11. **TRY TO MORTGAGE OUT**—it can put cash into your pocket while you take over an income-producing property.
12. **START WITH LOCAL SINGLE-FAMILY HOMES.** They are easy to buy and can get you started in income real estate quickly at low or zero cost.
13. **LOOK FOR SELLERS WITH BUILT-IN FINANCING** and you'll get started on zero cash sooner and easier.
14. **TURN YOUR REAL ESTATE HOLDINGS** into your private bank, borrowing against them to buy more properties.
15. **REMEMBER: *REAL ESTATE IS THE WORLD'S BEST BUSINESS!*** Follow these rules and success in real estate can be yours.

Finally, a reminder: My newsletters, *International Wealth Success* and *Money Watch Bulletin,* have many subscribers throughout the world. Many of these subscribers ask me business-related real estate questions. Since these subscribers have shown faith in me by subscribing to one or both newsletters, I try to answer their questions first. So, if your questions as a nonsubscriber are slow in being answered, please don't say I didn't remind you of this possibility!

And now, here's how and when you can contact me, as I've promised you several times in this book. If you have any questions about the business aspects of your real estate wealth building, you can call me from 8 A.M. to 10 P.M. (New York time) at 516-766-5850. Or fax me 24 hours a day at 516-766-5919. If you prefer e-mail, drop me a note at admin@iws-inc.com. However, I prefer a fax. My web site is: *www.iws-inc.com.* My postal mailing address is IWS, Inc., PO Box 186, Merrick, NY 11566-0186. Please remember that I try to help my newsletter subscribers first! Meanwhile, good luck in your real estate wealth search, my good friend!

Useful Real Estate Books, Reports, Training Courses, and Newsletters for Beginning and Experienced Wealth Builders

YOU CAN BUILD YOUR REAL ESTATE RICHES ON BORROWED MONEY faster! How? By getting more know-how about real estate. As has often been said, "Knowledge is power!" And Ralph Waldo Emerson said "Only an inventor knows how to borrow, and every person is or should be an inventor!"

Here are a number of sources of real estate techniques you'll find helpful and profitable.

Real Estate Investment and Management Books

The following books are available from John Wiley & Sons, Inc., 111 River Street, Hoboken, NJ 07030, 201-748-6000, *www.wiley.com.* Books listed, here range from beginner's guides to helpful dictionaries and comprehensive references.

Achenbach, George, *Goldmining in Foreclosure Properties,* 5 ed., paperback, $27.95.

Albrecht, Donna G., *Buying a Home When You're Single*, paperback, $14.95.

Berges, Steve, *The Complete Guide to Buying and Selling Apartment Buildings*, paperback, $29.95.

Berges, Steve, *The Complete Guide to Flipping Properties*, paperback, $19.95.

Boroson, Warren, and Ken Austin, *The Home Buyer's Inspection Guide: Everything You Need to Know to Save $$ and Get a Better House*, paperback, $19.95.

Carey, Chantal Howell, and Bill Carey, *Going Going Gone! Auctioning Your Home for Top Dollar*, paperback, $16.95

Eldred, Gary W., *The Complete Guide to Second Homes for Vacations, Retirement, and Investment*, paperback, $16.95.

Eldred, Gary W., *The 106 Common Mistakes Homebuyers Make (& How to Avoid Them)*, 3 ed., paperback, $16.95.

Irwin, Robert, and David L. Ganz, *The 90 Second Lawyer Guide to Buying Real Estate*, paperback, $19.95.

Lumley, James E. A., *Challenge Your Taxes: Homeowner's Guide to Reducing Property Taxes*, paperback, $19.95.

Lumley, James E. A., *Five Magic Paths to Making a Fortune in Real Estate*, 2 ed., paperback, $16.95.

Molloy, William J., *The Complete Home Buyer's Bible*, hardcover, $29.95.

Shemin, Robert, *Unlimited Riches: Making Your Fortune in Real Estate Investing*, hardcover, $24.95.

Shim, Jae K., Joel G. Siegel, and Stephen W. Hartman, *Dictionary of Real Estate*, paperback, $24.95.

Real Estate Self-Study Success Kits, Books, Reports, and Newsletters

The following success kits, books, reports, and newsletters are available from the publishing company of which Tyler G. Hicks is President. To obtain any of these publications, send a check or money order to the address listed below. You can call the phone number listed below to order by credit card. You can also order on the Internet or by fax to:

International Wealth Success, Inc. (IWS, Inc.), PO Box 186, Merrick, NY 11566-0186. Order on the Internet at: *www.iws-inc.com.* Order directly by telephone using a credit card at 516-766-5850. You can fax your orders 24/7 to 516-766-5919. An alternative web site you can use is: *www.iwsmoney.com.*

Success Kits

Single-Family Home Riches Kit by Tyler G. Hicks covers earning money from single-family homes (SFH) by owning them and renting them out, flipping them, leasing them to Section 8 tenants, etc. Topics include: 10 ways to get your SFH on zero cash using Other People's Money (OPM), where to find big cash-flow properties, how to buy low and sell high today, when—and where—to get zero-down finance, getting hard-money loans today, investing with no risk to your money, easy ways to make big flipping profits, fast financing methods for real estate startup, getting started with poor or no credit. Includes 4 big bonuses—*Home Buying Guide, Getting the Best Mortgage, Handbook of Adjustable-Rate Mortgages,* and *The TY Hicks Fast Financing Methods for Real Estate Startup and Expansion.* **\$150. 500 pages, 8.5 × 11 in., paperback.**

Multi-Family Home and Multi-Unit Estate Riches Kit by Tyler G. Hicks covers multi-family properties such as apartment houses, town-houses, garden apartments, condos and other residential income structures you might wish to invest in. Also discusses small- and medium-size office buildings you can own to build your real estate riches. Shows how and where to find and buy multi-unit properties for profitable income. Gives hundreds of lenders for multi-unit properties of various types. Focuses on zero-down methods you can use to buy multi-unit buildings, even though your credit may not be the best. Shows how to squeeze the maximum profit from a multi-unit building while providing your tenants with clean, neat, safe and comfortable housing or office space. This big Kit includes four big bonus reports to help you earn more in multi-unit properties. The bonuses include smart methods for creative zero-cash financing of multi-unit buildings. **\$150. 500 pages, 8.5 × 11 in., paperback.**

Fast Financing of Your Real Estate Fortune Success Kit shows you how to raise money for real estate deals. You can move ahead faster if you can finance your real estate quickly and easily. This Kit concentrates on getting the money you need for your real estate deals. The Kit gives you more than 2,000 lenders of real estate money all over the United States. It includes private lenders who may consider your real estate deal. And the Kit shows you how and where to find deals that return a big income to you but are easier to finance than you might think. **$99.50. 7 Speed-Read Books, 523 pages, 8.5 × 11 in., paperback.**

Financial Broker/Finder/Business Broker/Business Consultant Kit shows you how to start your own private business as a Financial Broker/Finder/Business Broker/Consultant. As a Financial Broker, you find business or real estate money for companies or individuals and you are paid a fee after the loan is obtained by your client. As a Finder, you are paid a fee for finding things (real estate, money, raw materials, etc.) for firms or people. As a Business Broker, you help in the buying or selling of a business—again for a fee. This big Kit shows you how to collect fees for the work you do for your clients. The Kit also contains typical agreements used in the business, tells you what fees to charge, gives you a prewritten news release to get free publicity for your business, and four colorful membership certificates (each 8 × 10 in.). **$99.50. 12 Speed-Read Books, 485 pages, 8.5 × 11 in., paperback, four membership cards.**

Foreclosures and Other Distressed Properties Kit shows you—with 6 audio cassette tapes and a comprehensive manual—how and where to find and buy foreclosed and other distressed properties of all types. Gives names, addresses, and other data about agencies offering foreclosed properties—often at bargain prices. Presents forms giving examples of actual foreclosure documents and paperwork. Shows how to evaluate properties you're considering buying. **$53.95. 150+ pages, 8.5 × 11 in., paperback, 6 audio cassette tapes.**

How to Build Your Real Estate Fortune Today in a Real Estate Investment Trust Kit shows you how to start a REIT to finance any type of real estate you want to invest in to earn money from. Gives you the exact steps to take to raise money from either private or public sources. Today's REITs raise millions for almost every type of real estate used by human beings—multi-family residential (apartment houses), factories, marinas, hotels, motels, shopping malls, nursing homes, hospitals, etc.

REITs can own these types of properties, lend on them (issue mortgages), or make a combination of these investments. Written by Tyler G. Hicks. **$100, 150+ pages, 8.5 × 11 in., paperback.**

Low-Lost Real Estate Loan Getters Kit shows the user how to get real estate loans for either a client or for themselves. Lists hundreds of active real estate lenders seeking to make first and/or junior mortgage loans for a variety of property types. Loan amounts range from a few thousand dollars to many millions, depending on the property, its location, and value. Presents typical application and agreement forms for use in securing real estate loans. No license is required to obtain loans for oneself using the data in this Kit. This big Kit provides step-by-step guidance for obtaining the real estate loan or loans of the user's choice. Written by Tyler G. Hicks. **$100, 150+ pages, 8.5 × 11 in., paperback.**

Real Estate Riches Success Kit shows you how to make big money in real estate as an income property owner, mortgage broker, mortgage banker, real estate investment trust operator, mortgage money broker, raw land investor, and industrial property owner. This is a general Kit covering many key aspects of real estate ownership, financing, and investment. Includes numerous financing sources for your real estate wealth building. The Kit also covers how to buy real estate for the lowest price. (Down payments of no cash can sometimes be arranged.) And the Kit also shows how to run your real estate for the biggest profits. Written by Tyler G. Hicks. **$99.50, 6 Speed-Read Books, 446 pages, 8.5 × 11 in., paperback.**

Mega-Money Methods Kit covers the raising of large amounts of money (multi-millions) for real estate and business projects of all types. Some of these projects may be offshore in overseas countries. The Kit shows how to prepare loan packages for very large loans, where to get financing for such loans, what fees to charge after the loan is obtained, plus much more. Using this Kit, the BWB should be able to prepare effective loan requests for large amounts of money for viable projects. The Kit also gives a list of offshore lenders for big real estate and business projects. Written by Tyler G. Hicks. **$100, 200+ pages, 8.5 × 11 in., paperback.**

Loans by Phone Kit shows you how and where to get real estate, business, and personal loans by telephone. With just 32 words and 15 seconds of time, you can determine if a lender is interested in the loan you seek for yourself or for someone who is your client—if you're working as a loan broker or a finder. This Kit gives you hundreds of telephone lenders. About half have toll-free 800 or similar numbers, meaning that your call is free of long-distance charges. Typical agreement forms are also included in the Kit. Written by Tyler G. Hicks. **$100, 150+ pages, 8.5 × 11 in., paperback.**

Zero-Cash Success Techniques Kit shows you how to get started in income real estate or in your own business venture with no cash of your own. This big Kit includes a special book by Ty Hicks entitled *Zero-Cash Takeovers of Real Estate and Business,* plus a 58-minute audio cassette tape by him entitled *Small Business Financing.* In the tape Ty talks to you, telling you how you can get started in income real estate or in your own business without cash and with few credit checks. **$99.50, 7 Speed-Read Books, 876 pages, 8.5 × 11 in., paperback; 58-minute audio cassette tape.**

Real Estate Books

Comprehensive Loan Sources for Business and Real Estate. Gives hundreds of lenders' names, addresses, telephone numbers, and types of loans made. **$25, 136 pages, 8.5 × 11 in., paperback.**

Directory of 2,500 Active Real Estate Lenders. Lists 2,500 names, addresses, and telephone numbers of direct lenders or sources of information on possible lenders for real estate of many types. Lists lenders nationwide for a variety of real estate projects—from single-family homes to multi-unit residential buildings. **$25, 197 pages, 8.5 × 11 in., paperback.**

Diversified Loan Sources for Business and Real Estate. Gives hundreds of lenders' names, addresses, telephone numbers, and lending guidelines for business and real estate loans of many different types. **$25, 136 pages, 8.5 × 11 in., paperback.**

How Anyone Can Prosper and Get Wealthy Trading Country Land by Frank Moss. Shows how to acquire wealth and have fun trading in country land. Covers supply and demand, starting your own home-based spare-time moneymaking business buying and selling wood-lands, estimating value, time/distance analysis, plus much more. Using this book, a person can get started in this lucrative part of today's real estate market. **$21.50, 100+ pages, 8.5 × 11 in., paperback.**

How to Be a Second Mortgage Loan Broker by Richard Brisky gives complete details on how to set up your office, find clients, locate lenders, negotiate with clients and lenders, what fees to charge, how to comply with any licensing laws in your area of business, what files to keep, plus much more. Using this book, a person can get started in this lucrative aspect of today's real estate market. **$25, 100 pages, 8.5 × 11 in., paperback.**

How to Create Your Own Real Estate Fortune by Jens Nielsen. Covers investment opportunities in real estate, leveraging, depreciation, tax rules, remodeling your purchases, buy-and-leaseback, understanding your financing, plus much more. **$17.50, 117 pages, 8.5 × 11 in., paperback.**

Rapid Real Estate and Business Loan-Getting Methods by Tyler G. Hicks gives innovative techniques to get loans, ways in which real estate can make you rich, getting free of the "9-to-5 grind," new steps to getting venture capital, smart-money ways to get loans, plus many other ideas for real estate and business financing. **$25.00, 96 pages, 8.5 × 11 in., paperback**

How to Make Your Fortune in Real Estate Second Mortgages by Tyler G. Hicks. Covers second mortgages, how a second mortgage finder works, registering your firm, running ads, finding capital, expanding the business, limited partnerships, plus much more. **$17.50, 100 pages, 8.5 × 11 in., paperback.**

How to Borrow Your Way to Real Estate Riches Using Government Sources, compiled by Tyler G. Hicks, lists numerous mortgage loans and guarantees, loan purposes, amounts, terms, financing charges, types of structures financed, loan-to-value ratio, special factors, plus much more. **$17.50, 88 pages, 8.5 × 11 in., paperback.**

Real Estate Reports

Here are seven real estate reports on various aspects of property financing. Each report measures 8.5 × 11 inches and presents essential information on getting money for the real estate transaction detailed in the report.

Neighborhood and Convenience Shopping Center Loan Package, Report M-1. Example of a typical successful loan package. $12.50, 40 pages.

Downtown Office Building Loan Package, M-2. Example of a successful loan package for an office building. $12.50, 24 pages.

Single-Family Home Foreclosure Business Plan, M-3. Shows how money could be raised to buy single-family home foreclosures and rent them out or resell them for a profit. $12.50, 24 pages.

Single-Family Home Income Property Business Plan, M-4. Shows how money could be made by owning a string of single-family homes that you rent to tenants for a profit. $12.50, 24 pages.

High-Rise Apartment Building Loan Package and Business Plan, M-5. Presents a comprehensive loan package and business plan for the financing and operation of a multi-family apartment building. $12.50, 24 pages.

Refinancing Proposal for a Multi-Family Apartment House, M-6. Shows how a large apartment house can be refinanced to enhance its competitive position in its marketplace. $12.50, 61 pages.

FHA Multi-Family Building Loan Package and Business Plan, M-7. Shows a typical loan package and business plan that complies with Agency requirements. $12.50, 24 pages.

Newsletters

International Wealth Success is Ty Hicks' monthly newsletter published 12 times a year. This 16-page newsletter covers loan and grant sources, real estate opportunities, business opportunities, import-export, mail order, and a variety of other topics on earning money in your own business. Every one-year or longer subscriber can run one free 60-word (or less) classified ad or a one-inch display ad free of charge in the newsletter each month. Ads can be for Money Wanted, Business Opportunities, or Money Available. The newsletter has worldwide circulation, giving readers and advertisers extremely broad coverage. Started in January 1967, the newsletter has been published continuously every month since that date. $24.00 per year, 16 pages plus additional inserts, 8.5 × 11 in.

Money Watch Bulletin gives a monthly coverage of 100+ active lenders for real estate, business, and personal use. The newsletter gives the lender's name, address, and telephone number. In some cases, the lender's funding guidelines are also given, along with other helpful information about the lender. All lender names were obtained during the last two weeks; the data is therefore right up to date. In addition, lender's names are supplied on self-stick labels on an occasional basis. Also covers venture capital, accounts receivable financing, government mortgage guarantees, as well as overseas and Canadian lenders. Institutions listed include banks, mortgage brokers, credit unions, private lenders, etc. $95.00 per year, 12 issues, 20 pages, 8.5 × 11 in.

Index

9 780471 464990